D0363537

The Black Plaque Guide to London

Previous books by Felix Barker

The Oliviers
(Hamish Hamilton, 1953)
The House that Stoll Built
(Frederick Muller, 1957)
The First Explorers
(with Anthea Barker) (Aldus, 1971)
London: 2,000 Years of a City and its People
(with Peter Jackson) (Cassell, 1974)
London as it might have been
(with Ralph Hyde) (John Murray, 1982)
Laurence Olivier, A Critical Study
(Spellmount, 1984)
Highgate Cemetery, Victorian Valhalla
(John Murray, 1984)

The
BLACK PLAQUE
GUIDE
to
LONDON

BY
FELIX BARKER
AND
DENISE SILVESTER-CARR

CONSTABLE · AND · COMPANY · LIMITED

First published in Great Britain 1987
by Constable and Company Ltd
10 Orange Street London WC2H 7EG
Copyright © 1987 by Felix Barker and Denise Silvester-Carr
Set in Monophoto Garamond 11pt by
Servis Filmsetting Ltd, Manchester
Printed in Great Britain by
BAS Printers Ltd, Over Wallop

British Library CIP data
Barker, Felix
The black plaque guide to London
1. Historic buildings–England–London
2. Crime and criminals–England–
London   3. London (England)–Description
–1981-
I. Title   II. Silvester-Carr, Denise
364.3'09421   DA689.H48

ISBN 0 09 465510 9

Contents

Introduction

ALL over London Blue Plaques tell us where the famous were born, lived and died. These memorials to the worthy were first put up by the Royal Society of Arts in 1866, were continued after 1901 by the London County Council and its successor, the Greater London Council, and still go up under the auspices of English Heritage.

As testaments to true blue pillars of society, they are all very fine, but they present a one-sided picture of London and a rather too generous view of its inhabitants. To redress the balance we have conceived the notion of seeking out dens of vice, abodes of love and the homes of the disreputable and marking them with Black Plaques; black, of course, because that is the livery of the Prince of Darkness; imaginary because presumably only satanists would want this kind of formal graffiti on their walls.

We invite you to regard the less than virtuous whose activities may not be so admirable but are frequently more entertaining. In doing so we are making the compass swing heavily to the opposite pole. The chronicle of evil is unremitting; human nature is seen constantly at its worst; virtue lies bleeding. A book so concerned with the infamous may well be denounced from the pulpit and burned by the public hangman if he is still around to do the job. As the Devil's Topographers we can expect little mercy.

In convict grey, and parading through the prison yard in alphabetical order, are adulterers, agitators, arsonists, assassins, bigamists, blackmailers, brothel-keepers, burglars, con-men, conspirators, deceivers, elopers, embezzlers, fanatics, forgers, gangsters, hoaxers, highwaymen, impostors, kidnappers, malcontents, plotters, pickpockets, poisoners, pornographers, procuresses, *provocateurs*, quacks, regicides, rioters, robbers, satanists, scandalmongers, seducers, sodomites, spies, swindlers, suicides, terrorists, traitors, transvestites, vandals, whoremasters.

To this desperate crew is added a sprinkling of murderers. These we have tried to keep to the minimum because they have been endlessly written about, but inevitably several three-star killers like Crippen, Wainwright, Seddon, 'Brides in the Bath' Smith and Jack the Ripper have knocked on their coffin lids and demanded a Black Plaque. We have also exhumed more obscure killers whose ingenuity or particularly flagrant conduct has appealed to us.

Altogether we reached a total of 189 people whose names we would like to see disfiguring 161 addresses. The earliest misdeed we record took place in 1196, the latest in 1987, but we make no claim that the list is exhaustive. We have played favourites in our choice of evil-doers, rejected villains whose offences seemed insufficiently rank; and many, no doubt, we have failed to sniff out.

One category of sinners creates problems simply because sin is so outdated a notion. We have included a considerable number of *horizontales* – prostitutes, courtesans, kept women and naughty ladies – who once would automatically have been stigmatised as immoral. For this we shall probably be impaled by suffragettes wielding hatpins who will rightly argue that these women should be held no more culpable than the men who exploited them.

Louisa Fairbrother is an example of double standards. The finger of nineteenth-century scorn was pointed at her because for years she was kept in a house close to his by the Duke of Cambridge, a first cousin of Queen Victoria, and by him she had two illegitimate children. Society regarded her as beyond the pale and, even after she and the Duke were married, she was never recognised by the Royal Family. Yet no one blamed the Duke for conducting this clandestine affair. We have put her name rather than his on a Mayfair Black Plaque because this reflects the moral attitudes prevailing in their lifetimes.

It may seem equally unfair (especially since the publication of their letters) to cite the Duchess of Windsor rather than the Duke as the instigator of the Abdication. This is the inevitable implication of naming her Marylebone flat as the place where their love affair developed. Regardless of responsibility, Bryanston Court seems to deserve a Black Plaque as the birthplace of the constitutional crisis.

Occasionally Black Plaques overlap Blue ones; the line between good and bad can be very thin; the virtuous sometimes transgress. Are not John Wilkes and Sir Francis Burdett admired champions of liberty? Yes, but Wilkes, a member of the Hell Fire Club, also stood accused of obscenity, blasphemy and sedition. He was hauled off to the Tower as was Burdett who, proclaiming the precepts of Magna

Carta, created an almighty fracas in Piccadilly. Lord Palmerston was a much revered Prime Minister but the plaque on his house conveniently forgets that in his eightieth year he was named in a divorce case with a former governess. The very first Blue Plaque in London commemorated Lord Byron in Holles Street; we counter with a Black one in Albany in remembrance of flaming rows with his mistress Caroline Lamb.

To maintain a historical perspective we have ignored the compassion which now often gives the benefit of the doubt to miscreants, deviants and criminals. Just as Blue Plaques take virtue as a matter of course, our Black Plaques accept old-fashioned standards of right and wrong. They are stern reminders of vice and villainy in times when the fear of hell fire stalked the land and when few allowances were made for moral cripples.

We have found that disapproval is often the result of excessive prejudice, and that many crimes when investigated prove less cut and dried than brief popular accounts suggest. When we think of Crippen we have a picture of a ruthless wife-murderer who runs off at short notice with his secretary. It is generally forgotten that he and Ethel le Neve had known each other for ten years, and that there was a cautious courtship of six before they became lovers.

Responsibility to the people we are putting in the pillory has rather altered our original intention which was to be lighthearted and, heaven help us, whimsical about evil-doers. We soon found that humour and evil made a bad mix. There is nothing inherently funny about a servant dropping her mistress's head over Hammersmith Bridge or a necrophile in Notting Hill killing a woman during intercourse. The best we can manage is a wry smile at the idea of Aleister Crowley, the Wickedest Man on Earth, striving to procreate an Anti-Christ by the Ultimate Orgasm in a Turkish Bath. It is difficult to keep a straight face when contemplating a jury, each man on his knees, peeping through a keyhole to establish what a witness could or could not have seen in a Belgravia divorce scandal.

While virtue is proud to proclaim itself, vice is frequently secretive. Finding the exact address where crimes and scandals occurred has often posed problems and required different methods of detection. Each area and each century has thrown up its own particular puzzle.

For an address before the seventeenth century the only hope was from clues provided by contemporary historians like John Stow, or by drawing on the painstaking researches of later topographers such as George and Peter Cunningham who had the advantage of working before a great deal of modern demolition. When we read that the notorious Moll Cutpurse lived in Fleet Street 'within two doors of the Globe Tavern over against the Conduit' we were able to go to a sixteenth-century map, locate inn and conduit, impose this on a modern map, and so discover the present site. The exact place where the Gunpowder Plot was hatched, now lost under Barry's nineteenth-century Houses of Parliament, was found in much the same way.

From the seventeenth century onwards parish rate books, notably in Westminster, have helped locate houses owned or leased by infamous persons. One of the most gratifying discoveries was a Soho address for Casanova. His biographers have searched in vain, yet it should not have been too difficult had they gone to the rate books. In his *Mémoires* Casanova says his landlady in Greek Street was Suzanne Mercier. We found her at what today is No. 47.

Another elusive character was Kitty Fisher, the scandalous eighteenth-century beauty, who carried on her trade in Carrington Street, Mayfair. That much was known. But where exactly did she live in that much-altered little street off Shepherd Market? She is not mentioned in the rate books, but from them we learnt that in the years 1763–5 a 'Mistress Martin' was in the fifth house on the collector's route. Martin was the name of Kitty's protector, but what clinched it was when we found the collector had noted in the margin that he was paid by someone called 'Fisher'.

Unfortunately not all rate books have been preserved: those for two important boroughs, Kensington and Lewisham, were incinerated during the last war. The loss of the Lewisham books prevented us from discovering the late nineteenth-century house in Jew's Walk, Sydenham, where Eleanor Marx killed herself. For finally locating it we have to thank a German journalist, who visited several houses in the road and from Eleanor's own descriptions of the view from her window identified her home as No. 7: a particular tree and a Victorian pillar box were deciding factors.

One address eluded us for months. It was particularly maddening because without it we couldn't include one of the most extraordinary swindlers of all time. Oscar Merril Hartzell, an American citizen who came to London early in the 1920s, carried out his massive deception of the gullible for ten years. But we could find no address for him in conventional sources and no file in the Public Record Office.

As a last resort we telephoned the Home Office, remembering that when the law finally caught up with him he had been sent back to the United States for trial. We asked Mr Plunkett in the Extraditions Office in Croydon if a deportation order carried an address. He wasn't sure. If it didn't, then how, we asked, did the police execute the order? Good question. Could anything be on file of someone deported not last week, or even last year, but fifty-three years ago? He was sceptical but would find out. A week later Mr Plunkett jubilantly reported back that the Home Office still had the records, and he gave us Hartzell's address in Knightsbridge. The Iowa State Historical Department confirmed and expanded on the information.

Since Richard Horwood published the first London map with individual house numbers in 1799, a great many streets have been renamed, renumbered and drastically rebuilt. Fortunately the Greater London Council had a section in its Department of Architecture and Civic Design in Vauxhall Bridge Road where files and detailed maps record progressive changes. These enabled us to pinpoint exact sites of buildings in streets such as Park Lane, which since it was numbered in the eighteenth century has been renumbered twice. In this way we found the renumbered Bond Street house of the impostor Olivia Serres and the Harley Street rendezvous of the outrageous Jane Digby and an Austrian diplomat.

Some living persons awarded Black Plaques may have hoped that their past misdeeds were buried or purged. We apologise if they are upset because we have not followed the same circumspect Blue Plaque rule that a person should be dead for twenty years before being given recognition. We also hope that in identifying houses where bad people had once lived we do not embarrass innocent residents at these addresses today. We make a strong plea that their privacy should not be invaded.

The original idea of Black Plaques for London came from Mr Louis Kirby, former Editor of the *London Evening Standard* in which some thirty of the present 189 examples appeared in abbreviated form. We are grateful to him and thank him for his permission to include photographs taken by *Standard* photographers, notably Denis Jones and Paul Massey, which help to illustrate this book.

When Black Plaques first appeared as a newspaper series there was a courteous protest from Ralph Wade who wrote to point out that plaques of this colour actually exist in Hampstead where they have been put up for many years on the houses of the great and good. We apologise for invading his territory with ugly reminders of Ethel le Neve, Thomas J. Wise, Peter Rachman and Emil Savundra.

People interested to discover more about individuals will find sources in the Personalised Bibliography. As well as such expected reference books as the *Dictionary of National Biography* and the *Survey of London*, we have drawn information from *Post Office Directories* (now *Kelly's*), *Names of Streets and Places in the Administrative County of London* (published by the LCC, and covering 1856–1954), Electoral Rolls, Census Returns, newspaper files, especially of *The Times*, and the *Murderers' Who's Who* by J.H.H. Gaute and Robin Odell (with excellent bibliography). We have constantly and gratefully kept within reach *Scenes of Murder* by David Cargill and Julian Holland, an invaluable topographical book which for legal reasons Heinemann withdrew on the eve of publication in 1964.

Local History libraries have come to our aid, and we would especially like to thank Julian Watson at Greenwich and John Coulter at Lewisham; librarians especially at Westminster, Chiswick, Hampstead and Holborn; David Webb of the Bishopsgate Institute and Bob Pike at Hither Green Library. We much appreciate assistance received from the Greater London Record Office and History Archives at Clerkenwell, the Guildhall Library, the India Office Library, and, as always, from the invaluable London Library.

We gratefully acknowledge help from Ralph Hyde, Keeper of Prints and Maps at Guildhall, and his opposite number, John Phillips, at the Greater London Record Office. Valuable suggestions and help have also come from A.S. Adams, Alan Brien, Susan Harris, Kendall McDonald, Nigel Swift, J.F. Whelpton and Lowell R. Wilbur, and keen scrutiny from Patricia Still.

It becomes increasingly clear that no book on London can be written without the help of Peter Jackson, to whom we are grateful for his many suggestions and for generously providing ideas for illustrations from his famous London collection.

To Anthea Barker we offer affectionate thanks for advice, for reading text and proofs, and for her long-suffering exposure to evil which has not yet sent her along the Primrose Path.

— 1 —

The Strand and Covent Garden

OUR journey down the paths of infamy starts at Charing Cross. In search of Black Plaques we travel along the Strand and back through Covent Garden to Whitehall. Thirteen buildings deserve the dark distinction of a plaque in this area but, unlike more residential districts we shall visit later, there are no discernible houses among them. For the last 150 years this part of London has been predominantly commercial.

After the Great Fire, a growing population moved west out of the City and in the late seventeenth century Covent Garden became briefly fashionable, and then, in the eighteenth century, disreputable. With the building of Aldwych and Kingsway in the early 1900s thousands of homes in the surrounding neighbourhood were destroyed. To discover the sites of many houses and lodgings once lived in by the notorious sets problems. Demolition and austere rebuilding make it hard to trace to their actual doors people like Nell Gwyn, Titus Oates and William Ireland, the Shakespeare forger.

Our starting point is in itself rather unexpected – Charing Cross Station – but this is somehow appropriate. Many journeys begin at railway stations, and for years Charing Cross has been regarded as the centre of London, the place from which all distances are measured.

On Friday, 6 May 1927, a trunk was deposited at the Left Luggage office at CHARING CROSS STATION. It was soon to be the most famous trunk in London.

Within a week a picture was in the papers along with a detailed description: 31 inches long, 23 inches deep and 19 inches wide; made of wickerwork and shiny black American cloth; black iron fittings; white canvas lining. The label with an address in Sussex looked innocent enough but the contents were not.

The weather was warm and by Tuesday, four days later, an unpleasant smell was traced to the trunk. An official who was summoned pulled a face. There was only one explanation, he told a colleague – a dead body. He was going to call the police.

A detective-sergeant, Leonard Burt, later to become a famous Commander at Scotland Yard, arrived at the station and removed the offending trunk to Westminster Mortuary where it was examined by the pathologist, Bernard Spilsbury. The contents were not a pretty sight. A woman's body had been cut up and the dismembered limbs wrapped in four paper parcels.

At first the 'Charing Cross Trunk Murder' appeared the perfect crime. What better way of anonymously disposing of a body? The police had only a few leads, but laundry marks on the clothes identified the woman as Minnie Bonati, aged 37. Separated from her husband, an Italian waiter, she had been a cook living at various addresses with different men. Newspaper appeals led to a trunk shop in Brixton, and produced a driver who had been hailed in the Vauxhall Bridge Road. He had driven round to 86 Rochester Row where he helped to load a heavy trunk into the front of his cab. This had been brought downstairs from an estate agent's office.

The office, just opposite Rochester Row Police Station, was a small one-man business rented two months earlier by someone called JOHN ROBINSON. The police issued a description: age, about 35; medium height, rather good-looking with a small moustache. This tallied with descriptions given by the taxi driver and the man who had sold the trunk.

It did not take long to trace Robinson to De Laune Street, Kennington, but he denied all knowledge of the murder. The police had searched the office but had no definite evidence to prove that Minnie Bonati had been killed or cut up there.

Detectives returned to Rochester Row and during a further search found a vital clue in the best tradition of detective fiction: a bloodstained matchstick. This was at the bottom of a wastepaper basket and they deduced that, having cut up the body, Robinson had scrupulously cleaned away all traces of his crime, but before, or while, doing so he had lit a cigarette. Carelessly he had thrown away the tell-tale match.

Robinson, a former clerk who had ambitiously started on his own as an estate agent, confessed that he had met Minnie Bonati at Victoria Station and taken her up to his office for sex. There was a quarrel, presumably about payment. To prevent her shouts being heard he had stifled them with a cushion and she had suffocated.

Had Robinson immediately gone to the police, reported what had happened and pleaded that he had no intention of killing her, he might have got away with manslaughter. But because of the callous, systematic cutting up of her body, the neat wrapping up of the pieces and the way he tried to dispose of the trunk he was found guilty of murder and hanged.

Three hundred yards from Charing Cross on the same side of the Strand is SHELL MEX HOUSE where KLAUS FUCHS was arrested. The climax of one of the most damaging cases of modern treachery was carried out with scientific detachment free of all drama.

A gloomy courtyard gives on to the entrance of the building where in 1950 the Ministry of Supply still retained their wartime premises. Here at 2.30 p.m. on 2 February of that year Fuchs, the German-born naturalised British physicist, had an appointment in the office of the Atomic Energy Division of the Ministry. It was a meeting which led to his fourteen-year sentence for espionage.

Fuchs, just 38, and Deputy Chief Officer at the Harwell Atomic Energy Establishment, came up to London by train from Didcot. His visit was arranged over the telephone and he freely agreed to go to Shell Mex House.

In December of the previous year he had been informed that he was known to have passed information to the Russians in New York. Fuchs confessed that he had been in touch with Soviet contacts from 1942 onwards – a period covering the conception, construction and explosion of the atom bomb. He had accepted £100 as a 'symbol of his subservience'.

The Shell Mex House rendezvous was fixed to save him being arrested at Harwell (where his staff knew nothing of the investigation). The time of the appointment was not strictly kept. Some technical difficulties caused a small delay. The Prime Minister, Mr Attlee, involved in a General Election, had to be informed, and the Attorney General, Sir Hartley Shawcross, returning from the north of England, had to decide on the exact form of the charge. So it was about 3.20 p.m when police and Fuchs faced each other. Only when he was charged before being taken to Bow Street did Fuchs seem fully conscious of what would happen to him, and his round, spectacled face went grey.

His crime of betraying secrets on four occasions between 1943 and 1947 was described by Lord Goddard at his trial as 'only thinly differentiated from high treason', and he was gaoled.

After serving nine years he earned full remission and was

released from Wakefield Prison on 22 June 1959. His British nationality had been removed on grounds of disloyalty and, though as a stateless person he could not be deported, he was put on a plane to East Berlin. He was appointed Deputy Director of the East German Institute for Nuclear Physics at Rossendorf, near Dresden, at a salary of £12,000 a year.

Our next plaque is at the SAVOY. Any international hotel has more scandals than the house detective would care to admit. Most are discreetly disposed of like soiled linen down the laundry chute. For the manager the ultimate nightmare comes when he has to call the police and an agitated hall porter rings through to announce that Fleet Street is camping out in the foyer.

There could be no question of covering up the incident that took place around 2 a.m. at the Savoy Hotel on 10 July 1923. Three shots were fired in Suite 41 on the fourth floor. To lend colour to the drama a wild thunderstorm was at its height but this did not prevent the head porter, John Beattie, who was passing the door, from hearing the shots. A few moments earlier he had been somewhat alarmed when a man had come out of the room, a scratch on his chin, and said to him: 'Look at my face! Look what she has done!' Before the door closed Beattie caught a glimpse of a petite dark woman in a white evening gown.

The porter ran back to the suite. Inside, the man, now lying on the floor, was suffering considerably more than a scratch. Blood was pouring from the head of ALI KAMEL FAHMY BEY. His wife, Marie-Marguerite, was putting down a pistol.

The night manager, Arthur Mariani, was summoned. According to him, Mme Fahmy gave him the sobbing explanation, 'Oh, sir, I have been married six months. They have been torture to me. I have suffered horribly.' Such dialogue, one feels, deserved the accompanying obbligato of a thunderclap.

The hotel tried not to shudder at headlines like 'FRENCH WIFE CHARGED WITH MURDER OF PLAYBOY EGYPTIAN HUSBAND', and 'SAVOY SHOOTING WHILE STORM RAGES'. These were inflammatory enough, but when Edward Marshall Hall came to defend Mme Fahmy he built up a picture of her marital life that was as melodramatic as the killing itself.

The murdered man was Egyptian of twenty-two. Whether he was really a prince is uncertain – Bey is an imprecise title – but undoubtedly he was extremely rich. He had met his future wife the year before in Paris – she was then Mme Laurent, a divorcée ten

The Savoy Hotel overlooking the Embankment. Mme Fahmy, left, a Moslem convert, shot her husband, an Egyptian prince, in a suite on the fourth floor.

years his senior – and had followed her to Deauville. They had lived together until she became a Moslem and they were able to marry.

They had arrived at the Savoy with a secretary, a valet and a maid, and at supper on the night of the shooting there had been a prolonged quarrel. They had gone to their room at 1.30 a.m.

Pale and dressed in deep mourning at her Old Bailey trial, Mme Fahmy looked suitably pathetic. She told of being forced to change her religion; of how Fahmy had been after her money; how he had hit her and kicked her, dislocated her jaw and had once locked her in a cabin on board ship. A policeman in charge of Mme Fahmy during her early detention, writing years later, described her husband as a 'brutal pervert who treated his wife like a white slave'. There were implications of a homosexual relationship between Fahmy and his secretary and the court was told of her husband's 'vicious and eccentric sexual appetites'.

Mme Fahmy, speaking in French through an interpreter (which may have accounted for the unconvincing dialogue), said that when she and her husband got to their suite he had threatened to kill her. As a precaution she had loaded a gun which he had given her. In doing so she put one shot through the window. The prince came to attack her and the gun had again gone off – this time killing him.

Marshall Hall produced this as evidence that Mme Fahmy was ignorant of guns. She had fired, he insisted, not in self-defence or intending to maim: she had pulled the trigger accidentally. The reason for the *third* shot seems to have been conveniently ignored. The artful defence of the renowned advocate secured Mme Fahmy's acquittal. The Savoy breathed again.

Recent research has revealed that two very surprising names, CÉSAR RITZ and AUGUSTE ESCOFFIER, may also be due for a Black Plaque at the Savoy.

Perhaps the best-known names in hotel history, Ritz, then aged 38, and Escoffier, 42, were brought to London by Richard D'Oyly Carte from Cannes for the opening of the Savoy in 1888. Nine years later Ritz, the manager, and Escoffier, the legendary chef, left the hotel. They were said to have resigned 'for personal reasons'. It is now believed that they were dismissed.

Copies of what appear to be signed confessions by the two men were found in the early 1980s. Escoffier admitted taking £8,000 in commissions and Ritz was accused of using the hotel to further his own private business enterprises. All this was hushed up by the Savoy to avoid a scandal.

Ritz and Escoffier went straight to their new hotel, the Carlton in the Haymarket, and Ritz started his world-wide syndicate which included the Ritz, Piccadilly. Both achieved great fame before Ritz, a manic depressive, died in a Swiss clinic in 1918 and Escoffier, more or less penniless, in Monte Carlo in 1938.

A quarter of a mile separates Shell Mex House where Fuchs was arrested and KING'S COLLEGE, also in the Strand, where four years earlier another traitor, ALAN NUNN MAY, was apprehended for giving information to a foreign power – microscopic samples of uranium were passed by him to a Russian agent in Canada. Fuchs had received £100; May, a few dollars and a bottle of whisky.

As in the Fuchs case (p. 15), there was no fuss, no guns, no melodrama. Dr Nunn May had been lecturing on nuclear physics on the cold late afternoon of 4 March 1946 when Chief Inspector William Whitehead of the Special Branch arrived at the college. Nunn May's actual confession had been made a fortnight earlier. The doctor was quite calm when he was confronted outside the lecture room. 'I was expecting something like this,' he said quietly. To avoid embarrassment he was asked to step out of King's for his formal arrest before being taken to Bow Street to be charged under the Official Secrets Act.

Nunn May made no comment then; pleaded guilty at his trial, and before being sentenced to ten years' imprisonment told the judge that he had nothing to say.

He was released from Wakefield Prison on 29 December 1952. For the next ten years he researched metal fatigue in Cambridge and then became a professor of physics in Ghana.

Eight houses down from the Strand at 55 NORFOLK STREET a young man, WILLIAM HENRY IRELAND, carried out a remarkable literary imposture. In February 1795 some manuscripts were put on display at this modest terraced building owned by his father, Samuel Ireland, an engraver and bibliophile. Norfolk Street became a place of pilgrimage. Among thousands who examined the manuscripts was the future Prince Regent. James Boswell went down on his knees, kissed the relics and thanked God that he had lived to see them.

The cause of the furore was the announcement a few months earlier that William Ireland, who was only 18, had discovered a collection of papers written by Shakespeare and also a lock of the playwright's hair. He said he had found them in an old chest in the house of a gentleman he had met. Among them were early drafts of *Kynge Leare* and *Hamblette*, love poems from Shakespeare to 'Anna Hatherewaye', and two unknown plays, *Vortigern* and *Henry II*.

Completely believing his son's story, the delighted Samuel Ireland exhibited the documents at Norfolk Street. They were inspected by seventeen leading literary experts who testified they were genuine. Sheridan, anxious to revive the fortunes of the Theatre Royal, Drury Lane, decided to stage *Vortigern*, the drama of a fifth-century British chief with an incestuous passion for his daughter.

Mrs Siddons refused to appear and the actor John Philip Kemble, Sheridan's manager, made no secret of the fact that he thought the play spurious. On the eve of the production a caustic inquiry into the play's authenticity was published. But the performance went ahead in a crowded theatre to an audience who found the language increasingly unconvincing. In Act V when Kemble, playing Vortigern, came to the ominous line 'And when this solemn mockery is o'er...' there was a burst of laughter. Ribaldry continued until the end of the play.

The mocking reception ended the credulity which had lasted for over a year. Driven to desperation the young Ireland confessed. He had obtained blank pages of ancient paper from booksellers and had purchased ink treated to simulate age. The two plays were to be forerunners of a complete cycle based on every reign not covered by Shakespeare – from William the Conqueror to Queen Elizabeth.

His confession made, Ireland disappeared for many years, and the rest of his life was spent in fairly mundane literary work. He was always proud to have pos-

William Ireland, 18-year-old Shakespeare forger.

sessed the skill to carry out the forgeries. He died at Sussex Place, St George's-in-the-Fields, in 1835.

All traces of the Norfolk Street house where William Ireland deceived London have disappeared with the street itself. Two parallel streets – Arundel Street and Surrey Street – still survive between the Strand and the Embankment but the intervening, now demolished Norfolk Street is covered by modern Arundel House.

Norfolk Street disappeared in 1972 but more devastating changes took place at this end of the Strand in Edwardian times following the building of Aldwych. Among the casualties was narrow little Wych Street, with overhanging Elizabethan buildings, which ran diagonally from St Clement Dane's in the Strand to join the south end of Drury Lane. This part of Drury Lane also went during the alterations along with countless houses, streets and alleys that were replaced by Bush House, Australia House and India House. Kingsway took a further toll.

Romantic legend always represents Nell Gwyn as selling oranges in Drury Lane. She may well have done so, and it is possible that the Cock and Magpie public house at 91 Drury Lane (one of the Aldwych casualties) was where she lived at one time. Her presumed birthplace in Coal Yard, higher up on the right, is now lost under Stukeley Street. Nell Gwyn always had an acquisitive eye for property. Sandford Manor, Fulham, is another house she may have owned, but we shall have to wait until we reach Pall Mall (p. 40) before awarding her a Black Plaque on her one incontestable and still visible address.

Travelling up Drury Lane there are also difficulties in finding the site of the lodgings lived in by that outrageous perjurer and conspirator TITUS OATES. They were in COCKPITT ALLEY (later Pitt Street), named after the Restoration theatre, and replaced on the right-hand side by the Peabody Estate. The house was in the centre of the courtyard that lies between Drury Lane and Wild Street.

Even before he rigged the anti-Popish plot that has made him infamous, Titus Oates showed dark promise by being expelled from Merchant Taylors' school and by running into debt at Cambridge. 'A great dunce', he came down without a degree, though he later bestowed one upon himself. He managed to 'slip into orders' and while a curate at All Saints, Hastings, he trumped up a false charge of sodomy against a local schoolmaster. He was then imprisoned but escaped and, to avoid arrest, took berth as a chaplain in a naval vessel bound for Tangier. From this post he was discharged for immorality of the kind he had imputed to the schoolmaster.

'In a word,' wrote a contemporary (who found one word insufficient) 'he was a most consummate cheat, blasphemer, vicious perjurer, impudent and saucy foul-mouthed wretch ...' These disqualifications did not prevent Oates rising from total obscurity to a position in which he was listened to by the Privy Council and the King. This he achieved in 1678 by fanning easily ignited suspicions against Roman Catholics. With another anti-Jesuit, Israel Tonge, he fabricated a plot against the Papists, warning Charles II that he was to be assassinated while walking his spaniels in St James's Park.

At his Drury Lane lodgings and while undergoing a cure for venereal disease, he invented an elaborate story of conspiracy that implicated Spanish Catholics, French Benedictines, Irish and English malcontents. Oates warned that there was to be a massacre of Protestants and (with a cunning use of fictitious detail) that silver bullets would be used to kill the King. Charles II would be replaced by the Catholic Duke of York and a Jesuit government established.

The King was sceptical, but for four years Oates sustained his story of 'a damnable and hellish plot contriv'd and carried out by Popish recusants'. Directly, or indirectly, he was responsible for the arrest and execution of some thirty-five 'suspects'. With great astuteness, a persuasive pulpit manner and limitless self-assurance he kept up the deceit until 1685 when his lies caught up with him and he was denounced and arrested at the Amsterdam Coffee House behind the Royal Exchange. Convicted of perjury, he was

Titus Oates in the pillory.

stripped of his canonical vestments, heavily fined and whipped from Aldgate to Tyburn. The sentence of perpetual imprisonment was only relieved by brief annual releases to stand in the pillory.

Oates remained in the King's Bench Prison, Southwark, for over three years, the first year in irons. Yet, not only did he survive but he managed to father an illegitimate child by his prison bedmaker. He secured his release almost as soon as William of Orange came to the throne. The Protestant King, who saw Oates as one of the instruments of his succession, granted him a pardon, and a pension of £10 a week.

Oates has come to be referred to almost admiringly as a scoundrel, a superior villain and the master of effrontery. He died in 1704, not in Cockpitt Alley, or his next lodgings in Lambeth, but at his final home in Axe Yard (now demolished), a small street in Westminster just south of modern Downing Street.

About 200 yards west of Drury Lane lived another man sentenced to stand in the pillory. But the penance was limited to an hour for EDMUND CURLL, an eighteenth-century publisher of pornographic books whose premises were at 2 BOW STREET, next to Will's Coffee House on the corner of Russell Street.

'The unspeakable Curll', who has been called the father of English pornographic publishing, first fell foul of the authorities in 1719 when he was in his early forties. The book that caused the trouble, a translation from the German, was *A Treatise on the use of Flogging in Venereal Affairs*. Curll protested it was not an immoral book; rather a warning to any who might follow the example of a man who had died as a result of voluntary flagellation in a Fleet Street brothel.

Curll was a great one for dressing up salacity in a blameless guise. His pamphlet-catalogue, *Curlicism Display'd*, though really an advertisement for his books, insisted on their worthy intentions: he contended flogging was a matter of serious concern; as for his volume *Eunuchism Display'd*, it had been written 'by a Person of Honour' and with castrati singing in opera at the Haymarket was surely justified.

A translation from the French in 1724 (which Curll sold but denied publishing) of *Venus in the Cloister or the Nun in her Smock*, along with the book on flogging, brought him to trial before the Court of King's Bench in Westminster Hall. The title was more alluring than the contents, which take the form of imaginary, far from erotic dialogue between two nuns.

Curll was released on bail and did not take the warning. From his press came *The Case of Seduction. . . the late proceedings at Paris against the Rev Abbé des Rues for committing Rapes upon 133 Virgins, written by Himself*. The 'scandalous and seditious' memoirs of a Government spy led to his re-arrest and sentence to the pillory. Curll escaped being pelted with rotten vegetables by arranging to have copies of a pamphlet distributed among the crowd stating that he was being unfairly punished. The memoirs, he insisted, were really a tribute to the memory of the late Queen Anne.

Curll, a tall thin man, white-faced and ungainly, seems not to have been merely a passive pornographer. He was a debauchee and, according to a contemporary, his translators 'lay three in a bed at the Pewter Platter inn in Holborn'. As well as No. 2 Bow Street (opposite the Globe public house), Curll had a shop next to St Dunstan's, Fleet Street, published one book from the Sign of the Pope's Head in Rose Street, Covent Garden, and had another bookshop in an alley off the Strand known as 'Curll's Court'. He died in 1747, two years after publishing *The Pleasures of Coition*.

Actors expect applause. If they are in a very bad play they know they risk being booed. But they may reasonably consider that being stabbed to death is going altogether too far. This, however, is what happened to the popular actor William Terriss, in MAIDEN LANE which runs parallel with the Strand to the south of Covent Garden.

The memorial to this seemingly extreme form of dramatic criticism should be placed by the old royal entrance with a coat of arms over the lintel which is next to the stage door of the Adelphi Theatre. At 7 p.m. on 16 December 1897 Terriss arrived here to play the star role in *Secret Service*, by William Gillette.

He had no warning of any kind, but inside the doorway a small-part actor in the company was waiting for him with a knife. RICHARD PRINCE was insanely convinced that he, not Terriss, should have the leading part. Prince was committed to Broadmoor where he died aged 71 in 1937.

Rather over a hundred years earlier another murder outside a theatre took place in the north-east corner of Covent Garden. Jealousy, but of a different kind, was again the motive.

On 7 April 1779 Martha Ray, mistress of the fourth Earl of Sandwich, was shot as she was getting into her carriage following a performance at COVENT GARDEN THEATRE (at the side of the present Royal Opera House). She was shot by a young clergyman, JAMES

HACKMAN, who had been in love with her for four years.

When she was eighteen Martha Ray, the daughter of a staymaker in Holywell Street, Clerkenwell, became the Earl's permanent mistress. He had separated from his wife. She lived in his home and bore him nine children.

Hackman, who came from Gosport, had been bought an army commission seven years before the tragedy, and it was while he was recruiting in Huntingdon that he was invited into Lord Sandwich's great Tudor house, Hinchingbrooke. Here he met Martha, a woman 'of great sweetness of manner', and apparently immediately fell in love with her. He was 20. She was 30. Her protector was 54.

The situation and ages of the three people suggest a classic triangle with a woman torn between an impecunious young lover and a wealthy older man. It is not easy to be sure about the exact balance of emotions that led to the tragedy because information is based on slightly suspect, conceivably forged, love letters published after the couple's deaths. They build up the romance with accounts of secret meetings when the two were thrown into each other's company and were snowed up for three weeks at Hinchingbrooke. There was apparently an ecstatic night in the village inn at Hockerill near Bishops Stortford.

It may have been a great love affair for both of them, but for Martha there were practical considerations. First she had a responsibility to her protector for whom she felt affection. There were her five surviving children to think of. As she had no financial settlement, a runaway marriage with a penniless young officer would have been a hazardous step.

The need to make up her mind was postponed because Hackman was posted to Ireland for two years though his twice weekly letters remained adoring. When he came home Martha's indecision was hardly lessened when he informed her that he was going to leave the Army and join the Church – a curious move for a man involved with another man's mistress. He was ordained in 1779, just six weeks before the shooting.

By what seemed to him incredible good fortune he was offered a living with a parsonage and a reasonable income at the Norfolk village of Wiverton and wrote to Martha: 'Now my happiness can be deferred no longer. Oh, consent to marry me directly!'

At the very moment when Hackman thought all his hopes would be realised fate took a hand in the person of Signora Galli, a woman who taught Martha singing and was also her close confidante. Acting in what she conceived to be Martha's best interest she got in

James Hackman and his mistress Martha Ray. The vignette below shows him shooting her in Covent Garden Piazza.

touch with Hackman and told him that Martha was tired of him and had taken another lover. The lie had immediate and terrible consequences.

In agonies of jealousy the newly ordained deacon came to London and waited one night outside the Admiralty where Sandwich was First Lord. He saw Martha get into her carriage and followed her to Covent Garden where she was about to attend

Dibdin's operetta *Love in a Village*. His mind made up, with two pistols in his pocket, and drinking brandy, he waited at the Bedford Coffee House in the piazza near the theatre.

Martha came out at eleven. She was in full evening dress, wearing jewellery and with a red rose in her bodice. Hackman pushed through the throng and pulled at her gown as she was getting into her carriage. He shot her through the head and turned the second gun on himself and, when it failed to kill him, attempted to beat out his brains with the butt of the pistol.

At the trial Hackman said he had intended to kill himself and then in an unpremeditated 'momentary frenzy' had shot Martha. The jury pronounced him guilty without retiring, but the judge, the famous Sir William Blackstone, the whole court, subsequent newspaper comment, and the public at large were generally sympathetic to Hackman, the desperately unhappy lover. Lord Sandwich offered to intervene for his life. But Hackman wanted to die and was accompanied to the gallows at Tyburn by the incorrigibly curious Boswell. Inconsolable, Lord Sandwich brought Martha's portrait from Hinchingbrooke to the Admiralty where it still hangs.

Set back at an angle from Garrick Street, the Lamb and Flag public house in ROSE STREET, Covent Garden, was the scene of a violent assault in 1679. The poet Dryden was making his way home from Will's Coffee House in Bow Street when he was waylaid by three ruffians who called him a rogue and the son of a whore. Then they knocked him down.

It was widely believed that the man behind the attack was the EARL OF ROCHESTER, the most profligate figure in the profligate age of the Restoration. His motive was revenge for an insult he considered he had received from the poet.

By the date of the crime, 18 December 1679 (annually commemorated by free drinks in the Dryden Room of the pub if the landlord is prompted), John Wilmot, second Earl of Rochester, was 32 and already worn out by debauchery. An ill man, he had less than eight months to live.

His short, scandalous career may be said to have got under way at Wadham College, Oxford, where he caught venereal disease and had his first homosexual experience with a don. At Padua during a Grand Tour arranged for him by Charles II he was initiated into the refinements of masochism. Returning to England aged seventeen he quickly established himself as a favourite at Court and acted as a 'pimp' (his own word) for Charles II. According to Dr Gilbert

Burnet, the contemporary historian very close to the Court, Rochester enjoyed 'the wildest frolics that a wanton wit could devise'. Burnet also noted: 'Drink was his ruin. He told me that for five years together he was continually drunk.'

Constantly engaged on campaigns of seduction, 'Rake Rochester' kidnapped a woman in a coach at Charing Cross (she later became his wife) but not surprisingly proved too promiscuous, unstable and unfaithful to be much of a husband.

Erotic poetry was his limited forte as a would-be literateur, and, hoping to emulate them, he made friends with men of the theatre – Etherage, Killigrew, Wycherley – and for a while was a patron of John Dryden, whose poetry he admired. But Dryden regarded him as a dangerous friend. He broke with Rochester and came under the patronage of the Earl of Mulgrave. This appears to have led directly to the Rose Street incident. During 1697 an anonymous satirical poem, *An Essay on Satyr*, was being circulated. The author was known to be Mulgrave but Dryden was suspected of being his collaborator. In the poem Rochester was referred to as having a tail and cloven feet. His wit seldom hit its target, according to the writer, and a final couplet went:

So lewdly dull his idle works appear,
The wretched texts deserve no comment here.

Fairly insulting stuff, but hardly, one might think, sufficiently abrasive to trigger off so violent a reprisal as the hiring of thugs. Rochester's responsibility was never proved though a reward of £50 was offered for information and he was highly suspect. A phrase in a letter he wrote would definitely seem to implicate him but this evidence has been challenged. One thing is certain. Whether it should go up outside the Lamb and Flag or, for more general reasons, elsewhere, the Earl of Rochester deserves his Black Plaque.

Highwaymen somehow seem out of place in London. They should be going about their unlawful business on Hounslow Heath or the Cambridge Road. But there have been exceptions. James Mclean, who lodged in St James's posing as an Irish squire, held up Horace Walpole in Hyde Park; Dick Turpin is remembered, if dimly, at the Red Lion, Whitechapel Road (p. 235); and CLAUDE DUVAL was arrested in CHANDOS STREET.

We don't know exactly how, but one January night in 1670,

The Lamb and Flag off Garrick Street where Dryden was attacked.

Was the Earl of Rochester responsible?

Duval came to be taken at the Hole-in-the-Wall public house (now the Marquis of Granby) on the corner of Bedfordbury. Unwisely he had ventured back to England from France where he had taken refuge when things became too hot for him. There was still a price on his head when he reached London and he was drunk.

Duval was the prototype of those gallant Gentlemen of the Road whom John Gay took as models for Macheath in *The Beggar's Opera*. Born in Normandy in 1643, he went to Paris when he was 14 and came to England at the Restoration in the service of the third Duke of Richmond. He did not long remain a footman; daring robberies soon made him a byword in Highgate, Islington and Holloway, and one exploit led to a road being named Duval Lane, Hampstead (now Platt's Lane). The following story smacks of romantic historical fiction but is vouched for by Macaulay:

> The highwayman holds up a lady's coach on the edge of the heath and while he is relieving her of booty worth £400 she, with remarkable coolness, plays on the flageolet. Entranced, Duval invites her to dance with him at the roadside which she does with her powerless husband looking on in fury. When Duval rides away he takes only £100.

There is a possible clue why Duval came to be at the Chandos Street tavern. The Hole-in-the-Wall (named after the still existing passageway alongside the Coliseum Theatre) was also known as Mother Mabberley's, and was run by a former mistress of the Duke of Buckingham. Both she and Duval would have been members of the coterie of returned Restoration exiles that included Buckingham and the Duke of Richmond.

Tried on six indictments, Duval was condemned to death. A number of great ladies are said to have interceded for his life (Charles II expressly declined a pardon) and his hanging led to demonstrations by crowds of all ranks, which were only stopped by a judge's order.

Duval was carried from Tyburn to St Giles-in-the-Fields and his body given an almost royal lying-in-state at the Tangier Tavern followed by a funeral at St Paul's, Covent Garden, with flambeaux lighting a long procession. He was buried under the central aisle of the church but no trace remains of the stone inscribed with the epitaph:

> *Here lies Du Vall: Reader, if man thou art,*
> *Look to thy purse; if female, to thy heart.*

From Chandos Street we cross the Strand to find what little survives of a street where, in July 1885, people queued to buy copies of the *Pall Mall Gazette*. 'The crowd raged and wrestled, fought with fist and feet, tooth and nail, clamouring for the sheets wet from the Presses . . .' wrote the triumphant editor as he watched the reaction to his series of articles, *The Maiden Tribute of Modern Babylon*. Interest in each sensational instalment was so great and distribution so difficult – W.H. Smith would not handle the paper – that copies bought for a penny could almost immediately be resold for twelve times the price.

The offices of the Gazette were at 2 NORTHUMBERLAND STREET, on the east side. Now demolished and replaced by a modern building, there is nothing to show where W.T. STEAD published what he ardently hoped would be a great exposé of Victorian immorality.

Stead, bearded, red-haired and excitable, involved himself in a dangerous charade for which he was sent to prison. Prison does not necessarily brand a campaigning journalist a villain. He might have been a hero had he not gone too far. He had a great story but he couldn't resist improving on the facts and falsifying them.

Child prostitution was the dominant sexual scandal of the times and the worst feature of the trade was the procuring of young virgins for private customers, for brothels and export abroad. Stead wrote with righteous relish about 'a London Minotaur' whose 'quantum of virgins from his procuresses was three a fortnight'.

Even with the co-operation of reformers, the authorities seemed powerless to curb this traffic. To supply evidence Stead decided to buy a girl of thirteen from her mother, have her certified as a virgin, and then introduced into a London brothel, and afterwards sent abroad to one in France. There was to be an important variation from actual fact: once the purchase was made and the medical examination completed, Stead would only pretend to put her into a brothel and when she arrived in Paris she would be taken to the Salvation Army.

The girl chosen was Eliza Armstrong who lived with her father and mother in a slum house in Marylebone. The transaction was carried out for Stead by a former brothel keeper, now a reformed woman converted by the Salvation Army. The parents were paid £5.

The 'purchase' and medical examination were real; but Eliza's removal for seduction to a notorious Poland Street address was a

Campaigning editor William Stead. His exposure of Victorian child prostitution brought crowds to the Northumberland Street offices of The Pall Mall Gazette.

charade; so too was her export abroad (leaving for Paris from Charing Cross where Stead acted the role of 'white slaver').

In his articles, eagerly snatched up in Northumberland Street, Stead called Eliza 'Lily' which was a reasonable precaution to hide her real identity: but he grossly exaggerated other details. He represented the girl's mother as a drunkard, the father as a wife-beater and their one-room home as a brothel. He stated that Mrs Armstrong *knew* she was selling Eliza for sexual purposes. He thought this vital to the story, but later in court the mother insisted that she understood the girl was to become a domestic servant.

During the three months of controversy that followed publication Stead was praised by some reformers but vilified by others. Most papers were against him, especially the rival *St James's Gazette* which condemned the articles as 'the vilest parcel of obscenity that has ever yet issued from the public press'.

Stead and those who had assisted him were charged at the Old Bailey with unlawfully taking an unmarried girl under the age of 16 out of the possession of her mother and father. They pleaded not guilty on the grounds that there was no criminal intent but this was brushed aside by the judge who said the issue was the actual abduction. Stead was given three months' imprisonment, a sentence in which he gloried ('I shall make no appeal . . . I will take my punishment and I shall not flinch') and celebrated each subsequent anniversary by travelling on his commuter train to London in his convict clothes. As a moralist Stead was a great actor.

As a campaigner he was an undoubted word-spinner. He followed up his London exposé by publishing in America *If Christ Came to Chicago* and *Satan's Invisible World Displayed* (about New York). But Stead forfeited much of the credit due to him for *The Maiden Tribute* by falling into the journalistic trap of excessive and unnecessary embellishment of facts. He died as dramatically as he wrote, drowned on the *Titanic*, a disaster he predicted but failed to avoid.

Across the top of Northumberland Avenue, and a few yards down Whitehall, facing the Whitehall Theatre, is a narrow alleyway. It leads into a small courtyard, a lost backwater in which can be discerned traces of buildings constructed after the Whitehall Palace fire of 1698. Around CRAIG'S COURT were half-a-dozen Georgian houses – all now rebuilt or refaced – which became the focus of unusual excitement when constables followed by sightseers arrived on a September morning in 1748.

The exact building where TERESIA CONSTANTIA PHILLIPS was then living is uncertain, but our Black Plaque will probably not be far out on the back of what is now the Old Shades public house. When the officer knocked, the crowd hoped Mrs Phillips would come to the door or at least appear at the window. There was great curiosity to see the author of a just published volume of memoirs. It was spiced with accounts of her seductions, liaisons, broken marriages, court cases and imprisonment.

Teresia, generally known as 'Con', was notorious but she could boast plausible family connections. Her father had been a captain in the Grenadiers and the godmother who brought her up was the Duchess of Bolton. Now nearly 40, Mrs Phillips was regarded as a formidable litigant. Apprehending her might cause trouble. Thirteen constables, she boasted, were sent to arrest her in Craig's Court.

They had orders to convey her to Newgate – the charge would seem to have been for debt – but Mrs Phillips managed to stand firm. She even capitalised on the proceedings. Observing the gathering in the courtyard she let it be known that she would gladly sell copies of her book *An Apology for the Conduct of Mrs Teresia Constantia Phillips*.

Special piquancy was given to the memoirs because, among accounts of many amours, Con related how, when she was little more than 12, she had been seduced by the young Lord Stanhope, now the fourth Earl of Chesterfield. This brief liaison twenty-seven years previously might have been of no great consequence had not Chesterfield become a distinguished statesman recently appointed a Secre-

Teresia Constantia Phillips. She sold her scandalous memoirs from her Whitehall window.

tary of State, and had he not already written the first in the series of famous letters of moral guidance to his natural son Philip.

In her so-called 'Apologia' Con not only related that she had been procured and deserted by Chesterfield, she told of her later marriage to escape debt, her next marriage to a Dutch merchant, a suit for bigamy, trials involving shooting and adultery and her disappearance to Paris with a lover. Another titled lover, she boasted, tried to stab himself when she threatened to leave him. Though he never admitted being Con's *first* seducer, Chesterfield had offered her £200 to keep his name out of her memoirs. She asked for £500 and when he refused she went ahead and published.

As the rate books do not mention her by name, Mrs Phillips does not appear to have remained long at Craig's Court. When next we hear of her she had retired from the immediate fray and had left London for Jamaica. Before her death in 1765 she married a further three times – an Irishman, a Scot and a French officer. During carnival time in Kingston she was elected Mistress of the Revels. It seems a suitable title.

2

Trafalgar Square to St James's

WHEN we cross Trafalgar Square and enter Pall Mall by way of Cockspur Street we are more or less following the line of the ancient highway which ran west from the village of Charing to St James's Palace and beyond. With the creation of Pall Mall as a street in 1661 and the development of the fields to the north into St James's Square during the following decade, both street and square became fashionable places in which to live. They also attracted royal and upper-class indiscretions.

Outside 116 PALL MALL (now the Institute of Directors) a man was shot dead on the Sunday evening of 12 February 1682. His killers were tracked down and the next month were executed on the same spot in a symbolic act of retribution. They were a CAPTAIN VRATZ, a Swede LIEUTENANT STERN, and a Pole named BOROSKI who actually carried the gun. But the person really responsible, COUNT CHARLES JOHN KONIGSMARCK, was tried and acquitted. It was an altogether very strange affair.

The murdered man was Thomas Thynne who had become extremely rich on inheriting Longleat in Wiltshire. On the night he was shot he was returning home after supper with the Duke of Monmouth. Although only in his mid-thirties Thynne was described as 'a well-battered rake' and in the previous summer, 1681, he had married a rich heiress of 14, Elizabeth, daughter of the Earl of Northumberland. Because of her age, the marriage was not consummated and she was sent abroad to stay in Hanover where it seems likely she once again met Count Konigsmarck whom she had first encountered when he had come to London a year or two before.

The Count, a naturalised Swede of German extraction, and a soldier of fortune, had decided that Elizabeth would make him a perfect wife. He does not seem to have been simply a fortune hunter; about 20, and with a fair amount of money, he may well

The Pall Mall attack on Thynne's coach by the confederates of Count Konigsmarck.

have been a gallant suitor. Elizabeth's guardians, however, refused permission. Perhaps they had heard of his previous affairs, including one in Venice with the Duchess of Southampton who travelled with him to France disguised as a boy. More probably they thought Thynne, the master of Longleat, was a better match. The Count returned to the Continent and shortly afterwards he heard that she had been married to Thynne.

Still determined to make Elizabeth his wife, Konigsmarck attempted to solve the impediment of her marriage by twice challenging Thynne to a duel. Thynne not unreasonably declined; if required to fight every man who made advances on their wives, few men would escape a duelling. But Konigsmarck refused to be thwarted and early in 1682 came back to England.

Six weeks after his arrival Captain Vratz, who was in the Count's service, and the two hired accomplices stopped Thynne's coach in Pall Mall. Pointing a blunderbuss through the coach window Boroski shot him dead.

There was an immediate hue-and-cry and the three men were caught within twenty-four hours. Their confessions implicated Konigsmarck, who was arrested at Gravesend when boarding a ship for Sweden in disguise. He was said to be so distraught that he 'started biting his clothes', but there seems to have been little need for him to be so demonstrative. He was subjected to only a superficial examination, shown every courtesy, and given an audience by Charles II at Whitehall. Konigsmarck was acquitted while Thynne's actual assailants were sentenced to death.

In the uproar of public protest that followed the trial, the Count quickly slipped out of the country leaving behind all sorts of wild rumours – political, religious, sexual – to explain the murder. It remains a celebrated historical whodunit that has resisted many latter-day solutions.

Thomas Thynne was buried in Westminster Abbey where his killing is depicted in bas-relief over his tomb. Konigsmarck died honourably in battle four years later. The child widow Elizabeth, clearly a great matrimonial catch, subsequently married the sixth Duke of Somerset and became an influential Whig hostess.

Turning out of Pall Mall, the scene of a modern tragedy confronts us. From one of the central windows on the first floor of the Libyan People's Bureau at 5 ST JAMES'S SQUARE shots were fired on a crowd which included anti-Gaddafi dissidents demonstrating outside. A woman police constable, Yvonne Fletcher, aged 25, was killed. She fell only a few yards from her police constable fiancé. The date was Tuesday, 17 April 1984. The time: 10.18 a.m.

The house had diplomatic immunity during the siege which lasted ten days while the whole square was closed off. The staff were given a deadline to surrender and on 27 April thirty people, including probably the UNNAMED GUNMAN, came out and were taken to Sunningdale en route to Heathrow for a flight to Tripoli. The funeral of Woman Police Constable Fletcher took place at Salisbury Cathedral a few hours later on the same day, and a memorial was raised to her in 1985 on the edge of the central gardens in St James's Square.

The gunman has not been identified. He may have been one of two people known to have escaped through a rear door before the building was sealed by the police or, more probably, was one of the two main suspects among eight non-diplomats whom the police had insufficient time or facilities to interrogate before they departed. The police desperately wanted to find the man guilty of killing their woman colleague but danger of reprisals against Britons in Tripoli frustrated their investigations.

Although it has a reasonably convincing classical facade, 21 ST JAMES'S SQUARE (now combined with No. 20 and owned by the Distillers Company) is actually a reconstruction of the seventeenth-century house which had the dubious distinction of being the residence of two mistresses of James II: ARABELLA CHURCHILL and CATHERINE SEDLEY.

When still Duke of York, James bought the house in trust for Arabella, sister of the Duke of Marlborough, and the liaison, persisting through his second marriage, resulted in four children. Arabella lived there for three years, and when the relationship cooled the house was given to his next favourite, Catherine Sedley.

The daughter of Sir Charles Sedley, rake and playwright, Catherine was young enough to be James's daughter. She came to the house (described by a neighbour as having walls 'of great height because none should look over them') in 1685. This was the year James became King and for a short while he gave up seeing her.

The following year, however, she resumed her role as his mistress, was created Countess of Dorchester, and gave birth to a daughter. At the end of the affair, when James was in exile, Catherine continued to live at No. 21. She married in 1696, vacated the house for several years but later returned with her husband, the Earl of Portmore. When she died there in 1717 the property passed to her daughter, the Duchess of Buckingham, in all probability her child by James II.

As well as Arabella and Catherine, James II had at least five mistresses, a pattern of behaviour which led Charles II to observe: 'I do not believe there are two men who love women more than I do, but my brother, devout as he is, loves them more.'

During the period that James II as Duke of York was maintaining these two ladies in St James's Square, his brother's mistress, NELL GWYN, was living less than a hundred yards away at 79 PALL MALL. Charles II arranged her move there in 1671.

The actress whose debut had taken place at the Theatre Royal, Drury Lane, six years earlier, was still only 21. She displayed great vivacity on the stage, and 'pretty, witty Nell', as Pepys called her, was especially effective when delivering risqué prologues and epilogues. It was after reciting a monologue wearing a hat the size of a cartwheel which, as she was very small, made her look particularly appealing, that King Charles took her to Whitehall for supper.

Her rival was the Duchess of Portsmouth but Nell, the 'indiscreetest and wildest creature that ever was in a court', was always his favourite mistress, maintained at great expense. It was a few months after the birth of Charles, her first son by the King, that she moved from a house in Lincoln's Inn Fields to Pall Mall. The story goes that she was angry at not being given the freehold immediately. When told that she had only a Crown lease, Nell is said to have returned the papers asserting that she would not accept the house until it was conveyed free to her by Parliament – giving as her reason that she had 'always conveyed free under the Crown'.

The property was fully settled on Nell in 1676, and remains the only ground site on the south side of Pall Mall not owned by the Crown. It was to have been inherited by her younger son, James Lord Beauclerk, but as he predeceased her, the property went to her elder son, Charles, Duke of St Albans.

Many houses are associated with Nell Gwyn, but 79 Pall Mall is her one indisputable address. The building we see today is not the actual house in which she lived for sixteen years until her death in 1687.

In 1770 the house was rebuilt, only to be demolished in 1866 when the present building was erected for the Eagle Star Insurance Company. Though deceptively similar, the blue plaque on the facade has been put up privately, not by the Greater London

*Nell Gwyn aged
about twenty.
Charles II gave her a
house on the site of
79 Pall Mall
(extreme right).*

Council. The colour needs, anyway, to be changed to black.

Next door is 80–82 PALL MALL (Schomberg House) with a skilfully reconstructed front to simulate the seventeenth-century original. Among several famous residents were the artist Gainsborough, and for a single year – 1760 – William Augustus, Duke of Cumberland, 'the Butcher of Culloden'. But it is not Cumberland but the dubious DR JAMES GRAHAM who qualifies for a Black Plaque.

Graham's extraordinary practices began in the central part of the house in 1781 at a time when Gainsborough was occupying the west side. In an age of quacks, Graham had no peer. In Pall Mall, this former Edinburgh medical student established the 'Temple of Health and Hymen' which he had previously opened in Adelphi Terrace. The main features were a piece of 'medico-Electrical Apparatus' and 'the grand celestial bed' for which Graham was most celebrated. The bed, supported by forty pillars of glittering glass, could be occupied (for a large fee) by couples hoping for children. Under a mirror-lined dome, covered in coloured sheets and to the sound of music, they would (Graham guaranteed) 'obtain the desire of their lives'; an heir was a certainty.

Among his assistants was a girl of about twenty – Emma Hart (the future Lady Hamilton) – to whom the doctor gave the title of Vestina, Goddess of Health. Emma helped Graham to demonstrate the beneficial effects of mud baths. Both immersed themselves in the liquid mud up to their chins and together must have presented an astonishing picture, the doctor in an enormous wig, and Emma with her hair elaborately dressed with powder, flowers and feathers and wearing two ropes of pearls on her neck and naked breasts.

At 'The Elisium', as Graham described his house after its redecoration in 1783, a 'very celebrated Lecture on Generation' was delivered by him from 'The Celestial Throne'. In 'The Suite of Apartments in this Elysian Palace' people were promised soul-transporting experiences. As a sporting alternative, and presumably in quite different rooms, cards were played. When legal action was taken, naming it as a common gaming house, attempts were made to bribe the prosecution witnesses.

Elixirs were on sale at huge prices, among them Imperial Pills, Electrical Aether and Nervous Aethereal Balsom (for decayed and worn-out constitutions). But these exalted remedies could not help the man who prescribed them. By 1787 Graham had become a religious fanatic. Styling himself 'The Servant of the Lord O.W.L.'

(the initials stood for 'Oh! Wonderful Love'), he was committed to a lunatic asylum. He died in Edinburgh in 1794.

Over a hundred years later that flamboyant, extravagant character HORATIO BOTTOMLEY moved into a building on the other side of the street. Between 1879 and 1912 the founder, editor and trenchant campaigner of *John Bull* had a luxurious apartment at 56a PALL MALL, now Quadrant House. In what was described as 'a den of iniquity' the arch-swindler enjoyed his period of greatest affluence. In a vividly coloured dressing gown, he breakfasted off kippers and champagne. Rarely far from his side was one of the mistresses; these he kept much as he did a string of racehorses at his sumptuous Sussex home.

Bottomley was born in 1860. His early years were spent in an orphanage from which he ran away to become an errand boy in a solicitor's office. The first of his many bankruptcies and charges of fraud followed his publication of a suburban weekly newspaper in Hackney. Undeterred, he floated a series of Australian gold mining companies and by the time he was 37 he had made £3,000,000. A company director owning fifty businesses, he had sixty-seven bankruptcy writs filed against him in five years.

John Bull, started in 1906 – so named because he said it suggested 'common sense, warm blood and no humbug' – was Bottomley's main claim to fame. He was a powerful journalist, the Member of Parliament for South Hackney and an eloquent speaker in public, but even though his magazine was highly successful he seemed unable to resist dishonesty. Competitions were rigged; there were countless minor swindles; big firms were attacked and intimidated until they bought advertising.

During the Great War the magazine helped to promote Bottomley's Victory Bond Club which amassed him £900,000, but when thousands of small investors, many of them struggling ex-servicemen, came to cash their certificates, they found their money had disappeared. His conviction for fraudulent conversion led to a sentence of seven years' imprisonment.

After his release in 1927 Bottomley fought back briefly. But within a few years he was reduced to drawing the old age pension, and in 1932 – the most ignominious experience of all – he appeared at the Windmill Theatre. A patiently enduring mistress, Peggy Primrose, found him the engagement.

Evening dress hanging on his shrunken figure, the once bombastic speaker walked slowly to the middle of the stage where

Schomberg House
(right) where the
Scottish quack, Dr.
James Graham, seen in
pursuit of a woman
(below), conducted
profitable potency
treatments using the
'Grand Celestial Bed'
(left) assisted by
Emma, the future
Lady Hamilton.

he struggled to tell stories of the past. But the old names and long-dead controversies meant nothing to an audience waiting impatiently for the nudes. They found him neither comic nor even particularly pathetic: just dull. The strain was too much; he collapsed. It was for all the world like the bathetic end to an Emil Jannings film of the period. Bottomley was 72 when he died on 28 May 1933.

If we leave Pall Mall for St James's Street, a turn on the left takes us into a pleasant little street which retains much of the Georgian charm that would have been familiar to JOHN CLELAND. The author of probably the most famous pornographic novel ever written, Cleland was living at 37 ST JAMES'S PLACE when *Memoirs of the Life of Fanny Hill* was published in 1749.

Variously described as 'the first masterpiece of English pornography', 'the best erotic work in the language' and 'a scandalously indecent book' (by the Dictionary of National Biography), *Fanny Hill* contains scenes of seduction, attempted rape, varied forms of intercourse, flagellation, lesbianism and homosexuality.

The fictitious autobiography of a Liverpool girl of low parentage who comes to London and at 15 starts a life of sin in a brothel was written by Cleland in the Fleet Prison. Aged 40, he was serving a sentence for debt after an unsuccessful career as a minor official in India and a period of drifting about Europe. He said he wrote the book out of boredom.

The author was paid only twenty guineas though the bookseller in St Paul's Churchyard to whom he sold the copyright is reputed to have made £10,000 from the sales. Cleland's main reward was to be summoned before the Privy Council whose President, the cultivated Lord Granville, was curious to discover how he had come to produce such a work. He escaped punishment by pleading that he had been forced to it by poverty.

The notoriety seems to have done Cleland no harm: he was awarded £100 a year by Granville, who apparently saw nothing in *Fanny Hill* to prevent the author being appointed a Government writer. Cleland's other literary works include plays and a learned book on philology.

After the summons he produced an expurgated edition but this was also suppressed, and like most later editions also excluded the notorious passage in which Fanny describes in great detail the behaviour of two homosexuals at Hampton Court.

Cleland would certainly have been bemused by the extraordinary subsequent history of his one excursion into erotica: endless editions, one of which resulted in a bookseller going to the pillory; piracies and court cases; fines and imprisonment for two itinerant booksellers who persuaded Massachusetts farmers to buy copies in 1819; a vogue among soldiers engaged in the American Civil War; seizure by the US Customs (though permitted in the State of New York since 1963); and the 1964 Bow Street test case when, after Mayflower Books, the paperback publishers, invited prosecution, 171 copies were destroyed on the order of the Chief Magistrate, Sir Robert Blundell. Unexpurgated British editions became available in 1985.

John Cleland lived to the good age of eighty and died in 1789. He ended his days in Petty France (the house lost under modern Queen Anne's Mansions) sustained by his pension, surrounded by a good library and occasionally visited by literary friends. Only the site of his house in St James's Place exists, and while later street numbering makes it impossible to be absolutely sure where it was, the best bet is the mansion block (No. 37 with No. 36) in the small cul-de-sac next to Duke's Hotel.

For a woman to pose as a man may not be illegal but it invites speculation, and a great deal of prurient curiosity was aroused in the late 1920s when it was revealed that a 'COLONEL BARKER', briefly resident at 73 LITTLE ST JAMES'S STREET, was really a woman.

No. 73 was – and remains – a block of small, elegant service flats, at least one of which was thought rather daring at that time for having a ceiling mirror over the alcove double bed. During her stay there a square-faced, rather jolly-looking woman with close-cropped hair was passing herself off as an ex-cavalry officer. She might have kept her secret from the public had she not been exposed by a court case in 1929.

The news that 'the Colonel' was a woman came as a surprise to a great many people, especially to a valet mutually shared with residents of the other flats. He declared that he had 'often held the towel for the Colonel when he was in the bath' but had never guessed he was not a man. He must, one feels, have been singularly unobservant.

The story of her masquerade, which lasted for more than thirty years, began with a childhood in Jersey, where she was a tomboy brought up by a well-to-do father who taught her cricket, boxing and fencing. She was twice married and had two children. Then about 1923 she decided to change her persona. She went to live at

Brighton under the name of 'Captain Sir Victor Barker, DSO'. Barker had been her maiden name.

The 'Captain' went through a form of marriage with a Miss Haward, a chemist's daughter, took male roles in a local repertory company, and later in Andover where she ran an antiques business she rode to hounds. In 1926 she left Miss Haward, came to London, promoted herself to Colonel, joined the National Fascist movement and, just before going to Little St James's Street, she and an actress lived as man and wife in Hertford Street, Mayfair.

Acting and subterfuge saw her through many crises. There was a court case concerning a forged firearms certificate. The 'Colonel' masked her real identity by appearing in the dock with bandaged eyes and alleging temporary blindness from war wounds. The hero of Flanders was acquitted.

Luck ran out and the Colonel's identity as a woman was revealed after six years' imposture when, in 1929, she appeared at the Old Bailey. In sentencing her to nine months' imprisonment (for false entry in the Brighton marriage register) the recorder described her as 'a mendacious and unscrupulous adventuress'.

After her release the 'Colonel', now calling herself Sir John Hill, roamed Camden Town walking with the aid of sticks (more war wounds, she explained), and became involved in a number of minor crimes. They included stealing £25 from a woman who was astonished when she discovered the sex of the person she had engaged as a manservant.

In the Second World War Barker served in the Home Guard and afterwards became a recluse in the little Suffolk village of Kessingland, where on her death in 1960 local people were amazed to learn the truth about the woman they had always known as Geoffrey Norton.

Turning down St James's we are faced with ST JAMES'S PALACE and, though unquestionably a Black Plaque needs to go up on the mellow walls of the royal apartments known as York House, it is hard to decide who was the villain responsible for the bloody deed that took place shortly after midnight on 31 May 1810. The question which has never been decided is whether ERNEST, DUKE OF CUMBERLAND, murdered his valet (as his enemies contended) or whether his valet, JOSEPH SELLIS, committed suicide after unsuccessfully trying to kill him (as the Duke maintained).

To solve the mystery we would need to have been in the Duke's bedroom on the first floor of the Palace overlooking Cleveland

Row when the Duke, brother of George IV and William IV, returned from a concert at the Hanover Square Rooms.

Two very debatable versions of what happened must be considered.

It may safely be accepted that the Duke took a drink before taking to his four-poster bed. He was, he said, awakened about 2.30 a.m. by what he thought at first was a bat. The next thing he knew he was being attacked by fierce blows from a razor-edged weapon that cut through his padded nightcap. He tried to ward them off, and with blood flowing from his hand and wrist called out for help. A valet named Cornelius Neale ran in to find the Duke's regimental sabre covered with blood lying by the doorway.

Doctors were called and the Duke asked for Sellis, his Corsican valet, who slept not far away. The Duke's housekeeper – Neale's wife – and a German servant went to rouse him and when they reached his room said they heard a gurgling sound and found Sellis lying on the bed with his throat cut and his head almost severed from his body.

At 10 a.m. a bulletin announced that the Duke was 'as well as could be expected' and the coroner and Chief Magistrate at Bow Street arrived to take depositions.

A quickly convened inquest that afternoon accepted the Duke's account that the intruder to his room had been Sellis who had tried to kill him and had then gone to his room and slit his throat. A verdict of suicide was returned by the jury.

The result far from satisfied Whigs and radicals who disliked the unpopular Duke, nor has it been accepted by sceptics who have investigated the evidence subsequently. They have preferred a very different interpretation. The most sensational version of what they think really happened is that there was a fight because Sellis found his wife in bed with the Duke, that the Duke overcame Sellis in a struggle and killed him to prevent him talking. Then he faked his own injuries.

An alternative and more recent version has Sellis attacking Cumberland because the Duke had seduced the valet's daughter and she had committed suicide when she found she was expecting a child.

These theories sound melodramatic but, given the Duke's account to be true, some reason has to be found to explain why Sellis attacked him. Could a mysterious document written seventeen years later by Charles Jones, the Duke's private secretary, confirm the Duke's guilt? Jones said that Cumberland told him he was forced to kill Sellis because 'the villain threatened to propagate a report and I had no alternative'.

Also it has never been clear how, if Sellis committed suicide, he managed to inflict such a terrible wound on his neck without removing his cravat and how his hands were found clean. There was bloodstained water in his basin but he could hardly have cut his own throat and then washed his hands before getting on to his bed to die.

Stories circulated at the time by newspaper articles led to a libel action which the Duke took (and won) against one writer. Twenty-two years later an even wilder story was spread that the Duke and the other valet, Neale, were involved in 'the grossest and most unnatural immorality', and that Sellis had discovered them and been murdered on the Duke's order. The perpetrator of this libel broke bail and fled before the jury brought in a verdict.

Recent writers have favoured the theory that the Duke was guilty and protected by a royal cover-up. This makes a better story. But it also implies that a formidable amount of perjured evidence was very quickly assembled.

— 3 —

Buckingham Palace through Victoria to Westminster

To put a Black Plaque on BUCKINGHAM PALACE and accuse a queen of spreading a scandalous rumour and compounding an injustice smacks of *lèse-majesté*. But in 1839 the young QUEEN VICTORIA made an extraordinary accusation against her mother's lady-in-waiting and insisted on a medical inspection to see if she were pregnant.

Five years earlier Lady Flora Hastings, a tall, quiet, rather plain woman of twenty-seven, had been appointed lady-in-waiting to Victoria's mother, the Duchess of Kent, in the hope that she might provide companionship for the Princess. But this had not been a success partly because Lady Flora worked closely with Sir John Conroy, Comptroller of the Duchess's household, a man whom Victoria grew up disliking intensely.

Throughout the Christmas of 1838 Lady Flora felt unwell and consulted the Queen's physician, Sir James Clark. He noted that her figure was unusually full and was unprofessional enough to tell one of the Queen's ladies that Lady Flora might be pregnant. This quickly got back to Victoria who, also noting her figure, seized on the information that while returning from a Scottish holiday Lady Flora and Conroy had travelled alone in a post-chaise.

'We have no doubt', Victoria wrote in her journal, 'that she is – to use the plain words – *with child*!' Later, referring to Conroy, she added: 'The horrid cause of all this is the Monster and Demon Incarnate . . .'

Instead of dealing discreetly with what she called 'this awkward business' Victoria insisted on Lady Flora being medically examined. But even after two doctors declared the suspicion quite unfounded, the Queen still behaved unwisely. Clark should really have been dismissed for his indiscretion and for urging Lady Flora 'to confess'; Victoria said it would be enough for him to make a private apology.

Lady Flora described the affair as a 'horrible conspiracy'. Her family were outraged, and, by the time the gossip had spread beyond the palace to the clubs and the press, Lord Hastings felt obliged to write a letter to the *Morning Post* to clear his sister's reputation.

At the time Victoria was only 19. With little experience of life and statecraft, her prejudice against Conroy may have caused her to be drawn into court politics and intrigue. She may have been given bad advice. Privately she appears to have been contrite and to have asked Lady Flora to forgive her, but publicly seems to have been curiously insensitive to the uproar she had provoked. Defiantly she recorded in her journal that she had been cheered at Windsor on her way to Sunday Service.

The episode ended tragically four months later with the sudden death of Lady Flora. A post-mortem revealed the true reason for her condition: she was suffering from an incurable liver disease.

If you look closely at the inside walls of the WESTMINSTER THEATRE in Palace Street near Buckingham Palace you can just discern the outline of the bricked-up windows of what was once the Pimlico Chapel. The man who built the chapel in 1766 and attracted fashionable London to hear him preach was DR WILLIAM DODD. Queen Charlotte and Horace Walpole were among those attending the passionately delivered sermons of the clergyman who, with his elaborately powdered wig and dandified manner, became known as 'the Macaroni Parson'. His star blazed briefly before extravagance and forgery – then a capital crime – led him to Tyburn.

Dodd's eloquence and flamboyant personality secured him advancement from a West Ham curacy in 1752 to the position of a Royal Chaplain at St James's Palace twelve years later. A house in Plaistow was exchanged for one in Pall Mall. When he came to build his Pimlico Chapel at the age of 37, his eye was firmly on the main chance: he chose a site conveniently close to Buckingham House which became a royal home in 1762.

The scholarly son of a Norfolk clergyman, Dodd was extremely industrious in the early years of his ministry. But success with society congregations tempted him into a luxurious way of life which he could not support. A frequenter of the pleasure gardens at Vauxhall and Ranelagh, he openly declared himself 'a votary of the god of dancing'. Sermons to the nobility in highly priced pews were the invariable prelude to expensive tavern suppers. He never repudiated a Press accusation of an affair with a married woman of twenty-three.

Debts started to mount and the Macaroni Parson's first serious mistake was to offer 'a thumping bribe' (Walpole's phrase) to the wife of the Lord Chancellor to secure him the fat living of St George's, Hanover Square. She told her husband. He reported to George III, and the King's outraged reaction was to deprive Dodd of his royal chaplaincy. A short absence abroad became expedient.

When he returned the Doctor found life more difficult. Increasingly desperate for money, he sold the Pimlico Chapel in 1776, and moved to Argyll Street. Here he committed his greatest folly by going to the City to raise £4,200 with a bond bearing the forged signature of the fifth Earl of Chesterfield, to whom he had once been tutor.

In the Wood Street Comptor for debtors Dodd came within some £400 of making restitution but, despite the intervention of powerful friends, he was put on trial for forgery. Dr Johnson wrote him a mitigating speech to read in court: 'I am sunk at once into poverty and scorn; my name and my crime fill the ballads – the sport of the thoughtless and the triumph of the wicked'. But even these rolling Johnsonian periods could not save him; nor could an unprecedented wave of public sympathy and a petition with 23,000 signatures. The Lord Chief Justice, the Privy Council and King were all appealed to in vain, and Dodd was executed in 1777.

Although she was one of the most famous English courtesans of the last century, CORA PEARL spent most of her life in Paris. After the age of 23 she came to this country only once and then briefly. London on that occasion did not put out the flags. She stayed at the GROSVENOR HOTEL in the autumn of 1870 but her reputation had travelled ahead of her. She was known to be under the protection of a French prince but was asked to leave.

Cora's real name was Emma Crouch and her early years were spent in Plymouth. She called herself Cora Pearl later when she found that the French had difficulty in pronouncing Crouch. Her father, Frederick Crouch, had some claim to fame as the writer of the song 'Kathleen Mavourneen' but she saw little of him as he deserted his family to go to America.

After schooling in France, Cora came home to stay with her grandmother in London where she was apprenticed to a milliner. In her *Memoirs*, written towards the end of her life and not to be entirely trusted, she says that she was first seduced by a diamond

Cora Pearl, mistress of Prince Napoleon, as Cupid in Orpheus in the Underworld. *She chose the Grosvenor Hotel for her London visit.*

merchant who met her on the way to church in Marylebone.

She was attracted to the Argyll Rooms in Great Windmill Street (on the present site of the Trocadero) and there she met Robert Bignall who ran the notorious Victorian night house and took her to Paris. Cora did not come back with him, and within a few years she had acquired a collection of admirers, lovers and protectors that reads like the *Almanach de Gotha*: William, Prince of Orange; the Duc de Morny; Ludovic, Duc de Gramont-Caderousse; the Duc de Rivoli; and Prince Achille Murat, who became her protector when he was only 17.

Sharing a house with another courtesan, Cora displayed what was described as 'the acme of sensual delights' with 'an almost superhuman knowledge of the art of love' and 'an inordinate talent for voluptuous eccentricities'. These attributes enabled her to keep a stable of sixty saddle and carriage horses and spend a fortune on equipage. In the Bois de Boulogne she shocked convention by riding astride.

With flaming red hair and a temper to match, Cora thrived on scandal. According to *Le Figaro* she introduced make-up to Paris in 1864, and when she appeared as Cupid in Offenbach's *Orpheus in the Underworld*, fashionable Paris including princes, dukes and the entire Jockey Club came to see her. They were not disappointed: she was virtually naked except for strategically placed diamonds.

Cora's outrageous behaviour did nothing to discourage admirers, three of whom were cousins of the Emperor Napoleon III – one, Prince Napoleon, her most influential and enduring lover. The Prince, nicknamed Plon-Plon and said to resemble a villain in a third-rate repertory company, set her up in a house in the rue de Chaillot so sumptuous that it was known as Les Petits Tuileries.

During the Siege of Paris in the Franco-Prussian War of 1870, she turned her house into a hospital, but on her royal lover's advice she left for London soon after the bombardment began.

In September of that year she arrived at the Grosvenor Hotel in Victoria. Travelling under another name, she had booked a suite of rooms on the first floor and paid a month in advance. But the secret of her identity was soon rumoured. She was approached by the manager who asked if she were Cora Pearl. When she said she was, he asked her to leave. Her advance payment was not refunded. 'That's how it is in England!' was her surprisingly acquiescent response to eviction.

Cora moved to another hotel, then to a house where Plon-Plon joined her. During her stay of about two months some time was spent riding in Sussex but it is unlikely that she would have been included in the visit Plon-Plon made to Camden Place, Chislehurst, where the Empress Eugenie was to spend her exile with his cousin Napoleon III.

The Continent soon called them back. But Plon-Plon was now poorer and without his former status. The affair waned and after Cora returned to Paris she took up with the young son of a wealthy butcher who spent a fortune on her. He went bankrupt and when she rejected him he tried to shoot himself at her house, an incident which turned people against her.

Her fortunes in decline, Cora was forced to sell her house and her silver and resort to the last refuge of the notorious – writing her memoirs. She died of cancer in a third-floor flat in the rue de Bassano in 1886, aged about 50.

It is from her memoirs that we learn of Cora's one ascertainable London address. But this creates a difficulty. Another Grosvenor Hotel existed at this date in Park Street, Mayfair. It would seem more likely, however, that the hotel at Victoria, near the Continental railway station, built in the grand French Second Empire style, would have been Cora's choice.

Two small Queen Anne houses – 8 and 9 SMITH SQUARE – have a deceptive look of calm elegance. With separate front doors under a shared portico, they were occupied between the wars as one building on which a Black Plaque could hardly be more appropriate. Here the Blackshirts – the British Union of Fascists – were launched in 1932 when this was the home of SIR OSWALD MOSLEY.

It is hard to associate this corner house in the square with the friend of Hitler and Mussolini, the frenzied orator who with his bodyguards caused ugly East End riots against the Jews. A

Sir Oswald Mosley. Violent Blackshirt oratory contrasts with the serenity of his Smith Square home.

political black sheep, Mosley was to be interned in 1940 for three years.

Smith Square really belongs to the earlier, untainted period of Mosley's life – the golden years when, after Winchester and Sandhurst, a gallant World War I record, election as MP for Harrow and marriage to Lord Curzon's daughter, he seemed assured of a brilliant future. But early in the 1930s all his dazzling opportunities were wrecked by his fatal association with the totalitarian leaders.

The party he founded was initially dedicated to Parliamentary reform, slum clearance and the abolition of unemployment; but it lost its way. With their sinister uniforms and theory of a single party, Mosley's Blackshirts turned the East End into an ugly battlefield.

The windows of the Smith Square house rattled with the protests of wrathful adversaries. Outside Nos. 8 and 9, as well as at the Union's headquarters in Great George Street not far away, banners read:

Hitler and Mosley what are they for?
Thuggery, buggery, hunger and war!

Until 1939 it was just possible to regard the British Union of Fascists as something distasteful and un-British; but with the declaration of war Mosley's continued advocacy of peace with Hitler assumed the complexion of treachery. He and his second wife, Diana Mitford, were detained 'for custodial not punitive purposes' until 1943, when they were released from Holloway.

After the war Mosley reconstructed his party under the name of the Union Movement, but cast only a pale shadow. Meetings became rarer after 1950 and the end was spelt out clearly when the Union's leader lost his deposit at North Kensington in the 1955 General Election.

Sir Oswald Mosley's death in 1980 left the unresolved enigma of how a man of great potential ability could have been so lacking in political judgement and so insensitive to public feelings.

To the north of Smith Square at 1-19 WESTMINSTER MANSIONS, at the intersection of Tufton Street and Great Peter Street, lived COLONEL THOMAS BLOOD. While occupying a corner house on what was then Bowling Alley he may well have planned his theft of the Crown Jewels in 1671.

Col. Blood, born in 1618 the son of an Irish blacksmith, was an adventurer with a 'villainous unmerciful look' whose sanguinary name has done nothing to diminish his reputation. But his life was one in which daring was frequently confounded by failure: a frustrated attack on Dublin Castle to capture it from the Royalists in 1663; the attempted murder of the Duke of Ormonde, dragged from his coach in St James's Street; even a thwarted shooting of Charles II while he was bathing in the

The 'dangerously insinuating' Colonel Blood.

Thames at Battersea, an assassination prevented, Blood explained piously, because his arm was checked by the 'awe of majesty'.

In the seventeenth century the Crown Jewels and Royal Regalia were kept in the Martin Tower at the Tower of London, and were in the charge of an elderly custodian, Talbot Edwards. Blood ingratiated himself with Edwards and his wife, first approaching them dressed as a parson. He was invited to dine some days later and while being shown the jewels he threw a cloak over his host's head and clubbed him down. He then seized the crown, crushing it under his cloak. A confederate took the orb while a third man attempted to get away with the sceptre.

The plan might have succeeded but for the chance arrival home on leave of Edwards's son, a soldier, who raised the alarm and, firing shots, pursued Blood and his accomplices as they ran across the drawbridge. They were captured before they could escape on waiting horses.

Blood was strangely calm. 'It was a bold attempt' he said, adding enigmatically, 'but it was for a Crown'. What did this mean? And why was so grave a crime not followed by hanging or at least imprisonment? Instead Blood was personally interviewed by the King at Whitehall and was not only pardoned but given back his forfeited land in Ireland which yielded £500 a year.

The first published account of the attempted theft appeared in 1680, nine years after the event and in the year of Blood's death. The crime remains as mystifying today as it was then. The pardoning in the late seventeenth century of obviously guilty men such as Blood,

Konigsmarck and Titus Oates seems to be part of the pattern of double-dealing and political intrigue. One explanation – hardly plausible, but the best – is that Charles II had secretly instructed Blood to steal the jewels, hence Blood's double-edged remark on capture that he had acted 'for a Crown'. The theory is that he was to have sold the jewels on behalf of the King, whose income was being severely restricted by Parliament.

Blood's house has long since gone, but the site, pinpointed by the London topographer George H. Cunningham, is today a mansion block with an entrance in Great Peter Street. So well-placed a Westminster home, and his burial in the Westminster graveyard of either Christ Church or St Margaret's, suggests that at his death at the age of 62 Blood was a person of standing. Evelyn's assessment that he was 'dangerously insinuating' would seem well founded.

An earlier attempt on the Royal Regalia took place at Westminster nearly four hundred years before. A travelling merchant, RICHARD DE PODLICOTE, broke into the CHAPEL OF THE PYX off the cloisters of Westminster Abbey and, assisted by ten monks, escaped with about £75,000 worth of jewellery.

The theft took place in April 1303 while Edward I was away from London on his campaign against the rebellious Scottish leader William Wallace. It needed to be carefully planned because the Royal Treasury, perhaps the oldest surviving chamber in the Abbey, was virtually impregnable.

Preparations were carried to the lengths of growing a clump of flax in the cloister garden under which the treasure could be hidden until carried in leather panniers to the Thames and taken across to Lambeth by boat.

Somehow Podlicote broke in and prised open chests and coffers. The Coronation Crown and three other crowns were left behind, scattered on the floor, apparently because they were thought too difficult to dispose of.

Part of the haul – gold and silver vessels – was hidden in Kentish Town by a St Giles's linen-draper who was a receiver. Podlicote was caught with the jewellery still on him. The sub-prior and sacristan who were among the conspiring monks were imprisoned and it is said that King Edward's vengeance on Podlicote involved nailing his flayed skin to the chapel door and to this day remnants of his skin appear to have survived.

To safeguard the sovereign's private treasure (but not the Coron-

*Robbery of the Royal
Treasury. Manuscript
drawing of the fourteenth-
century robber Richard de
Podlicote. The door to the
Chapel of the Pyx (right)
was installed immediately
afterwards for added
security.*

ation Regalia), a Jewel Tower that still survives was built just under fifty years later as part of the Palace of Westminster. The Crown Jewels themselves were permanently moved to the Tower of London in the Middle Ages, first housed in the Martin Tower (where Blood struck) and then transferred to the Wakefield Tower (the present Jewel House) in 1870.

As wicked deeds go the Gunpowder Plot takes a lot of beating, yet London has nothing to mark the attempt in 1604 to blow up Parliament, kill King James I and send five hundred MPs to their deaths.

GUY FAWKES should obviously have a very Black Plaque indeed. The question is where. Fawkes came from Yorkshire and had no London address. Most of the other conspirators were 'gentlemen of good houses' but those houses were also outside London. St Paul's Churchyard, where five of them went to the scaffold, is hardly appropriate and too far from the scene. The little pedimented building on the Lambeth shore where the gunpowder was hidden disappeared in the last century.

Fawkes and his seven fellow conspirators would best be remembered at the Houses of Parliament in OLD PALACE YARD with a plaque on the wall immediately north of the gateway into State Officers Court. This is the nearest site to the house which Thomas Percy, cousin of the Earl of Northumberland, rented as a base for operations.

Only a matter of yards from the then House of Lords, this was one of many private houses existing in the seventeenth century with courtyards and alleyways leading to the river. Here Percy took up residence with Fawkes who, under a false name and dressed in a white smock, acted as his servant. From the nearby river stairs they took a boat across to Lambeth and by night secretly ferried back thirty-six barrels of gunpowder.

The house disappeared in the fire of 1834: perhaps before. Certainly it was obliterated by Barry's Houses of Parliament. But its position at the southern end of the Parliament buildings can be located almost exactly from an early nineteenth-century plan made by the antiquary William Capon which is in the library of the Society of Antiquaries.

The actual happening is too well known to need more than a brief description. The conspirators' first idea was to dig a tunnel under the House of Lords, but this difficult operation was abandoned when a ground level crypt immediately beneath the

Peers' chamber became available. Here the gunpowder was concealed by firewood.

All was ready for the spring Opening of Parliament but that year a severe outbreak of plague led to a postponement until 5 November. During the summer some of the dispersed conspirators had qualms about killing not only the King but five hundred innocent men. Ten days before Parliament assembled a warning letter was sent to one of the peers warning him of 'a terrible blow'.

Not until the day before the Opening was the King informed and a search ordered. When Sir Thomas Knyvet, a Westminster magistrate, went into the crypt at midnight, he found the gunpowder under the faggots, and arrested Fawkes who had stayed behind to fuse the charge. Fawkes, a tall red-bearded fellow in his thirties, was taken before the King, to whom he explained that 'a desperate deed requires a desperate remedy'. He withstood 'uttermost torture' for three days while his confederates escaped. During their pursuit two were killed and eight stood trial for 'the greatest treasons that ever were plotted in England'. Their sentences of death were inevitable and their decapitated heads were set up 'to become a prey for the fowls of the air'.

These are the ascertainable facts of the Gunpowder Plot as it has come down to us. Some doubts remain. The ostensible motive – that these Papist malcontents were determined on the death of the Protestant King – seems clear, but so much of the evidence is based on suspect testimony that there is reason to believe that the details were embroidered to make anti-Catholic propaganda.

Another crime at the Palace of Westminster took place in the LOBBY OF THE HOUSE OF COMMONS when Spencer Perceval, the Prime Minister, was murdered by JOHN BELLINGHAM.

It was a deliberate assassination of an unspectacular statesman by someone who thought he had a grievance. When he could not get a petition before Parliament, Bellingham gave advance warning that he felt 'under the imperious necessity of executing justice'. At the time the shooting caused considerable Government apprehension, but the excitement was short-lived when it was perceived that the crime was not part of a wider conspiracy.

Only a week separated the killing and the execution of the killer. Almost as quickly the deed was erased from public memory, and has been forgotten by history.

At about a quarter past five on the afternoon of 11 May 1812, Spencer Perceval was on his way to the Commons to answer

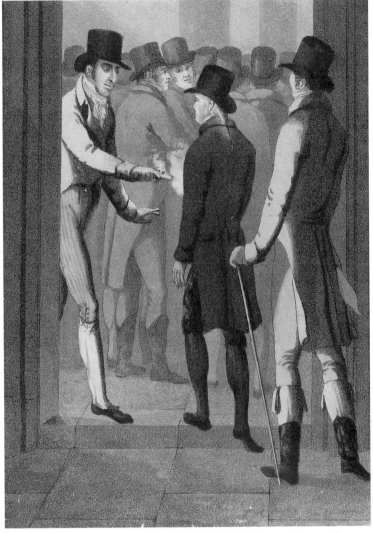

Murder at the House. Calmly, Bellingham shoots the Prime Minister Spencer Perceval in the Lobby of the House of Commons.

questions about some very dull Orders in Council affecting foreign trade. He was with two companions. They passed through the Lobby which, in the old Houses of Parliament, was not where it is today but nearer the main public entrance, opposite the south end of Westminster Hall. From behind double doors where he was waiting unnoticed a tall raw-boned man of about forty with a thin face stepped forward, drew a pistol and shot Perceval in the left breast. He fell to the ground crying 'Murder!' and was dead even before he could be carried to the Speaker's apartments.

Bellingham remained where he was. He made no attempt to escape. When he was seized, he simply said: 'My name is Bellingham; it is a private injury – I know what I have done – it was a denial of justice on the part of the Government.'

His grievance, which had grown into an obsession, went back over a period of eight years. During part of this time he had been working in Archangel where he had run foul of two Russian firms and had been arrested. He insisted that his interests had not been adequately represented by the English Ambassador, who had refused to interfere with Russian law.

In a vain search for redress Bellingham petitioned the Prince Regent and Spencer Perceval. When his protests got nowhere he purchased a pair of pistols and, after a few preliminary visits to Westminster from his lodgings in Milman Street, carried out the deed.

Fearing at first some political uprising, the Cabinet went to the extreme lengths of ordering all mail to be stopped that night. Bellingham was taken to Newgate under strong military escort, and on the day of his execution the military were stationed at Islington and London Bridge and the whole volunteer corps of London ordered to be under arms.

Bellingham, who declined to plead insanity, went to the scaffold protesting about his treatment in Russia, and his public execution caused sufficient interest for Byron to rent a window to watch. He wrote: 'On Monday, after sitting up all night, I saw Bellingham launched into eternity and —— launched into the country.' The dashes refer to Lady Caroline Lamb, an allusion which becomes clearer on page 70.

The champion of liberty ... the enemy of corrupt authority ... an acclaimed Lord Mayor of London chaired through the streets ... the people's favourite. This is how JOHN WILKES emerges from the pages of eighteenth-century history. But there was another side to the man whom George III called 'that devil Wilkes'.

It may seem invidious to focus on the year 1763 when he was accused of obscenity, blasphemy and sedition and was taken to the Tower, but Wilkes, the passionate advocate of free speech, would not expect the more scandalous aspects of his life to be whitewashed.

The Westminster house where Wilkes was living when the storm broke was 13 GREAT GEORGE STREET. This has been swallowed up by the Royal Institution of Chartered Surveyors, but still preserved in Alfred Waterhouse's redbrick building, after the demolition of No. 13 in 1900, are Georgian mantelpieces and carvings which were there in Wilkes's time.

Born in Clerkenwell in 1725, John Wilkes had fearsome features and a sinister squint but boasted he could talk away his face with a pretty woman within an hour. Combining political audacity as publisher of the *North Briton* with licentious pleasure, he was an early member of the Hell Fire Club. Accounts of the club's erotic, anti-religious revels at Medmenham Abbey on the Thames near High Wycombe have become exaggerated but it was for the 'Medmenham Monks' that Wilkes published an indecent poem, *An Essay on Woman*. He may or may not also have been the pseudonymous author – 'Pego Borewell Esq' – of this parody of Pope's *Essay on Man*. The satire starts:

Awake my Fanny, leave all meaner things
This morn shall prove what rapture swiving brings.

The poem contained a good deal of fairly obvious obscenity of a kind which would have passed muster at the end of a carousal by the Hell Fire Club. Twelve copies were run off for members on Wilkes's private press at Great George Street. Unfortunately some discarded proof sheets – and then a complete copy – came into the hands of the Government adversaries whom Wilkes had attacked in the celebrated issue No. 45 of the *North Briton*, the periodical in which for more than a year he had attacked and satirised the Government and King George III.

It was just the ammunition they needed. The 15th of November, 1763, was a serious day for Wilkes. The Commons passed a motion declaring that 'Number 45' (in which both King and Parliament were ruthlessly pilloried over their handling of foreign affairs) was a 'false, scandalous and seditious libel'. They ordered the journal to be burnt by the common hangman at the Royal Exchange. In the Lords the Earl of Sandwich read out *An Essay on Woman* with considerable relish and to rowdy interruptions. Attempts to stop him were lustily countered by shouts of 'Go on, go on!'

Though he denied authorship of the poem and its anti-clerical notes, Wilkes stood accused of perpetrating a 'most scandalous, obscene and impious libel'. He faced expulsion from the House of Commons where he was MP for Aylesbury, as well as being outlawed.

To add to his difficulties , on the following day Wilkes received a challenge to a duel in Hyde Park from an MP whom he had attacked in the *North Briton*. He accepted and fell, wounded by a shot in the groin. As he lay recovering in Great George Street he was brought news that Pitt was vilifying him in the House as 'the blasphemer of his God and the libeller of his King'. He was also accused of malingering to avoid prosecution, but when he took refuge in France it was not out of cowardice but to gain time.

While abroad he was outlawed – for publication of 'Number 45', not his alleged authorship of the poem. On his return four years later in 1768 he surrendered himself to the King's Bench and after a short time in prison was discharged.

Immediately Wilkes resumed his campaigns of agitation, organising his constant battles with authority first from Prince's Court (now Old Queen Street) near his previous Westminster address, then from Fulham and Kensington Gore, and finally from Mayfair.

The 'Friend to Liberty' (as his memorial inscription in the Grosvenor Chapel calls him) died insolvent in 1795 aged 70 at 35 Grosvenor Square, a house on the corner of South Audley Street.

Near the Post Office at the bottom of Whitehall is a dusty-looking building with a shop on the ground floor. No. 38 PARLIAMENT STREET has a rather neglected appearance. But in the 1920s it probably had a far smarter air, and the proximity of Government offices was calculated to impress those who called on very delicate business – the business of acquiring honours.

Waiting to welcome them behind the doors of the *Whitehall Gazette* – a suitably dignified title – was the editor, who had the resonant name of J. MAUNDY GREGORY. Dressed with formality, he exuded charm. The son of a Hampshire clergyman, Maundy Gregory had been at Oxford (without getting a degree); then he had been a schoolmaster; he had also been an actor, an added help in the part he had to play as a person of influence in royal and government circles.

The visitor would be impressed by personally signed photo-graphs of King George V and the Duke of York. He was offered a cigarette from a silver case with an inscription which indicated that it was a present from the King. The names of Lord Birkenhead and the exiled King George II of Greece were dropped into the conversation; his friendship with Sir John Hanbury-Williams, a senior member of the Royal Household, was also mentioned. And now, asked Maundy Gregory, how could he be of assistance to his visitor?

The answer might be veiled or forthright. Bluntly it came down to one thing: the caller wanted to see his name in the Honours List, and he had heard that Mr Gregory could help in that direction.

Pausing only to take a telephone call announced by his secretary as 'No. 10 on the line, sir' (it truthfully was – No. 10 Hyde Park Terrace, his Bayswater home), J. Maundy Gregory named the exact honour that could be expected and when. But these things, he murmured, cost money. He would require £10,000 to arrange a knighthood, £30,000 for a baronetcy and up to £100,000 or even more for a peerage.

His visitor – perhaps a hard-faced man who had done well out of the war – paid up and left happily. This dubious form of brokerage continued successfully until 1925 but was severely curtailed by the Honours (Prevention of Abuses) Act. This meant that Maundy Gregory had to devise another method of making titles pay. Through his well-placed contacts he often knew in advance who was in line for a particular title and approached them. They paid him for a title which was *already* decided.

Determined to put a stop to these swindles John Davidson, Chairman of the Conservative Party, arranged for Albert Bennett, the party's assistant treasurer, to insinuate himself into Gregory's confidence. As soon as Bennett learned the names of Gregory's clients, he passed them back to Davidson who made sure that none received the expected title.

Gregory became desperate, and in 1933 unwisely offered to obtain a knighthood for a retired naval officer in return for £10,000. Lieut.-Cdr. E.W. Billyard-Leake, an unambitious friend of Lord Louis Mountbatten, went straight to the police. Maundy Gregory was taken to Bow Street and charged with fraud.

Fearing that in court he might reveal past Government corruption over honours, Gregory was approached while awaiting trial and told that in return for his silence he could go abroad after his sentence with a sum of money and a quarterly pension. He was paid £30,000 and it has long been assumed it was the Conservative Party that found the sum to keep him quiet. It is now known that Baldwin quite cynically approached Ramsay MacDonald, who was then Prime Minister, with the request that Sir Julien Cahn, sportsman and philanthropist, should be made a baronet. Cahn would pay the £30,000 needed for Gregory's silence.

MacDonald wanted to refuse. But recalling that, as well as Tories, such Labour personalities as J.H. Clynes and Arthur Henderson were implicated, he conceded. 'The dunghill had to be cleared away without delay' he decided.

Maundy Gregory served two months in Wormwood Scrubs, and then was driven by a friend of Davidson to Dover. Accommodation in France had been reserved for him. He kept his side of the bargain, remaining silent until his death in a Gestapo hospital in Paris in 1941.

Further up Whitehall on a morning of black frost a country executed a king. The wrongs and rights of the beheading of Charles I on 30 January 1649 are still fiercely argued.

Whatever the verdict in the endless debate of King versus Parliament, the occasion was an ugly one. Whitehall was packed, with every window filled and people climbing on to roofs for a view, when Charles stepped on to the scaffold that had been erected outside the BANQUETING HOUSE.

As the axe fell there was a general reaction of horror. As someone in the crowd recorded: 'There was such a dismal universal groan amongst the thousands of people who were in sight of it, as it were with one consent, as I have never heard before and desire I may not hear again.'

The Black Plaque should be set above the doorway of the present extension to the left of Inigo Jones's building. Formerly a narrow two-storey annex with a sloping roof abutted the Banqueting House. From a first-floor window Charles most probably approached his death.

Harder to decide is what name, if any, should be put on the Black Plaque as the person most culpable.

The immediate instrument was the executioner. As there were two men on the scaffold masked with heavy visors to prevent identification, he may well not have been Richard Brandon, the common hangman of London, to whom the beheading is generally ascribed. Whoever it was, he would, anyway, have been acting under orders, and the execution has to be regarded as a logical sequence of events following the death sentence pronounced by the judge, Richard Bradshawe. The judge, in turn, was acting on the verdict of the 68 jurymen, themselves representing 135 commis-

Who killed the King?
Most representations of his death show the
executioner masked to hide his identity. The man
holding head and axe may be General Fairfax.

sioners ordered to this duty by Parliament. Behind Parliament are all those electors with Parliamentary sympathies and especially those who voluntarily took up arms against the Royalists.

It has sometimes been contended that the 59 signatories to the Death Warrant deserve special censure. Of these, 15 died before the Restoration; others disappeared or escaped abroad; and 6 signatories were among the surviving 29 'regicides' tried in 1660, of whom

10 in all were executed. Oliver Cromwell who died in 1658 served a grisly posthumous sentence: with three other 'regicides' he was exhumed in 1661 and his body hung on Tyburn gallows; his head was then displayed on a pole over Westminster Hall until 1681; after this an embalmed head, alleged to be Cromwell's, started on a macabre journey which, a hundred years later, included exhibition in Bond Street.

Deciding who was responsible for the judicial murder of Charles I is even more difficult than fixing the guilt of modern war criminals. A Black Plaque is too small to accommodate all the accused: a more convenient alternative is to use the legal formula for a person unknown – QUIDAM IGNOTUS.

Almost opposite the Banqueting House in Whitehall is MELBOURNE HOUSE (renamed Dover House and now the Scottish Office) with windows looking out at the back over Horse Guards Parade. Here towards the end of March, 1812, Lord Byron limped up the stone stairway in the domed hall on his first visit to LADY CAROLINE LAMB.

This was the prelude to Caroline's tempestuous affair with the poet which was to scandalise London in an age not easily shocked. She had first seen him a week or two earlier at a ball. Her reaction was to note in her diary that Byron, then aged 25, looked 'mad, bad and dangerous to know'. A few days later she had contrived an actual meeting at Holland House when he asked if he might call on her.

By Regency standards or, for that matter, by those of the present, an affair between a peer and a young married society woman would not be considered unusual or particularly wicked. Today Byron might be regarded as a womaniser but hardly an excessive one. But his fame as a poet and his death while fighting for Greek liberty are inextricably bound up in the legend of Byron the great and 'dangerous' lover. The affair has acquired historic renown.

In the same month that he met Caroline Lamb, Byron achieved literary fame with the publication and enormous success of *Childe Harold*. The poet Samuel Rogers lent her a copy and tried to cool her interest by warning her that the author had a club foot and bit his nails. 'If he was as ugly as Aesop, I must know him,' she replied.

Caroline was 27 and married to William Lamb, later Lord Melbourne, Queen Victoria's Prime Minister. Lamb's parents lived on the ground floor of the Whitehall house; Caroline, her patient husband and their young son occupied the spacious upper floors. It

Behind the big window of Melbourne House overlooking Horse Guards Lady Caroline Lamb entertained Lord Byron.

had been her custom to invite friends in for dancing practice at noon, but after Byron's early visits this stopped because his leg prevented his taking part. They both preferred cosy meetings behind closed doors when she read aloud from the books he brought her.

Each was captivated by the other. Byron was enchanted by her boyish charm, her short fair curls, her impetuosity; she by his romantic good looks, his sudden fame. On his third visit he arrived with a rose and a carnation (she still possessed them twelve years later when he died) and all discretion was abandoned.

Meetings were constant. Letters flew between Melbourne House and 8 St James's Street where he was lodging. Their passionate relationship reached its crescendo in April when their behaviour was so indiscreet that it became the talk of the town. 'Wild and imprudent' the Duchess of Devonshire called Caroline's conduct, and before long stories were flying around of her eccentric demonstrations: following Byron's carriage on foot; besieging his lodgings dressed as a page; and threatening to stab herself.

Caroline's mother, Lady Bessborough, and the Lamb family were extremely worried. Her mother-in-law Lady Melbourne (even though she had been involved in a famous liaison for years) was shocked. But nothing anyone could say could curb 'Caro' or subdue the irrepressible emotions Byron had released in her. Her love was so intense that she was quickly jealous and frequent quarrels began to warn Byron of his folly. He was finding the relationship too conspicuous, too ardent to sustain, and too restricting to his other interests.

Early in May when the affair was hardly two months old he wrote in light-hearted remonstrance, 'People talk as if there were no other absurdities in London'. Her love regarded as 'an absurdity'! Caroline's fury can be imagined. But she failed to heed the warning of his next sentence. 'This dream, this delirium must pass away ...' Perhaps she preferred simply to ignore Byron's slowly growing disaffection which was to lead to a crisis two years later at an address which we shall visit when we reach Piccadilly.

Piccadilly, Park Lane and Mayfair

T HE creation by Nash of the Regent Street Quadrant involved the demolition of a number of small houses on the north side of Piccadilly. Among them was 23 PICCADILLY, (now renumbered, its site just east of the Bank of Scotland). Here a child was born in circumstances of great secrecy on or about 30 January 1801. The mother was EMMA, LADY HAMILTON and the girl, christened Horatia, was her illegitimate daughter by Lord Nelson. She had been conceived the previous spring on a cruise during which his ship HMS *Foudroyant* had called at Malta and Syracuse.

Nelson's affair with the wife of the elderly Sir William Hamilton, British Envoy at the Neapolitan Court, had been an open secret – anyway in the Mediterranean and at the Admiralty – for some two years. Emma was sourly referred to as 'that Hamilton woman' by Nelson's midshipman stepson writing home to his mother. When Nelson came back to England in November 1800 the fact that he travelled with the Hamiltons did not escape press innuendoes. Her pregnancy was noted. 'Lady Hamilton has arrived in the very nick of time in this country', said the *Morning Post*, adding 'It was owing to her ladyship's activity that Lord Nelson's fleet was so *victualled* at Syracuse'. The relationship soon became a much lampooned scandal caricatured by Gillray.

But Nelson's position, the reputation of the Hamiltons and Lady Nelson's *amour propre* demanded formal discretion. When Nelson left to take part in the Battle of Copenhagen the following January, knowing that the birth was imminent, he and Emma arranged a code involving a 'Mrs Thompson' and a 'godchild' which they carefully used in all letters.

The fictitious 'Mrs Thompson' was a widow – a Mrs Gibson – to whose house, 9 Little Tichfield Street, Marylebone, Horatia was taken from Piccadilly about a week after her birth. Emma always

Emma, Lady Hamilton.

Dido in Despair, *Gillray's view of a gross and pregnant Lady Hamilton watching Nelson sailing away to assume command of the Channel fleet. A complacent Sir William Hamilton sleeps in the bed behind her. This caricature was published in the week Horatia was born.*

spoke of her as her godchild when she was brought by Mrs Gibson for visits to Piccadilly or taken down to Nelson's house at Merton. Nelson pretended she was adopted when, home on leave, he went to see her by the sea or played with her on the carpet at lodgings in Sloane Street. Even after the deaths of Sir William Hamilton, of Emma (when Horatia was 14), and of Lady Nelson, the secret was kept.

Horatia lived to be 80. First she was called Miss Thompson; then (by Nelson's wish) Horatia Nelson Nelson; and after her marriage in 1822 to a clergyman – later the vicar of Tenterden, Kent – she became Mrs Philip Ward. Obviously suspecting her real parentage, she died in 1881 apparently without discovering the whole truth. Her tombstone in Pinner churchyard describes her as 'the adopted daughter of Vice-Admiral Lord Nelson'.

If we accept Lady Caroline Lamb's first impression that he was 'bad', an assessment sedulously repeated by posterity, LORD BYRON has to have a Black Plaque somewhere. There is no lack of possibilities.

We have already discovered him in adultery at Melbourne House (p. 70); in the same year, 1812, Caroline surprised him with another woman in his lodgings at St James's Street, and that autumn he had begun his affair with Lady Oxford at Eywood in Herefordshire. The following summer his half-sister Augusta Leigh stayed with him at 4 Bennet Street, St James's. Augusta's daughter Medora always believed she was conceived there in July 1813. In 1815 he embarked on a disastrous year's marriage with Annabella Milbanke at 13 Piccadilly Terrace (near Apsley House and now demolished).

But the choice for our Plaque falls most aptly on an eighteenth-century mansion which lies back from Piccadilly in a courtyard about two hundred yards from the Circus. This is ALBANY, to which in March 1814 Byron moved from cramped lodgings in Bennet Street to take up residence in APARTMENT 2A. He could afford to: *The Corsair*, published by John Murray the previous month, had sold 10,000 copies on the first day.

In this outwardly peaceful backwater which he occupied for almost a year, Byron fought out his final battles with Lady Caroline Lamb. For two years the affair started at Melbourne House had been kept going by Caroline with varying degrees of neurotic frenzy. There was an attempted suicide with a sword, a tearing off of her clothes in his Bennet Street rooms, hiding in a shop in Pall Mall and at a surgeon's house in Kensington, burning pictures of him and stabbing herself at a party.

In May and June of 1814, Caroline was back on the attack, writing furious letters, demanding the return of presents she had given him, wildly invading Albany. 'It is impossible,' he wrote to Lady Melbourne; 'She comes at all times, at any time, and the moment the door is open in she walks. I can't throw her out of the window . . .', adding two days later, 'All bolts, bars and silence can do to keep her away are done daily and hourly'.

Albany. Byron's apartments in this residential backwater were furiously invaded by Lady Caroline Lamb.

Lord Byron.

Caroline still got in, and once, when Byron was not there, scrawled 'Remember me' across the first page of a book.

To which Byron replied:

Remember thee! Ay, doubt it not:
Thy husband too shall think of thee.
By neither shalt thou be forgot,
Thou *false* to him, thou *fiend* to me!

This was in June. The next month they met a short way down Piccadilly in Burlington House at a masked ball in honour of the Duke of Wellington. Byron, wearing a monk's habit, got rather drunk. Caroline sought him out in a private room where she paraded before him making rude gestures and, ignoring his protests, displayed her green pantaloons.

They probably never saw each other again. But there was a strange final encounter. In the late summer of 1824 Caroline and her husband were taking the air by Brocket Hall, their estate near Welwyn, when by complete coincidence and to her great distress Byron's hearse passed them on its way to his burial in Nottinghamshire.

The next turning to the right along Piccadilly is Old Bond Street where many buildings still retain their early features above alluring shops. The upper part of a big double-fronted building with a pale green wash – now 37-38 OLD BOND STREET – probably looks much as it did when MRS OLIVIA SERRES lived there in 1805.

Mrs Serres was a woman with illusions of grandeur, and though this is not in itself a crime, it was to lead her into debt and imprisonment.

Mrs Serres, who called herself Princess Olive of Cumberland, was born the daughter of a house-painter in Warwick in 1772. She would seem to have had a reasonably uneventful upbringing but her marriage to a marine painter, John Thomas Serres, was an unhappy one. She herself was a painter of talent and exhibited at the Royal Academy when she was living at what was then 33 Old Bond Street. Shortly afterwards she published a book appropriately called *Flights of Fancy*.

It may have been her appointment as landscape painter to the Prince of Wales (the future George IV) that gave rise to her fantasy of royal birth. In 1817 Mrs Serres decided that she was not the daughter of Robert Wilmot, the house-painter of Warwick, but the child of Henry, Duke of Cumberland, George III's brother. At first she was content to call herself the Duke's illegitimate child, but three years later her pretensions extended.

She wrote to George IV asserting that she was in fact the Duke's legitimate daughter and signed herself Princess Olive. She took to travelling around London in a carriage bearing the royal arms, accompanied by servants in royal livery. This was a costly business and, as her expenses mounted, Mrs Serres resorted to forgery. One counterfeit document which she produced was a will purporting to have been made by George III bequeathing her £15,000.

Though these claims strained credulity, the affairs of the later Hanoverians were so tangled that the House of Commons agreed to an investigation. Robert Peel, then Home Secretary, discredited the documents but, though obliged to give up her royal arms and livery, Mrs Serres was not finished yet.

In her most elaborate story she claimed to be a princess of Poland (was she not the secret granddaughter of King Stanislas Augustus?). She said that her mother, Stanislas's illegitimate daughter, had been courted in England at the age of 18 by both the Duke of Cumberland and the Earl of Warwick. The Earl had given way; her mother had married the Duke in London; and she was, she asserted, the child of that marriage. How, then, did she explain her upbringing by the Warwick house-painter? Well, ten days after her birth, she had been spirited away from the royal birthplace and substituted for the house-painter's stillborn daughter . . .

All these claims supported by spurious documents ran Mrs Serres into serious debt and, despite a plea of royal privilege, she was arrested. For the next thirteen years Mrs Serres had to live 'within the rule of the King's Bench' (that is, the King's Bench Prison, the residential institution for debtors in Southwark). She was buried at St James's, Piccadilly, in 1834.

Her claims extended into the next generation. After her death her elder daughter carried on the fight. Mrs Anthony Ryves (who styled herself Princess Lavinia of Cumberland), of Maitland Park, Haverstock Hill, wrote an *Appeal for Royalty* in the form of an open letter to Queen Victoria. When she took her case to court in 1866 seventy documents were examined and a special jury declared them to have forged signatures.

London has been involved in a number of sieges. Because of a loss of life, the Siege of the Iranian Embassy (p. 198), the Libyan People's Bureau (p. 38) and the Siege of Sidney Street (p.238) have been serious affairs. Others, such as the Siege of Piccadilly (p. 85) and the Siege of Brewer Street (p. 143), have had elements of absurdity. The Siege of Bond Street on the night of 7 October 1801 was more of a demonstration.

The brief boisterous attack on 148 NEW BOND STREET (site of the Hermès shop in the Time-Life building) was due to the cantankerous LORD CAMELFORD, a dangerous and eccentric character who took an almost insane delight in involving himself in fights.

Thomas Pitt, second Lord Camelford, and cousin of George III's Prime Minister, was only 26 at the time of the affray, but by then he had already left a trail of unruly behaviour. As a young man in the Navy, he had been put ashore from a ship for insubordination; he had challenged one of his officers to a duel; he had shot another in a quarrel over seniority; and he had been court-martialled for mutiny.

His career as a roaring boy in London came after his accession to the Camelford title at 18 when he inherited vast estates in Cornwall and £20,000 a year. Rather than live at Camelford House, the fine family mansion at the north end of Park Lane, Camelford took lodgings over a shop in Bond Street: it was far more convenient to his favourite resort, the Prince of Wales Coffee House in Conduit Street. Dressed sometimes like a beau, and sometimes like a yokel, he strolled through Mayfair accompanied by his footman – a black prizefighter – looking for trouble and taunting the dandified Bond Street Loungers.

To mark temporary peace with France following the Treaty of Amiens, London decided to celebrate and it was in character for Camelford to declare that he considered the truce to be a patched up affair and that he would take no part in the illuminations that were general throughout the West End. He ordered that his house should be kept in darkness. Not a candle was to be lit.

Brooding behind closed shutters in his first floor drawing-room, he heard the exultant and cheering mob come close and a shout of 'Lights! Lights!' Stones were flung. A tattoo was beaten on his door knocker. Camelford's anger rose with the jeers and insults from the street. Seizing a bludgeon he went downstairs, opened the front door and set about his attackers. When the bludgeon was knocked from his hand he drew his sword.

Outnumbered, Camelford was kicked into the gutter, but rescued by his servants who dragged him back into the house. He next appeared at an upstairs window brandishing a pistol at the crowd which dispersed.

Lord Camelford. The short life of a roaring boy ended in a Kensington duel.

Within two and a half years Camelford was dead. He was shot near Holland House in a duel which he had provoked with a former friend, an army officer whom he knew to be a far better shot. It was almost as if he had a death wish. The intervening years had been packed with incident, the most mysterious being a visit he made to France under a false name. It has been suggested that he was a secret agent on a government mission either to kill or kidnap Napoleon Bonaparte.

After the fatal duel in March 1804 Lord Camelford was buried at St Anne's, Soho, and it is planned to exhume his body from the vaults. An autopsy is to be carried out in the hope of finding an explanation for his only partly explained death at the age of 29.

For another example of how vanity can lead to self-deception we have only to go a little further north. In the 1850s a shop was opened at what is now 50 NEW BOND STREET (Chappells, the music publishers; formerly No. 47) with large letters across the front carrying the enticing promise: 'Beautiful for Ever'. In the window were cosmetics, some with oriental names, and with prices as high as 200 guineas.

Inside the shop SARAH RACHEL LEVENSON, a woman whose unattractive appearance was no advertisement for her trade, offered many other beauty aids. There was 'The Royal Arabian Toilet of Beauty as Arranged by Madam Rachel for the Sultana of

Turkey' and 'Dew of Sahara for Removing Wrinkles': prices from 100 to 1,000 guineas. Obviously a snip at 20 guineas were bottles of Jordan Water 'brought by swift dromedaries from the River Jordan'. (When Mrs Levenson was later asked in court if she really believed the water came from the Jordan, she replied the water came from the East. 'That is very indefinite,' said the prosecuting counsel. 'From the East might mean Wapping.')

These exotic aids were enough to draw a rich and gullible clientele to the Bond Street shop.

Less than a decade earlier Sarah Levenson had been a fortune-teller going round East End pubs. She contracted fever near the docks and in hospital all her hair had to be cut off. A doctor provided a remedy and Mrs Levenson saw how easy it would be to capitalise on women's anxieties. So began the profitable business which by 1858 was earning her the then enormous sum of £20,000 a year.

Had she been content with this, Sarah Levenson might never have found herself at the Old Bailey. But greed encouraged her to exploit the vanity of one of her customers, Mrs Mary Borrodaile, widow of an Indian Army colonel. She told Mrs Borrodaile that a nobleman, Lord Ranelagh, had caught a glimpse of her while she was taking a beauty bath and had fallen in love with her. Madam Rachel forged love letters from the Earl to 'My own beloved Mary', and in the hope of captivating Ranelagh the widow paid her £1,000 for beauty treatments.

Before she had finished, Madam Rachel had extracted £5,300 from Mrs Borrodaile. This was achieved without the credulous widow ever meeting or even seeing Ranelagh who, when the fraud came to trial, described the story as too ridiculous for words. The sentence on Sarah Levenson was five years' imprisonment. After serving her time she returned to start her deceits all over again. During a second five years in gaol, she died.

On our way back towards Piccadilly, a brief pause should be made at 17 BRUTON STREET, at what is now the side of Berkeley Square House. A tablet by the entrance of the Lombard North Central bank records that Queen Elizabeth II was born here on 21 April 1926. It says nothing whatsoever about the much hyphenated WILLIAM POLE-TYLNEY-LONG-WELLESLEY. It is hardly to be wondered at.

The nephew of the Duke of Wellington, who took the house in 1832, was a very bad hat indeed. Few men when they die can have had an obituary like the one in the *Morning Chronicle*. It said he was

> redeemed by no single virtue, adorned by no single grace, his life gone out without even a single flicker of repentance; his 'retirement' was that of one who was deservedly avoided by all men.

As a young man William Pole-Wellesley was hastily sent back from the Peninsular War where, as a member of Wellington's staff, he was totally preoccupied with horses, gambling and women. He never looked forward.

Pressed for money, he contrived a meeting with a rich heiress, Catherine Tylney-Long, whose names and hyphens he added to his own, and whose fortune and family home, Wanstead House, Essex, he dissipated. Debts incurred by lavish parties forced him to sell this magnificent Palladian mansion at a catastrophic loss of £26,000 and it was subsequently demolished.

William then disappeared to Italy where he seduced Helena Bligh, wife of a Coldstream Guards officer, on the slopes of Mount Vesuvius. He had a child by her, which may well have caused his wife to have the heart attack from which she died. He married Helena but deserted her and left her the penniless occupant of the workhouse.

William's treatment of his wife had lost him custody of his three legitimate children who, as they had money, he spent his time kidnapping. In his campaign to retrieve them he threatened to kill their guardian, the Duke of Wellington, and issued a pamphlet accusing him of an affair with Mrs Arbuthnot. He charged his wife's sisters, who were bringing them up, with incest.

When his elder son of 14 was at Eton William enticed him to London, using him as a decoy to attract the younger son, to whom he promised cigars and jewellery. Next he tried to kidnap his daughter, an exploit which resulted in his imprisonment in the Fleet Prison. He managed to spirit his younger son away to Calais where he took the royal apartments at an hotel, employed a dozen servants and ran up debts of £29,000 in less than a year. He was further imprisoned in Boulogne. When a legal adviser was sent to France by Wellington to see if he could prevent William from appropriating his son's money, William countered by accusing the lawyer of seducing the boy.

All this left William little time to spend in the fine Bruton Street house which was the despair of the rate collector who wearily recorded: 'All lost. Gone away'. It remained empty for six years. On his return to London, William, by now the fourth Earl of Mornington, subsisted on a £10 a week allowance from the long-suffering Duke of Wellington. He died, unmourned, in lodgings in Thayer Street, Marylebone, in 1857.

No.17 Bruton Street, where the Bowes-Lyon family lived from 1921 to 1937, and where the Queen was born, was demolished in 1937.

While living at Albany and in St James's, Byron was never far from the offices of his publisher, John Murray, and after his death 50 ALBEMARLE STREET was the scene of an act of literary vandalism posterity finds hard to forgive. In the fireplace of the drawing-room on the first floor the poet's unpublished *Memoirs* were destroyed.

Of the seven people present, those directly responsible were JOHN MURRAY, JOHN CAM HOBHOUSE, Byron's executor, COLONEL FRANCIS DOYLE, representing Lady Byron's interests, and WILMOT HORTON, Byron's cousin. Their action was opposed by Thomas Moore, the Irish poet and close friend to whom Byron had entrusted the manuscript, and by Henry Luttrell, another Irish friend of Byron. The publisher's son, a boy of 16, was called in to witness the burning.

The destruction took place one month, less a day, after Byron's death from fever at Missolonghi where he had been taking a romantic, though vain, part in the war of Greek Independence. When the news reached England on 14 May 1824 a group of friends and others immediately concerned themselves with what should be done about the memoirs he had written some six years earlier. The chief advocate for their preservation was Moore to whom Byron had handed over the papers in Venice in 1821. Moore had given them to Murray in return for £2,000 on the understanding that, if Byron died before him, he should edit them. Though he had not seen the memoirs, Byron's even older friend Hobhouse took the view that they would be damaging to the poet's memory and should be destroyed. Lady Byron had declined to learn what they contained and, strangely, the prospective publisher, John Murray, had also not read them but feared they might contain salacious details. Those friends of Moore who had seen the manuscript took the view that while there were 'some indelicate passages' these were hardly scandalous recollections that demanded destruction.

On the morning of 18 May the main antagonists – Moore and his

No 50 Albemarle Street. In the long drawing room behind the first floor windows Byron's Memoirs *were burnt at the instigation of his publisher, John Murray (above).*

ally Luttrell, Hobhouse and his ally Murray – assembled in Albemarle Street where they were joined by Col. Doyle, Lady Byron's confidant, and Wilmot Horton. Moore and Luttrell argued passionately for the papers but, after wavering, Doyle and Horton sided with Murray and Hobhouse. The young John Murray entered the room during the violent disagreement, and (as he recalled over sixty years later) watched Doyle and Horton tear up the manuscript which they tossed into the small iron grate under a noble marble mantelpiece where it went up in flames.

The visitor who called at 73 PICCADILLY (now the Midland Bank at No. 79-80) on the corner of Stratton Street on 6 April 1810 was told the owner was 'not at home'. Assuming this to be the usual polite fiction, the Serjeant-at-Arms of the House of Commons went back to Westminster for advice. He was instructed by the Speaker to return once again with the warrant for the arrest of SIR FRANCIS BURDETT. He was to 'take into custody the body of the said Sir Francis Burdett' and deliver him to the Tower of London.

The difficulty was that Sir Francis was not prepared to have his body taken into custody. He had his reasons handy. He quoted Magna Carta.

Sir Francis Burdett. They called out the Guard for his Piccadilly arrest.

The violently radical MP for Westminster had recently written an open letter in Cobbett's *Political Register* objecting to restrictions on reporting in the House which he held to be an attack on the freedom of the press. As a result he faced arrest for alleged breach of privilege.

Faced with Burdett's assertion that the warrant was illegal, the Speaker, Charles Abbot, decided to make an open arrest and called out the Army. At midday on Saturday, 11 April, a troop of Life Guards rode up Piccadilly and cleared a space in the crowd who were buying hastily printed broadsheets, and cheering Sir Francis who was at his window.

The military commander was not prepared to disperse the crowd until a magistrate arrived to read the Riot Act. Then he cordoned off Piccadilly from Dover Street to Bolton Street. Taking the line that this impeded his lawful access, Sir Francis retaliated by invoking the law that protects citizens against invasion of privacy. He summoned a sheriff of London to order the soldiers away, and the sheriff, recalling ancient procedure, decided to marshal a *posse comitatus* (for which any male over the age of 15 may be summoned to prevent unlawful disorder). Backed by a token posse, he required the military to withdraw one hundred paces from the front of the house.

Sunday morning dawned with a well-provisioned Sir Francis behind a stout front door which the Serjeant-at-Arms was nervous about breaking down. Delighted at a chance to discomfort authority, the ever-increasing crowd jeered and smashed bottles with which they pelted the patrolling soldiers. When they refused to disperse a further detachment of Life Guards was ordered to Piccadilly. As if on the night before a battle, tents were erected in Green Park and camp fires lit.

Monday brought orders from Whitehall that Sir Francis was to be arrested, if necessary by force. The Foot Guards were drawn up in front of the house. With mounted cavalry as a second line of defence against the mob, all eyes now turned on the Serjeant-at-Arms. Since the front door would not give way to anything but an axe or a battering ram, he decided to use a ladder. This was placed against the sill of the first floor drawing-room window and he sent up his deputy. The window was obligingly opened – only to be brought down on the finger of the climber.

The only remaining alternative was an assault by way of the area steps on the basement door and windows. Once inside, and escorted by a detachment of Foot Guards, the Serjeant-at-Arms went up to the drawing-room where Sir Francis and his family were calmly waiting and where, if we can believe it, he was reading Magna Carta to his young son.

When Sir Francis stepped into his carriage bound for the Tower, Piccadilly might have been a parade ground. Taking no chances with the crowd, the Order of March was

Two squadrons 15th Light Dragoons
Two troops Life Guards
Sir Francis Burdett and the Serjeant-at-Arms
Two troops Life Guards

Two battalions Foot Guards in open order
   flanking the carriage
One troop 15th Light Dragoons

Everything else could only be an anticlimax. Sir Francis Burdett simply lodged at the Tower for six weeks until, with the prorogation of Parliament in June, the warrant ceased to be in force. A huge crowd awaited his release on Tower Hill but Sir Francis decided on a discreet exit by a side door. He crossed the river by boat and travelled quietly to Wimbledon where he had a country house.

If actors have a bad name, they can put much of the blame on EDMUND KEAN who spent nine years of his unruly life – 1815 to 1824 – at 12 CLARGES STREET. Kean was a mountebank prototype-cast for the role of tippling lecher. An office block, facing No.34, has recently replaced the terrace house where he lived at the height of his fame and when he was having an affair with the wife of a City Alderman. This led to a case of 'crim-con', short for 'criminal conversation', a legal euphemism for adultery.

One regular mistress was not enough for Kean. Legend insists that he needed sex before a performance to stimulate him and that he once satisfied himself with three women before going on to play Richard III.

The illegitimate child of an alcoholic father who went mad and committed suicide, Kean, born about 1790, spent his boyhood performing in barns, taverns and fairs; for nine years he toured the provinces; his first great success came in 1813, by which time he was already debauched, his personality split between professional megalomania and a sense of social inferiority.

Public notoriety burst on him when Alderman Robert Cox, a member of the Drury Lane committee, sued him for adultery with his wife. The affair had been going on for several years and because Cox had previously been complaisant, his claim for £2,000 damages was reduced to an award of £800. But Kean's love letters were read out in court, obscene ballads sold in the streets, and he was attacked in *The Times* which encouraged audiences to protest against 'that obscene little personage'. But his aplomb and refusal to accept defeat saw him through the trial and several subsequent nights of uproar. He died at Richmond in 1833, six weeks after collapsing while playing Othello at Covent Garden on the line: 'Villain be sure thou prove my love a whore'.

In the second half of the eigthteenth century CHARLOTTE HAYES ran an establishment known as 'The Cloisters'. It was a misleading name. No cathedral calm prevailed, for this was London's most notorious brothel, and so successful was it that she and her husband, DENNIS O'KELLY, made enough money to live in considerable style at a tactful distance from her place of work.

At a time when Mayfair had just become highly fashionable, they acquired two adjoining houses, 91 and 92 PICCADILLY. Here, just west of Half Moon Street, Lord Egremont, godson of George II and a great racehorse owner, was their close neighbour.

Their place of business was in King's Place, an alley between Pall Mall and King Street, where the activities of the 'priestess of the Cyprian Deity', as Charlotte Hayes styled herself, could be kept conveniently separate from the house where O'Kelly entertained his racing friends.

O'Kelly was born in Ireland and came to London about 1748 where he started work as a sedan-chairman. He had much going for him: good looks and personality, fine hands and an engaging Irish accent. He mixed happily with people on all levels of society and was very popular with women, one of whom, a countess living in Hanover Square, first employed him as her chairman and then took him as a lover. When her husband found out, O'Kelly lost himself for some while in the shadowy world of pleasure houses and Vauxhall Gardens. Though he had rich and famous acquaintances he ran into debt, and was sent to the Fleet Prison. This is where he met, and probably married, Charlotte Hayes.

The pair were released under an amnesty granted in 1760 on the accession of George III, and between them they raised enough backing to take the King's Place premises. Charlotte's 'Cloisters' appear to have owed something to the influence of the 'Medmenham Monks' and her 'nuns' to have had training in similar practices. 'The Cloisters' catered for both men and women and prices for elderly clients with particular requirements were high: fifty guineas a night.

Intrigued by something she was told about Polynesian courting rituals, and with little idea of even where Polynesia was, Charlotte devised the 'Polynesian Feast of Venus'. At the first enactment of the ceremony several members of the nobility and five MPs were present to watch the erotic display by twelve nymphs who were supposed to be 'spotless virgins'. She herself took the part of 'Queen Oberea'.

While Charlotte looked after her customers at 'The Cloisters',

The Piccadilly houses of the O'Kellys were immediately to the left of the tavern on the corner of Half Moon Street. Paul Sandby shows them with bow windows. In the rare print below, The Eclipse Macarony, *Colonel O'Kelly in macaroni costume is seen on his famous horse.*

O'Kelly was running a race gang and was more concerned with the turf and gambling. He bought a share in a yearling from William Wildman, a Leadenhall butcher, for 650 guineas. This was Eclipse which, when he bought out Wildman, won eighteen races in two years ('Eclipse first and the rest nowhere' was O'Kelly's famous prediction) and retired unbeaten to become one of racing's most famous sires. The stud fees for Eclipse were fifty guineas, equal to those charged by Charlotte for comparable services in King's Place.

The affluence and life-style of Charlotte and O'Kelly (who now called himself 'Colonel') were such that by the early 1770s they had acquired not only the house in Piccadilly but another at Clay Hill, near Banstead. A decade later they purchased the even more splendid Canons, near Stanmore, Middlesex. Sin had certainly paid.

The one ambition denied to O'Kelly – membership of the fiercely snobbish Jockey Club – could not be purchased. Dennis died in 1787 at 91-92 Piccadilly. Charlotte outlived him, and there is no record of how long she ran 'The Cloisters'. She went mad and died in 1811.

While Eclipse is remembered long after the erotic junketings of 'The Cloisters' have been forgotten, one faintly absurd story lingers on about the Piccadilly house. One of the great attractions for visitors was Col. O'Kelly's parrot, a bird whose educational achievements were an ability to recite and to whistle the 104th Psalm. Even Queen Oberea couldn't compete with that.

The Naval and Military Club – the 'In and Out' – at 94 PICCADILLY has a Blue Plaque recalling blandly that it was formerly a royal residence and then the home of LORD PALMERSTON. There is nothing to indicate that while living there in 1863 the Prime Minister was cited in a sensational divorce case. He was almost 80 at the time.

The house was built a hundred years earlier by the second Earl of Egremont, whose son was the O'Kellys' neighbour (p. 88). Before the Palmerston affair, No. 94 had known another embarrassment while occupied by Adolphus, Duke of Cambridge. On a visit to her uncle, Queen Victoria was attacked in the courtyard by a lunatic.

Palmerston was accused of having an affair with a former governess. She was Margaret O'Kane, the wife of Timothy O'Kane, an Irish journalist, and she went to Cambridge House ostensibly on a political errand for her husband. O'Kane charged Palmerston with making love to her on this and other occasions.

No 94 Piccadilly. The house, now a club, as it looked when owned by Lord Palmerston. Nearing 80, and Prime Minister while living here, Palmerston was cited for adultery with a governess.

He claimed £20,000 damages and, when Palmerston denied the allegations, O'Kane cited him in a divorce petition.

'In town and the country nothing was talked about for days than the Palmerston case', wrote Lord Clarendon to Lord Cowley in Paris: 'The lady has been a governess and an actress and good looking, and said not to make unnecessary difficulties'. The joke round the clubs was 'while the lady was certainly Kane, was Palmerston Abel?' Another gossip, William Hardman, said: 'The potent septuagenarian nobleman proved irresistible to the easy virtued governess. Hence a connection which resulted in various letters, sundry banknotes and equivalent copulation'. Gladstone was worried by the scandal. So was Disraeli but for a different reason: he feared it would make Palmerston more popular.

Palmerston extricated himself on a technicality because Margaret O'Kane claimed she had never been legally married to the journalist. She also denied the charges. O'Kane was asked to supply details of the marriage but because he did not comply the case was dismissed.

When he died two years later Palmerston was buried in Westminster Abbey.

What did the detective see? What, from his uncomfortable, not to say ludicrous, position under the drawing-room sofa, did he hear? And what did Lord Cardigan, the future hero of Balaclava, really get up to with Lady William Paget when they returned that night from the opera?

These questions take us round the corner to 10 QUEEN STREET on a May night in 1843 when LORD WILLIAM PAGET employed a detective to spy on his wife. Seldom have a husband's motives been more dubious; rarely can a private investigator have found himself so precariously concealed; and few similar situations can have had a greater flavour of French farce.

The dramatis personae are:

Lord William Paget, spendthrift second son of the first Marquess of Anglesey. Aged 40. Imprisoned for debt at 26; signed a promise to his father to reform and stay abroad; broke his promise; again found himself in debt and had to be rescued from King's Bench to save the family name. After being MP for Caernarvon he got himself adopted for Andover, knowing that as an MP he couldn't be imprisoned for debt. Over ten years his father estimated he paid £26,916 of William's debts. In 1827 he married *Lady*

William Paget, formerly Fanny Rottenburgh, daughter of a general. Took refuge from her husband's behaviour in an affair with a Frenchman in Pau, a flirtation with a Lieutenant Packenham, and whatever may have followed the opera performance she attended with

Lord Cardigan, James Thomas Brudenall, seventh Earl of Cardigan, Commander of the 11th Hussars. Estranged from his wife. A martinet, he once had an officer arrested for putting a bottle instead of a decanter on the mess table. Fought a duel on Wimbledon Common with a writer who criticised him. Was to take his private yacht to the war in the Crimea. When Paget heard that Cardigan's relationship with Lady William was 'the object of much distressing comment', he got in touch with

Frederick Winter, a disreputable detective, who was later to state that Paget promised him £100 a year for three years if he could produce evidence against Cardigan.

Before Lady William and Cardigan returned from the opera, Winter took up his observation post under the sofa in the first floor drawing-room. After a short discussion by the couple about the performance Winter reported that he heard a noise 'as of the pulling down of a blind . . . then kissing . . .'

Probably finding himself a bit cramped, Winter moved from under the sofa on his stomach which placed him in a strategic position to observe their activities. He particularly noted the heels of Lord Cardigan's boots and the straps under them as he lay uppermost.

'There, that's some of the seeds of misery,' said Cardigan as he got off the sofa. It is not recorded if Lady William took this as a compliment.

As soon as he could, the detective got away and went to Berkeley Square where Paget was waiting anxiously for news. After hearing Winter's story he went straight round to Queen Street, upbraided his wife as 'the most infamous whore that ever breathed' and, she said, physically assaulted her.

Paget brought a case against Cardigan, but the court had no difficulty in perceiving that he was suing confident that Cardigan would pay up rather than face the disgrace of divorce proceedings. Here he underestimated the future leader of the Light Brigade. Cardigan showed that he could deny an adultery charge with all the resolution with which he was shortly to lead a military one.

He decided to fight, and the enemy was clearly intimidated. On the first day of the trial Winter, on whose evidence Paget depended, failed to turn up in court. At a later hearing his testimony showed him so untrustworthy that the jury returned a verdict for Lord Cardigan without retiring. The sole object of Paget's action, declared the Solicitor-General, had been 'to extract money from a wealthy nobleman'.

Round the corner from Queen Street and opposite Crewe House is 38a CURZON STREET (now offices of the Lombard North Central bank). On this site in the middle of the eighteenth century was the May Fair Chapel where ALEXANDER KEITH, a parson of dubious credentials, did a roaring trade in illegal marriages. In the twenty years after 1733 some 7,000 clandestine weddings were performed without banns or licences, first by Keith and then after his imprisonment by his four assistants. He 'constructed a very bishopric of revenue', wrote Horace Walpole.

Among those who took advantage of these extremely lax nuptials was Elizabeth Gunning, one of three beautiful Irish sisters, on to whose finger, and carrying informality to its limits, James, sixth Duke of Hamilton, slipped a curtain ring. This he had impatiently prised from a bed-curtain in Chesterfield House before rushing his future bride a few yards down Curzon Street to the chapel for a wedding which took place half an hour after midnight.

This was characteristic of the way in which ceremonies were performed by the Revd Mr Keith who came from Scotland and was not always sober. He or his assistants married, among many others, Bysshe Shelley, grandfather of the poet, and the philandering bigamist Edward Wortley Montagu, son of the celebrated letter-writer, Lady Mary. The advantages of these marriages to the participants included being married without declaring names; antedating them to legitimise offspring; a woman's avoidance of debt by hiring a temporary husband.

These abuses (which were also practised in the Fleet Prison) led to Keith being taken to court and excommunicated in 1742, and being committed to prison 'for the contempt of the Holy and Mother Church'. While he was in prison his assistants carried on the business in another chapel fitted up a few yards from the original one.

A Marriage Act – forbidding clandestine unions – was passed in 1754, precipitating sixty-one accelerated Curzon Street weddings on the day before it came into operation. By this time Keith had done excellently from his curious trade. As well as his Mayfair marriages, during the first eleven of the fourteen years he spent in prison (where he died in 1758), he is reckoned to have performed 1,000 illegal marriages annually.

Murder in Mayfair is not a common occurrence. The area is too well-bred for anything so unseemly. So it caused no little stir on 16 April 1871 when a Frenchwoman, Mme Reil, was found choked to death at her house, 13 PARK LANE (now 14 Old Park Lane, part of the Pan Am office on the corner of Brick Street). People recalled that thirty years had elapsed since the last Mayfair murder in nearby Norfolk Street (p. 98). They trusted this sort of thing would not become a habit.

The murder could not even claim to be fashionable. It was committed by Mme Reil's cook, MARGUERITE DIBLANC. The one redeeming feature was that the Frenchwoman, a widow in her mid-forties, appeared to be the mistress of Lord Lucan, the Commander-in-Chief in the Crimea, who lived a few hundred yards away in South Street. That at least introduced a touch of distinction.

Otherwise it was a sordid run-of-the-mill business. Mme Reil, who had a reputation for being a difficult employer, had accused her cook Marguerite, a Belgian woman of 29, of listening at doors. She said that she drank. And so Marguerite had been dismissed with a week's pay. When she had demanded a month's pay, her mistress had told her that she must work out her notice.

On Sunday, 8 April, Mme Reil disappeared. She was seen by a maid who took up breakfast but not again until the evening of the following day when her daughter searched the house with a friend. They came to the pantry which they found locked. The daughter opened it and found her mother's body with a rope round her neck. The cook was nowhere in the house.

Several days later Marguerite Diblanc was arrested in Paris. She confessed she had killed her mistress out of resentment and the police found money on her which she had stolen from Mme Reil's safe.

Though Marguerite was found guilty, the jury considered she had been unduly provoked by Mme Reil. They recommended clemency and the death sentence was commuted.

Everything about WHITAKER WRIGHT – and this includes his death – was larger than life. Born in Cheshire in 1845, he emigrated to the United States when he was 21, and ten years as a mining prospector turned him into a dollar millionaire. Enormously wealthy when he returned to England in 1889, Wright floated four companies with a capital of eight million pounds.

In London his home was 18 PARK LANE, an imposing stucco mansion (now replaced by an extension of the Londonderry Hotel: it was the twin of the still surviving 17 Old Park Lane). At his country house, Lea Park, Godalming, he had stables for fifty horses and a billiard room with an unusual setting. It was built *under* the ornamental lake he had created.

Known as the biggest business man in Britain, Wright had a finger in a dozen enterprises – among them the Lake View and Star Goldmine in Australia and the Bakerloo Line of the London Underground. When his corporate company, the London and Globe, crashed in 1900, the Official Receiver discovered that the previous year's books showed a profit of nearly half a million pounds when in fact there had been a deficit of £1,600,000.

At the beginning of this century it was not an offence to issue a false balance sheet but Wright was prosecuted under the Larceny Act of 1861. Before he could be brought to court he left England for France and America with a young woman – so young that they travelled, presumably as father and daughter, under the names of Mr and Miss Andreoni.

It took a long time to trace and extradite him, and it was not until three years after the collapse that he went on trial, accused of transferring capital from one company to another to give the necessary appearance of assets.

He was sentenced to seven years' penal servitude but never reached prison. A few minutes after the trial, while waiting to be taken away by his warders, he stood chatting to his friends and legal advisers. He asked to be excused for a moment. When he returned he had a capsule of cyanide in his mouth but lit up a cigar. He took out his gold watch and one or two other personal possessions which he gave to friends. 'I shall not be needing these where I am going,' he said, and bit on the capsule.

On 19 April 1872 a brief, virtually incomprehensible, announcement appeared in *The London Gazette*:

> 'The presentation of Lady Twiss at the Drawing-room attended by her in 1869 is cancelled.'

What caused this retrospective 'cancellation' by the Lord Chamberlain of an event which had taken place at Buckingham Palace three years before? What had LADY TWISS, wife of an eminent, respectable lawyer, done to merit her presentation being officially effaced from history?

The paragraph focused attention on a large house at 19 PARK LANE (demolished; the Hilton Hotel is on the site), reminding passers-by of the scandal in 1872 when Lady Twiss had been accused by a solicitor named ALEXANDER CHAFFERS of being an immoral woman. We have to decide which of the two people – Marie Twiss or Chaffers – should be named on our Black Plaque.

Lady Twiss was the wife of Sir Travers Twiss who was aged 63, Queen's Advocate General, a former Regius Professor of Civil Law at Oxford and a recognised authority on international and ecclesiastical law. They had married in 1861 by special licence abroad when his bride had given her maiden name as Marie van Lynseele. She was understood to be the orphaned daughter of a major-general in the Polish Army.

During the next decade Travers Twiss followed a career of ever-increasing prestige, practising in the ecclesiastical courts (he was Chancellor of the Diocese of London), and was knighted in 1868. During this time Lady Twiss was twice presented at Court.

Shortly after her second presentation in 1869, the Lord Chamberlain, the official responsible for Court invitations, received an astonishing letter. The solicitor Alexander Chaffers wrote saying that before her marriage Lady Twiss had been a common prostitute. He stated that she had frequented London night houses and other places of ill repute.

Later he went before the Chief Magistrate at Bow Street and swore a deposition so damaging that Sir Travers and Lady Twiss decided to bring a criminal action against him for 'dangerous, false and malicious libels'.

Conducting his own defence at the Sessions House, Newington Causeway, the solicitor declared that Lady Twiss was not of Polish origin or the daughter of a high-ranking officer; she was a Belgian prostitute named Marie Gelas, the daughter of a carpenter. She had been a London streetwalker and an *habituée* of the notorious Argyll Rooms. Chaffers said she had been Twiss's mistress before their marriage and that he himself had paid her £1 and committed misconduct with her in Courtrai and Ghent. He supplied dates and a list of her clients.

Lady Twiss emphatically denied all these accusations, and among witnesses who testified for her was a former maid who said that Chaffers had tried to bribe her to give defamatory evidence. He was also accused of trying to blackmail Lady Twiss. During seven days of complicated and conflicting testimony, it was stated in her defence that Marie Gelas and Marie van Lynseele were two different persons. There had been a confusion of identity.

When the hearing resumed on the eighth day Lady Twiss was not in court. After some delay and consultations, her counsel informed the bench: 'Your Worship, Lady Twiss had decided not to appear again. My information is that she has left London . . .'

The news caused a sensation, not greatly reduced by her counsel's submission that she had found the cross-examination too hard to bear. The magistrate, however, showed sympathy to Lady Twiss, telling Chaffers: 'You will probably for the rest of your life be an object-lesson of contempt to all honest and well-thinking men.' But he had no alternative but to dismiss the libel case against the solicitor. Inevitable inferences were drawn from Lady Twiss's disappearance.

Sir Travers immediately resigned as Queen's Advocate General, relinquished all his other official positions and ceased to practise. He died aged 88 at 9 Whittingstall Road, Fulham, without making any public comment on the affair. It is not known if he saw his wife again, if she ever returned to England, or crossed the threshold of 19 Park Lane. Nor do we know if the Lord Chamberlain had additional information about this strange affair to justify the damning insertion in *The London Gazette*.

The first of Mayfair's only two notable murders was a below-stairs affair, or rather, as in the case of Marguerite Diblanc (p. 95), the killer was a servant and a foreigner.

Early on a May morning in 1840 Lord William Russell, a widower of 72, was found in bed with his throat cut at his home 14 NORFOLK STREET (where No. 16 Dunraven Street now stands), off Park Lane. The discovery caused a considerable sensation because Lord William was the brother of both the fifth and sixth Dukes of Bedford and his nephew was Lord John Russell, then Secretary of State for the Colonies. The Commissioner of Police was immediately called in. Queen Victoria was gravely informed of the news by Prince Albert at noon.

There were signs of a break-in; furniture was disturbed and, as gold coins, jewellery and silver plate were missing, the first impression was that Lord William had been killed by a burglar. But suspicion gradually fell on FRANÇOIS COURVOISIER, his valet, a smooth ingratiating young Swiss of 23. The police arrested him and he was sent to trial; but, as the missing valuables had not been found, the evidence against him was weak and largely circumstantial.

The question of whether he was guilty was widely debated, and there was betting in the London clubs on the outcome. On the day before the jury were due to give their verdict, the odds were heavily on Courvoisier's acquittal. Then chance intervened.

The same day in the small Hotel Dieppe, off Leicester Square, the part-proprietor, Joseph Vincent, happened to be reading a French newspaper article on the case. He showed the paper to his cousin, Charlotte Poilaine, who managed the hotel where her husband was Vincent's partner, but she was busy and did not read the paper until later when she suddenly remembered an incident which had occurred six weeks earlier. A young Swiss, who had once worked briefly at the hotel, had come to visit her. He had asked if she would take care of a brown-paper parcel for him. She had agreed.

Mrs Poilaine and Vincent realised there was no time to lose. The parcel was opened and found to contain Lord William's missing silver. The police acted with frantic overnight speed. They had so few hours left if they were to present evidence that would prevent the jury bringing in a not guilty verdict which could never be rescinded.

To identify the man who had brought the parcel to the hotel, Mrs Poilaine was rushed to Newgate where she picked out Courvoisier among the men exercising in the prison yard. The following day she appeared in court, and gave evidence which completely changed the jury's decision and secured his conviction.

The swiftness of the last-minute police action and the dramatic climax to the case created so much public interest that when Courvoisier was publicly executed at Newgate, the hanging was said to have attracted 100,000 people.

Many eighteenth-century houses in the north part of Mayfair have been replaced by Edwardian mansions, and this has happened in several streets of ponderous terraces between Park Lane and Grosvenor Square. Originally 13 GREEN STREET (where No. 19 now stands) would have resembled the pleasant Georgian No. 61 across the street. It is a house like this we should have in mind when we imagine THOMAS, LORD COCHRANE taking up residence a few days before the sequence of extraordinary events that were to blight his career.

One February morning in 1814 – the year before Waterloo – Cochrane was called on at his new home in Green Street by a man wearing the uniform and insignia of a military aide-de-camp under his greatcoat. The visitor's name was CHARLES RANDOM DE BERENGER. He was closely involved in the conspiracy with which Cochrane and others were later to be charged.

Berenger had just arrived from Dover after delivering a forged letter to the Port Admiral at Deal, stating that Bonaparte had been killed by Cossacks ('who immediately slaid him and divided his body between them'). Travelling to London he spread the news that the French were defeated and the Allies in Paris.

The effect of Berenger's news was the immediate rise in the value of shares on the Stock Exchange. Thomas, Lord Cochrane, who had bought £130,000 worth of stock only a few days before, made £2,470. His uncle and others enjoyed even greater coups. They were arrested and tried for rigging the market.

At the trial Berenger admitted spreading the false rumour. He said Cochrane had suggested that he inform the Port Admiral of the British victory, urging that it would be an 'incalculable value should he telegraph up the news'. Cochrane did not deny that Berenger had then come to London to see him at Green Street and said that it was true Berenger had been given civilian clothes before he left. When Berenger was arrested he had on him some pound notes that were proved to have come from Cochrane.

This evidence was sufficiently damaging for all the accused to be found guilty of conspiracy. Cochrane received twelve months imprisonment, was fined £1,000, and expelled as a Member of Parliament. He was also ordered to stand in the pillory – though he never suffered that part of the ordeal.

In the year of his downfall Cochrane is depicted by a satarist as half-expelled naval hero, half-disgraced civilian.

As the law then existed, Cochrane as an accused person was unable to give evidence, but afterwards in an autobiography and in endless statements, he consistently denied his guilt. While Berenger confessed, Cochrane refuted more or less everything except that Berenger had come to Green Street. He devoted the next eighteen years to clearing himself.

In the end he received a pardon from William IV. This was in 1832, by which date he had come into the title of tenth Earl of Dundonald and was living in Hanover Lodge, Regent's Park; he had served with courage and distinction in a South American war; and his constantly reiterated assertion that the evidence against him had been false or circumstantial gathered strength as the actual events receded into the past.

The conflicting evidence makes the whole story extremely complicated, and several latter-day writers have been inclined to give Cochrane the benefit of a great many doubts. Even if he were not directly responsible for instigating the fraud, the others who profited were certainly guilty. There is a multitude of strange coincidences that are hard to explain. If nothing else it must be said that Thomas Cochrane, Admiral the Earl of Dundonald, kept very dubious company.

In the second half of the eighteenth century an extremely rich widow, the Countess of Strathmore, had the ill hap to marry an adventurer who had a streak of villainy and a talent for romantic flourishes. At the age of 27, with a fortune of over a million pounds and a fine house at 40 GROSVENOR SQUARE, Lady Strathmore had a number of suitors, but CAPTAIN ANDREW STONEY won the day.

During the next eleven years the widow saw the consequence of her folly as Stoney went through her money, treated her violently and took a mistress. The climax came when, after she sued him for divorce, he kidnapped her in Oxford Street and she was carried off screaming in a coach for the north. Later at his trial it was alleged that among other horrors she was imprisoned 'in a dark passage, frozen almost to death' along with a grunting herd of hogs, pigs and swine.

Clearly this was no way to treat a member of the Bowes-Lyon family, and an ancestor of Queen Elizabeth, the Queen Mother.

The extraordinary sequence of events began in 1777, a year after the death of John Lyon, ninth Earl of Strathmore, when his widow, the former Mary Eleanor Bowes, fell under the spell of Stoney, a half-pay officer from Ireland. As part of a campaign to impress the countess, he challenged the editor of the *Morning Post* to a duel for publishing defamatory paragraphs about her. This 'affair of honour' was a put-up job, intended to impress Eleanor. It did. She married the seemingly gallant and impetuous Stoney four days later.

As a precaution against his acquiring all her money, the Countess at first put her property in trust, but this she revoked when Stoney became upset. In the next few years Stoney's extravagance caused so much overspending that in 1781 they had to leave Grosvenor Square. The marriage went slowly downhill with Stoney's repeated violence and greed. When he took a mistress she had grounds for a divorce.

Faced with the loss of his extravagant life-style, Stoney collected a band of conspirators who dogged his wife's footsteps in various disguises. She took fright but her precautions failed. One day in November 1781 she was visiting a shop at the corner of Oxford Street and Tottenham Court Road when she was taken by surprise and confronted by a constable (in Stoney's pay) who said he had a warrant for her arrest and orders to take her to the Lord Chief Justice, Lord Mansfield, at Highgate.

When they reached Highgate, Stoney appeared and, realising she had been duped, a now violently protesting Lady Strathmore was forcibly taken on an eight-day journey north to Durham. The purpose of the kidnapping was to prevent her proceeding with the divorce. Perhaps Stoney may also have had some vague hope that – as with the old duel – she might be dazzled by his impetuosity and so stop the case. But now the Countess was a great deal wiser.

At the trial Stoney claimed that there was mutual forgiveness and that they had cohabited; this the Countess strongly denied and produced plenty of witnesses with hair-raising accounts – they included the pig story – of her treatment on the road. At times they have the flavour of a rustic comedy by Oliver Goldsmith. The landlord of the Red Lion at Barnet testified that Lady Strathmore had appeared at the window of her coach shouting 'Murder, murder, help for God's sake! Murder, murder!' An ostler at Stilton told of her escaping, running down the road and being bundled back into a chaise. It is hard to know whether to believe further stories of her being hidden in a cow house, being threatened by Stoney with a strait-jacket and being so ill-used that she could not stand or walk downstairs.

All nine conspirators were found guilty, and after serving a sentence of three years, Stoney went back to prison. He was in

King's Bench when the Countess died in 1800 and was buried in Westminster Abbey in the gown she had worn at her wedding to the Earl of Strathmore. Stoney died in 1810 seemingly while still in prison.

No. 40 Grosvenor Square, demolished, is now part of the Britannia Hotel.

5

Inner Mayfair

I<small>T</small> may not be strictly cause and effect, but it looks very much as if, when the Court moved west from Whitehall after the fire of 1698, royal mistresses travelled in the same direction. The later Stuarts installed their favourites in Pall Mall and St James's Square (p. 39), but the Hanoverians, residing in Kensington and then Buckingham Palace, found Mayfair more convenient. As well as offering their ladies a good address, the area appealed to the large assortment of royal dukes for whom having a mistress was not only second nature but a first priority.

It cannot be a coincidence that in the eighteenth and nineteenth centuries eight women intimately connected with the English royal family, and three involved with foreign royalty, were living in this increasingly fashionable part of London. Not all were moved there by their lovers; some, like Kitty Fisher, were already there when royalty knocked; others, like Lillie Langtry, arrived after the affairs were over but were left well provided for. Grosvenor Square accommodated three of them – two royal brothers successively welcomed at one house. Even a note of domesticity was struck by a cousin of Queen Victoria who lived in Piccadilly and for over forty years maintained his mistress a matter of 500 yards away.

With the constrictions of arranged marriages, and the prohibitions of choice dictated by the Royal Marriage Act, to say nothing of their natural inclinations, many of the men can hardly be blamed. Nor can their partners who, robbed of status and in the teeth of convention, were sometimes touchingly loyal. To put Black Plaques on their houses and to attach the names of the mistresses rather than their lovers might appear unwarranted. But, as we shall see, the behaviour of many of the women was pretty scandalous.

The pace was set by BARONESS MELUSINE VON DER SCHULENBURG. A maid of honour at the Court of Hanover, Melusine had been

George I's mistress for more than twenty years, and the mother of two of his daughters, when she accompanied him to England on his accession in 1714. With them came the Baroness Sophia Kielmannsegge, suspected, probably wrongly, of also being George's mistress. This situation was to cause Horace Walpole to comment 'that the mob of London were highly diverted at the importation of so uncommon a seraglio'.

After many years in apartments in St James's Palace and Kensington Palace, Melusine moved into a house at what is now 43 GROSVENOR SQUARE. The square had only just been completed, and in 1728 she was the first occupant of this house on the south side. From her windows, this tall thin woman nicknamed 'The Maypole' looked out on the equestrian statue of her recently dead royal lover.

Created the Duchess of Kendal in 1719, she had an unflattering reputation as a rapacious woman 'who would have sold the king's honour for a shilling advance to the best bidder'. She received considerable sums for arranging honours and favours. But her rapacity seemingly paid dividends; as well as an income from the King of £7,500 a year, she was reputedly paid £5,000 for securing a title for Henry St John, whose son – the Jacobite first Viscount Bolingbroke – paid her double that amount to arrange his restoration (p. 144). She profited from the South Sea Bubble and, after obtaining a concession to mint copper coins for Ireland, she made a good thing out of selling the contract to a Birmingham manufacturer. Wheeling and dealing in her sixties, she profitably negotiated the marriage of Petronella, her illegitimate daughter by George I, to her next door neighbour, the letter-writing fourth Earl of Chesterfield (p. 34). Petronella was 40 but an heiress and, content with the financial and political value of the marriage, Chesterfield apparently celebrated the wedding by taking a new mistress: Petronella stayed at No. 43 with her mother.

Until her death aged 77 in 1743 Melusine also owned Kendal House, on the river at Isleworth. No. 43 Grosvenor Square, half-way between South Audley Street and Carlos Place, existed until 1967 when the Britannia Hotel was built on the site.

In 1764 and some years after Lord Chesterfield had left for South Audley Street, 45 GROSVENOR SQUARE (now rebuilt as luxury apartments) became the home of HENRIETTA VERNON. This was the year of her marriage to Sir Richard Grosvenor, the immensely rich ground landlord whose uncle had built the square. It is said that his behaviour gave his wife 'no slight grounds for alienation' and

Melusine von
der Schulenberg

Henrietta Grosvenor

Laura Bell

Maria Fitzherbert

Catherine 'Skittles' Walters

Lillie Langtry

Kitty Fisher

Lola Montez

Louisa Fairbrother
in the role of
Abdallah in a
Lyceum pantomime

Elizabeth Howard

Mary 'Perdita' Robinson

Henrietta responded in full measure by embarking on an affair with George III's brother, Edward Duke of York and then, two years after Edward's death, she became involved even more tempestuously with his brother, Henry Duke of Cumberland. The first affair was brief but the second had the whole of London talking when their love letters were intercepted and published.

It is from the journals of Henrietta's aunt, Lady Mary Coke, that we hear of her relationship with 'the weak and debauched' Prince Henry. Lady Mary noted that on a four-day journey from London to the Grosvenor estates at Eaton in Cheshire the Duke of Cumberland met Henrietta at every inn on the road. He was there 'some hours before her, and marked two bedchambers with chalk which, her ladyship understanding, made choice of one of them where she lay; the other was always engaged for the Duke who pretended to be a Welsh gentleman and always left the inn at six o'clock in the morning.'

The Middlesex Journal got hold of the letters between Henrietta and the Duke, probably from a disloyal servant, and her husband, himself a far from model partner, decided to sue. Rumour had it that there were attempts to buy him off, but the case, heard in 1770, resulted in damages of £10,000. Cumberland couldn't pay but his brother, the King, came to his rescue.

She was deserted soon after by Cumberland, and banished from Grosvenor Square by her husband, but Henrietta's memorial, a strange one, remains in the family. Her portrait by Gainsborough was cut in half by her enraged husband and only the upper half – the head and torso – survives at Eaton, the property of her descendant, the sixth Duke of Westminster.

Some eighty years after Henrietta Grosvenor had so generously entertained two royal dukes, eyebrows were raised with the arrival at 15 GROSVENOR SQUARE of a married couple, Captain and Mrs Augustus Frederick Thistlethwaite. The Captain had a respectable background; he was the grandson of the Bishop of Norwich, and the wedding in January 1852 was a very seemly event at St George's, Hanover Square. But gossip started when it was realised that in her recent past Mrs Thistlethwaite had been LAURA BELL.

Laura had first achieved notoriety two years before when, as a twenty-two-year-old shop assistant from Ireland, she had caught the eye of Prince Jung Bahadoor of Nepal. The Prince (an ancestor of the present King of Nepal) was then prime minister of his country and came to London on a diplomatic mission with two of his brothers, a retinue of twenty-six, and with the sum of £30,000 specifically allocated for spending.

As well as his official business which included audiences with Queen Victoria, the Prince devoted much of his three months' stay to high living and visits to pleasure resorts like Vauxhall Gardens. During this time the Prince met Laura Bell: how is uncertain, but it is possible that with her pretty eyes in a doll-like face she attracted his attention when she was working in Jay's Mourning House in Regent Street. Both Sir Robert Peel and the Duke of Cambridge died while he was in London and protocol would have required the purchase of mourning bands.

It is said that at the conclusion of their brief affair, Prince Bahadoor gave Laura £250,000. It is also alleged that when this became known in his own country, it caused such a strain in relations with Nepal that the British Government repaid the money. Both accounts are probably greatly exaggerated and no amount of research has produced evidence of any such sum being sent to Katmandu.

What is certain is that Laura was treated so generously that she was able to set herself up in Wilton Crescent, and was seen daily in her open phaeton in Hyde Park chatting with the fashionable and disreputable set who gathered around the Achilles statue. These visits to the park led to her meeting with Captain Thistlethwaite and their marriage within sixteen months of her Nepalese lover's departure.

When she and the Captain moved to Grosvenor Square Laura said goodbye to her previous life. She was extravagant, started to drink too freely and there were frequent quarrels with her husband. But now people started to talk about Laura Bell for quite different reasons. She reformed. No. 15 was opened for prayer meetings and she particularly welcomed women from whose ranks she had recently risen. Mr Gladstone, a zealous reformer of prostitutes, became a close ally. When her large house became too small for her congregations she preached and conducted salvation missions at the Regent Street Polytechnic and Exeter Hall in the Strand.

Laura's marriage ended dramatically in 1887. The servants in Grosvenor Square were not unduly surprised when a shot was heard above stairs; this was often their master's eccentric way of summoning them. But on this occasion they arrived to find Thistlethwaite dead, a bullet through his head. Whether the shot accidentally ricocheted from the ceiling or it was suicide was never established.

With a large inheritance, his widow moved from the north side of Grosvenor Square to Woodbine Cottage, on the corner of West End Lane, Hampstead, where she became a benefactor of many charities. When Laura Bell died in 1894 the exotic affair with a foreign prince was nearly half a century in the past. The penitent survivor left her home as 'a Retreat for clergymen of all denominations, true believers in my God and Saviour, and literary men'. No. 15 Grosvenor Square has been rebuilt as expensive flats.

From Grosvenor Square we take a zigzag course along Upper Brook Street with a north turn into Park Street to look for the house where MRS FITZHERBERT secretly married the future George IV. The actual house, 64 PARK STREET, no longer exists; on the site today is 129–131 Park Street, just before the corner of Oxford Street.

The address is of some consequence in the story of Mayfair's misalliances because the marriage was actually invalid. Under the terms of the Royal Marriage Act of 1772 the Prince of Wales had broken the law by marrying without his father's permission. He also risked a constitutional crisis because Mrs Fitzherbert was a Roman Catholic. Under the 1701 Act of Settlement, this meant he would be unable to inherit the throne.

So there was a marriage ceremony but no marriage. Mrs Fitzherbert was pronounced his wife but was never more than his mistress.

This matrimonial tangle came about four years after the twice widowed Maria Fitzherbert, a rich and graceful woman of twenty-nine, first met the Prince. Six years her junior, and fancying himself desperately in love, he went through a pantomime of stabbing himself at Carlton House when she first rejected him. Only reluctantly did she agree to the marriage.

The ceremony took place at dusk on the evening of 15 December 1785 in the drawing-room of the Park Street house with the door locked once the Prince had arrived and Mrs Fitzherbert's uncle and younger brother assembled as witnesses. The marriage was performed by an Anglican curate who, recently released from the Fleet debtors' prison, was encouraged to risk the consequences for payment of £500 and the promise of a future bishopric.

So started the curious relationship that survived the Prince's constitutional marriage in 1795 to Princess Caroline (p. 261). After only a temporary separation they were reunited (apparently with the sanction of Rome). A break came about 1803 after she was

'Wife or no wife' was Gillray's title for his cartoon of the secret marriage.
Edmund Burke performs the ceremony, Charles James Fox gives the bride
away and Lord North, the chief minister of the day, conveniently sleeps.

snubbed at a Carlton House banquet, but despite all the vicissitudes and the Prince Regent's countless liaisons, Mrs Fitzherbert remained the woman to whom he was most sincerely attached and whose miniature he was wearing round his neck on his death-bed in 1830. She died at Brighton seven years later.

One street away to the west (and just under a century after the Park Street marriage) the mistress of another Prince of Wales took up her residence in Mayfair. She was LILLIE LANGTRY, whose house at 17 Norfolk Street is now replaced by a late Victorian brick mansion, renumbered and renamed as 19 DUNRAVEN STREET.

The much loved actress, known as 'the Jersey Lily', moved there from Eaton Place in 1877 after leaving her husband and when her celebrated affair with Bertie, the future Edward VII, was on the wane. She and the Prince of Wales remained friendly and continued to mix in the same circles.

Among her new suitors were Leopold, the Prince's youngest brother, and the King of the Belgians whose curious habit was to arrive at nine in the morning. Another royal suitor was also from abroad. He was the Crown Prince Rudolf of Austria (later to die in that mysterious business at Mayerling). Rudolf, who was 19, was fascinated by Mrs Langtry's recent connection with his royal cousin. On a visit to London, he would give his tutor the slip and walk over to Norfolk Street from Claridge's where he was staying, bringing Lillie flowers and invitations. The idea of being a successor to the Prince of Wales lent piquancy to his pursuit, but Mrs Langtry gently deflected his advances.

A great beauty with pale golden hair, Lillie Langtry at 25 had a far more attractive alternative. He was the German-born anglophile, Prince Louis of Battenberg, a good-looking young officer who, on leave from the Royal Navy, was encouraged by Bertie to have a romance with his former mistress. He remained her devoted and discreet lover until naval duties took him round the world.

As a result of the Norfolk Street liaison, Lillie had a child early in 1881, Jeanne Marie, who was twenty before she accidentally discovered that Prince Louis was her father. By this time he had long been married to Queen Victoria's favourite granddaughter, Princess Victoria of Hesse, by whom he had a son, the future Lord Louis Mountbatten. The girl reproached her mother but Lillie retorted that instead of being bitter she should be thankful. Which did she prefer – to be (as she had mistakenly thought) the daughter of a drunken Irishman, Edward Langtry, or (as she now discovered) the daughter of a prince?

Jeanne Marie's daughter, Mary Malcolm, the former television announcer, is happy to acknowledge that as well as having the Jersey Lily for a grandmother she had a royal grandfather who became the first Marquess of Milford Haven, an Admiral of the Fleet and First Sea Lord.

At the bottom of Park Street, on the corner of the aptly named Rex Place, is another house, 15 SOUTH STREET, with which Bertie was familiar first as Prince of Wales and later in more staid circumstances as King. Pre-empting us, there is already a blue plaque on which the owner, CATHERINE WALTERS, ('SKITTLES'), is described as 'The last great Victorian Courtesan'. Like Nell Gwyn's in Pall Mall, this is an unofficial, privately erected plaque: the GLC always kept its fingers clean.

'Last' may refer to the fact that she lived there well into this century and did not die until 1920. Born in Liverpool (where she got her nickname 'Skittles' from helping at a skittle alley in a slum public house), Catherine Walters arrived in London in the late 1850s and while still in her teens acquired a series of protectors.

Like Laura Bell (p. 108) Skittles found Hyde Park an excellent parade ground for an aspiring courtesan and she is described as being a dazzling centre of attraction when she made her evening appearances in a phaeton driving a pair of perfectly matched ponies. These excursions led to love affairs with Lord Hartington, later eighth Duke of Devonshire, and the poet and traveller, Wilfrid Scawen Blunt.

It is difficult to decide whether Skittles had a lasting affair with the Prince of Wales, or indeed any relationship that justifies her place among the royal Mayfair mistresses. Stories about her are as difficult to substantiate as they are about Bertie, who is always painted as an insatiable womaniser. We know that she provided the amusing and light-hearted company that appealed to him. During meetings at South Street it is said that the conversation sometimes rose above horses and racing to growing German imperialism. Bertie disliked his nephew the Kaiser: Skittles had more intimate memories of Wilhelm as Crown Prince.

If they were lovers, as well as friends, she was careful to keep discreetly in the background, something very much to his liking as it avoided the kind of publicity which so upset his mother, the Queen. Though Skittles may never have had any prominent part in his life, it would hardly have been in Bertie's nature to pass up an amorous opportunity. There would have come a time for talk about horses and Germany to stop.

Sometime before his affair with Henrietta Grosvenor (p. 103) and his early death at the age of 28, Edward Duke of York went on what a contemporary satirist described as a fishing expedition in 'Kitty's Stream'. The metaphor clarified means that George III's brother went to 5 CARRINGTON STREET, off Shepherd Market, where he spent the night with KITTY FISHER. To extend the image, she swallowed his bait but declined to take his hook again. The story goes that her known charge was £100 and that when the Duke handed her £50 at breakfast, she contemptuously put the note between two pieces of bread and ate it. He need not, she said, bother to came back.

Kitty's price was steep, but then this legendary eighteenth-century *horizontale*, a favourite model of Sir Joshua Reynolds, was not without well-placed customers and never lacking in good introductions. She is said to have had six lovers from the House of Lords alone. She belongs not only to legend but also to nursery rhyme for when that careless 'Lucy Locket lost her pocket', she is the Kitty Fisher who 'found it'.

Born in Soho about 1738, Catherine Maria Fisher started life as a milliner. An army general moved her into his Leicester Square house, and when he went abroad Kitty was set up in an elegant apartment in a small Mayfair cul-de-sac called Carrington Street.

Though Kitty charged a lot for her favours, she lived lavishly to match, and she provoked endless stories. One of them told how, while entertaining the diminutive Lord Montford, and finding herself double-booked with Lord Sandwich, she smuggled the pygmy Montford out of her bedroom under her hoopskirt.

Her success with men led Henry, tenth Earl of Pembroke, aide-de-camp to the King, to settle £1,000 a year on her, and another admirer to have her painted by Reynolds. Her one recorded failure seems to have been with Casanova (p. 146) who declined to sleep with her though offered a cut rate of ten guineas.

Kitty's scandalous career lasted only six years. In 1765 she married John Norris, a former MP, a rich man with a large house, Hemsted, at Benenden in Kent. She died of consumption five months later and was buried in the Norris vault in Benenden churchyard in her wedding dress. She was 29.

The house where she ate the £50 note was fifth on the west side of Carrington Street (traced by an annotation to the eighteenth-century rate book): today the rear of a large apartment block is on the site.

The plight endured by the royal family because of marriage restrictions has a special poignancy in the extraordinary way of life forced on George, second Duke of Cambridge, nephew of both George IV and William IV. He wanted to marry a Covent Garden actress, LOUISA FAIRBROTHER, but she had to remain his mistress for years and even after they were married they lived separately in Mayfair: Louisa at 6 QUEEN STREET, which remains unchanged to this day; the Duke in Piccadilly. Two of their three children were illegitimate. She could never take his name.

They were forced into this clandestine arrangement because, although the Duke was only distantly in line to the throne, he was bound by the Royal Marriage Act. There was no way his cousin, Queen Victoria, would give him permission to marry the woman he loved.

Louisa was a commoner, born in Bow Street, the daughter of a theatrical printer. So Prince George of Cambridge set up the Mayfair ménage.

Louisa bore him three sons: George (born 1843), Adolphus (born 1846) and Augustus (born June 1847). The month of the youngest son's birth is significant because in January of the same year the Duke and Louisa were secretly married at St John's, Clerkenwell. It seems that they were determined that at least Augustus should be legitimate. But even with conventions observed, the marriage was held to be morganatic. Their children were barred from succession to the throne and, instead of being the Duchess of Cambridge, Louisa was styled Mrs FitzGeorge.

They retained the two households and there was no question of her going to any of the functions it was his duty to attend as a Field Marshal, founder of the Royal Military College of Music and, for almost forty years, Commander-in-Chief of the British Forces. She was never formally recognised by the royal family who apparently never received or ever met her. The Duke's sister, the excitable Princess Mary Adelaide of Teck (Queen Mary's mother), got as far as catching a glimpse of her in the street, when she is said to have nearly fallen from her carriage with curiosity.

None of the children seems to have been adversely affected by their unconventional start in life. George became a colonel in the Royal Welch Fusiliers, Adolphus a knighted rear-admiral, and the boy born, if not conceived, in wedlock, became Sir Augustus FitzGeorge, ADC to the Prince of Wales. The daughters of both George and Adolphus have a number of living descendants.

Queen Victoria remained on excellent terms with her cousin, and when Louisa died in 1890 sent him a letter of condolence. 'Dear Louisa would have been so pleased' the Duke wrote in his diary. When he died in 1904 he was at last able to join her permanently in the same vault in Kensal Green.

The international adventuress LOLA MONTEZ who arrived at 27 HALF MOON STREET in April 1848 does not conform to the general pattern of Mayfair's royal mistresses. An exotic bird of passage, she was in London on several occasions but this time reporters had a particular reason to besiege her door. George Augustus Sala, king of the newspaper gossips, was among those who called at her lodgings (now an extension of the Green Park Hotel). It is not, after all, every day that a woman comes to London fresh from precipitating a foreign revolution and the abdication of a king.

'Lola Montez is on every lip and in everybody's eye' wrote one journalist. In fact, the dark-haired, fascinating dancer had been good copy for years, her notorious exploits paragraphed in newspapers all over the world. To this day she has remained a figure of unusual interest thanks to her unreliable memoirs and numerous highly coloured biographies only slightly inhibited by accuracy.

Lola Montez was born plain Eliza Gilbert in Limerick in 1818. We can cheerfully disregard her claim (made in a letter she wrote to *The Times* in 1847) that she was the only daughter of a Spanish officer in the service of Don Carlos, and (lopping five years off her age) that her birthplace was Seville in 1823.

By the time she arrived in Mayfair, her career already included a marriage (the first of three), and lovers as varied as Franz Liszt and Prince Henry of Reuss. To her list of affairs may possibly be added Tsar Nicholas I of Russia (who she said gave her diamonds) and the elder Alexander Dumas (who coached her for her appearance at a trial after a journalist lover was killed in a duel in the Bois de Boulogne).

Her early marriage was to Thomas James, an Indian Army lieutenant with whom she eloped. When this came to grief Lola turned to the stage and, capitalising on the dark Hispanic looks of so many West of Ireland women, she took a short not very intensive training as a Spanish dancer. She was once booed in Warsaw, and she frankly admitted her dancing was not at all good. Her London debut in 1843, billed as Donna Lola Montez of the Teatro Real, Seville, was disconcertingly interrupted by a disgruntled and rejected lover, Lord Ranelagh, who shouted out from the stalls of the Haymarket Theatre, 'Why! It's Betty James!'

King Ludwig I of Bavaria, the most important of all her conquests, was not so critical. When she appeared in Munich three years later she may have danced an imprecise fandango, but he was captivated. Aged 60, he wrote to a friend that Lola made him feel 'like a youth of 20'. The King was happy to pay for this rejuvenation. He built Lola a palatial house to her own design, gave her a large allowance and created her Countess Maria von Landsfeld. This outraged Bavarian aristocracy, but it was her interference in politics that caused the greatest resentment and sparked off student demonstrations. When she asked the King to close the university, personal animosity against her boiled over. Revolution broke out and Ludwig was forced to abdicate. Lola avoided this final crisis by hurriedly making a tactical withdrawal across the frontier to Switzerland before seeking the comparative calm of Half Moon Street.

The calm was shortlived. Never one to remain long out of the headlines, Lola was married in the following year at St George's, Hanover Square, an event which Disraeli writing to his sister described as a sensation. Her allowance of £1,500 from Ludwig was doubtless insufficient and so she happily accepted the proposal of Gerald Heald, a young army officer of twenty-one with an income of some £7,000 a year.

Unfortunately Heald's aunt decided to investigate Lola's background and her discoveries led her to believe that Lola's divorce from Thomas James seven years earlier had only been a legal separation. Lola was arrested one August morning in 1849 as she stepped into her carriage in Half Moon Street and was taken to Marlborough Street where she was charged with bigamy. News of her arrest brought crowds to the court and those unable to get in waited on the pavement outside, curious for a glimpse of Lola who appeared in a close-fitting black dress and straw bonnet.

A court reporter from *The Times* ungallantly described her as 'rather plump' and he said that though her age was given as 24 she 'had the look of a woman of at least 30'. Heald, tall with small downy moustachios and whiskers, held her hand, which he several times pressed to his lips. She was granted bail, but they remained in the courthouse for some while to avoid the press of people outside.

The Times secured a scoop by publishing a copy of the 1842 divorce proceedings in which it was stated that Lola's marriage had been terminated 'on the usual terms'. This was a legal separation and did not mean that the parties had the right to remarry; for that an Act of Parliament was required at this date.

Once again Lola decided to be on the move. She did not answer her bail and was next heard of in Naples on her way to Egypt. Two years later she returned to the stage, and when she made her New York debut in 1851, Heald had disappeared. She said he had been drowned.

Though lacking the full flavour of her European progress, the last ten years of Lola's life were full of incident. She was married for a third time (to Patrick Purdy Hull, the editor of a San Francisco newspaper) and then took up with a German who accidentally shot himself. She lived in a Nevada mining camp, went to Australia where her dancing was critically received, came back to Europe for a while, acted in New York State, and when she was 40 went back to Ireland before embarking on a lecture tour in England.

Interest in her lurid life at first made her appearances sufficiently popular for her to rival Phineas T. Barnum who was touring the country with his freak shows, but on the platform of the St James's Hall in London in 1859, her lecture, *Era* reported, lacked personal interest and was like 'the speech of a long-winded American ambassador at a Mansion House dinner'. Lola Montez died of a stroke in New York in 1861, aged 42, and is buried in Greenwood Cemetery where the tombstone carries the name she had at birth – Eliza Gilbert.

While Europe was in a ferment in 1848 with revolutions brewing in more than a dozen countries, Mayfair became a refuge where participants could prepare for future action. At exactly the time Lola Montez arrived in Half Moon Street after quickening the Bavarian uprising, another royal mistress, ELIZABETH HOWARD, took part in plans for a French *coup d'état*. At a house only a few hundred yards away, at 9 BERKELEY STREET, she raised money from her own private resources to help her lover, Louis Napoleon, become President and then Emperor of France.

That a woman of only twenty-six, apparently of fairly humble origins, was in a position to lend him some £13,000, suggests that Elizabeth must have been astute in her previous affairs. Stories that she was the daughter of a cobbler, born in a garret, and at one time a Wapping barmaid, are almost certainly fictitious. She was probably born the daughter of a brewer called Haryett at Brighton in 1822.

In her teens Elizabeth became the mistress of Jem Mason, the jockey who won the first Grand National in 1839, and of a gambler who gave her money. She had a child by a major in the Life Guards who deserted her. Among subsequent protectors were the Duke of Beaufort and the Earl of Malmesbury. One of them had given her a house in Italy, at Civita Vecchia, on which she was able to raise the money needed by Louis Napoleon.

In 1846 when she was consorting with the Count d'Orsay, Elizabeth met the future Emperor at Gore House in Kensington. This was soon after Louis Napoleon's escape from the Fortress of Ham in France where he had been imprisoned after an abortive Bonapartist uprising. Elizabeth is said to have been a beauty with fair hair, fine classical features and lovely shoulders. She moved into Berkeley Street while Louis Napoleon took the lease of a house in King Street, off St James's Square.

The loan on the Civita Vecchia property enabled Louis to return to France, where he, as titular head of the Bonapartists, wrested authority from the Bourbons. He won election to the French Chamber, and so to the Presidency. Three years later he became Emperor. Elizabeth followed him to France where their affair caused scandal; but, though grateful for her financial help, at the end of a four-year relationship the Emperor married Eugénie de Montijo.

There were compensations. Like Lola, Elizabeth was created a Countess – la Comtesse de Beauregard. Her son was made a Count and she received £220,000. In 1854 she married a Cornishman, from whom she was divorced before returning to France to die, aged 43, in an eighteenth-century chateau with a large estate near Versailles. Appropriately enough, Madame de Pompadour had lived in the same district.

Following an eastward route we come, finally, to the Regent Street limits of Mayfair. Chronologically MARY ROBINSON – another mistress of the future George IV – should appear earlier than Mrs Fitzherbert (p. 110) because the ardently romantic Prince of Wales was only 17 when he fell in love with the actress whom he set up at, or near, 15 CORK STREET.

In December 1779 the Prince went to Drury Lane for a command performance of Garrick's version of *The Winter's Tale* and was immediately enchanted by the slim, lovely girl playing Perdita. He stared at her as if mesmerised and from his box paid her flattering compliments which she could hear on stage. The next day she received a letter addressed to 'Perdita' and signed 'Florizel', King Polixenes' son in the play.

The Prince's two earlier romances were immediately forgotten. If he knew that Mary Robinson had already been secretly married to a clerk and had given birth to a child in King's Bench Prison, he did not appear to care. That she had been compromised by Lord Lyttelton and a number of rakes seemed a matter of equal indifference. They first met secretly in the grounds at Kew. A lock of his hair and some extremely indiscreet letters (which later had to be bought back for £5,000) arrived at her door. When the Prince promised his Perdita £20,000 a year as soon as he was 21, she was happy to give up the stage and move into Cork Street as his mistress.

The exact site of the house which she called 'neat but by no means splendid' can only be conjectured. It must have been on the west side because the rear gardens of Burlington Street backed on to the east. The houses were unnumbered. But a possible clue in the rate books – the name 'George Robinson' – seems too apt an elision of their two names to be a coincidence. This would make their lovers' retreat by Cork Street Mews, just before the junction of Burlington Gardens.

Then as subsequently, the Prince was fickle. Within a year he took a fancy to the divorced wife of a doctor. Abruptly he wrote to tell Mary they must 'meet no more' and ignored her entreaties. Seriously in debt, and apparently responsible for the Cork Street establishment, she was finally given a settlement and a £500 annuity.

Latterly Mary Robinson is said to have been closely associated with Charles James Fox (who arranged her pension), Richard Brinsley Sheridan, and also with Colonel Banastre Tarleton, hero and scourge of the Carolinas in the American War of Independence, before she became partially paralysed. Her illness gave her the enforced opportunity to write poems, plays, and four volumes of memoirs from her home at 13 St James's Place, where she occasionally received her former lover. She died at Englefield in 1800 and was buried nearby in Old Windsor churchyard.

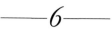

Bloomsbury and Fitzrovia

B Y tradition Bloomsbury is the spiritual home of the intellectual, the haunt of the unconventional, the refuge of the exiled cosmopolitan. Little wonder then that Bloomsbury had a special appeal for a brilliant foreigner with no national ties, an imprecise code of loyalties, and a polytheistic view of religion. Ignatz Trebitsch was at various stages in his life known as Ludwig Tolnai, Dr Leo Tandler, Hermann Ruh and Tsao Kun. In England he became IGNATIUS TIMOTHY TREBICH-LINCOLN, Liberal MP for Darlington.

The man who signed himself I.T.T. Lincoln (taking his name from the American President) was ordained an Anglican deacon in Canada and later a Buddhist monk in China. He was a forger, spy, *agent provocateur*, traitor, and this is to name only some of the misdeeds of the man who at one time made his home at 51 TORRINGTON SQUARE, Bloomsbury, but roamed the world in a restless pursuit of new experiences.

Few Members of Parliament can have had a more extraordinary life and less customary origins. He was born at Paks, south of Budapest, in 1879 to an intensely religious Jewish couple, and left home at the age of 18 on the proceeds of a watch stolen from his sister. He travelled all over Europe and then went to Canada where he studied theology at McGill University.

Forsaking his Jewish upbringing he first embraced Presbyterianism, but it was as an Anglican that he arrived in Britain in 1904 and was interviewed by the Archbishop of Canterbury who appointed him curate to the parish of Appledore in Kent. He quickly tired of this rural work and decided to extend his horizons. Ignatius seems to have had a knack for knowing the right people. The Quaker industrialist Seebohm Rowntree gave him a commission to investigate social conditions in Europe and it was with papers signed by Sir Edward Grey, the Foreign Secretary, that he set out on this work.

This entrée to high places increased his appetite for money and power, and when he got back to England in 1909 he decided to stand for Parliament. Within eight months of being naturalized he was elected MP for Darlington.

Until then Ignatius Trebich-Lincoln, as he now called himself, seems to have had a career of high-minded probity. Westminster brought a dramatic change. The theologian turned politician. The spiritual life was abandoned in favour of high finance, which led to bankruptcy. In an attempt to retrieve his fortunes he left Darlington for London and 51 Torrington Square, having first tried unsuccessfully to recoup his losses at the gaming tables in Monte Carlo.

The outbreak of the 1914–18 war gave Trebich-Lincoln a new outlet for his seemingly limitless energies. He offered to act as a double agent in Germany, but Naval Intelligence turned down his very complicated proposals to pretend to spy for the Germans, and report back to Britain.

Now desperately short of money he forged Rowntree's name on a guarantee for a loan, and when the forgery was discovered, fled to America. There he wrote anti-British articles claiming to be a German spy.

The Admiralty, anxious to have him extradited, asked the US authorities to arrest Trebich-Lincoln. He escaped from a prison in New York but was re-arrested and brought back to England to face the forgery charge at the Old Bailey. He served a three-year sentence, and when released in 1919 was stripped of his British citizenship and expelled.

He went to Germany and, claiming he was a former anti-British spy, he wrote for magazines and also became involved in an abortive *coup d'état* to make the Kaiser's son the new ruler of Germany.

As the years passed Trebich-Lincoln's exploits grew more and more hectic. In Vienna he was arrested for forgery; while hiding in Italy he was investigated by the League of Nations, suspected of monarchist conspiracies; and while trying to get into America was arrested by the FBI. Soon the Far East was the only part of the world where the name of Trebich-Lincoln was not at every frontier barrier. Here immigration officials were not so vigilant and we next hear of him implicated in plots to overthrow Oriental rulers, and being sent by the Chinese to Europe as roving ambassador to raise money and buy arms. During the 1920s he became Ludwig Tolnai and Dr Tandler to suit his various roles. After visits to Java, Ceylon and Manchuria, he changed his name to Hermann Ruh, seemingly an adequate cloak to get him into San Francisco where he joined a Buddhist community. It was as Tsao Kun that he became a monk at a monastery near Peking in 1931, perhaps the last of all the changes of identity he needed to prevent arrests for world-wide illegalities.

The last part of Trebich-Lincoln's life was so full of self-admitted fictions that his obituaries – even those in *The Times* and *New York Times* – must be regarded as suspect. Was he, for instance, a Fifth Columnist broadcasting from a Japanese radio station in Tibet just before he died? For this, or any other assertion, no claim of accuracy is made here. Perhaps all we dare accept is the report of his death – in a French hospital in Shanghai on 9 October 1942.

Research is hindered not simply because Ignatius Trebich-Lincoln changed his name frequently and travelled as extensively as he told lies; all his descendants changed their names too – not surprisingly in view of his background and since one of his sons was hanged for murder; the records of his Old Bailey trial were destroyed; and his Torrington Square house, eight doors down from Byng Place, is now buried under the University of London.

For a few dramatic moments on a June night in 1907 Bloomsbury was transformed into a Little Chicago. A cab pulled up outside Russell Square underground station and a red-haired woman shouted to her companion, 'There he is . . . Kill him, Charlie!' The man jumped from the cab, his gun blazing. The woman's former lover collapsed wounded on the pavement in Bernard Street. The gunman ran round the corner and turned on the approaching police . . .

This was London's last and most sensational encounter with MAY CHURCHILL, better known as 'Chicago May', who in her late years was also called the 'Queen of the Underworld'. At the time of the incident she was lodging at 107 GOWER STREET where the police found a small arsenal of weapons and a collection of blackmail letters.

'Chicago May' had an array of aliases that make even Trebich-Lincoln look like a beginner. They were (in alphabetical order) May Avery, Mary Brown, May Lambert (her name at birth), May Latimer, Margaret Smith, Lillian White, May Williams, May Wilson and Rose Wilson. All of these she found useful in eluding detection when playing the 'Badger Game', a blackmailing enterprise which she successfully imported from America.

The Bloomsbury shoot-out on Saturday, 15 June 1907, was the climax of a life which started with May Lambert's birth in Ireland about 1876. She had emigrated with her family to America, where after a period on the stage and a short-lived marriage she went to Chicago. There she became associated with 'Dutch Gus' and 'Kid McManus', names which help sustain the slightly unreal gangster quality of the whole story.

After working Chicago, New York and Philadelphia, May and her partners decided that London was ripe for the 'Badger Game'. This activity required May to slip 'Mickey Finns' into the glasses of unsuspecting men whom she picked up in hotels. The Metropole in Northumberland Avenue (still identifiable with a canopy over the door and now part of the Ministry of Defence) was her favourite haunt.

The victim was encouraged to order drinks and when he was off his guard May dropped in a mixture of alcohol and chloral hydrate. The half-stupefied man was got to his room and when he awoke May was on the bed by his side. There would be an agitated knock on the door. Enter the confederate with the alarming warning that May's husband had found out they had been together. He was threatening legal action and it would need a large sum to 'fix' him.

It was an age-old device but when the police searched her Gower Street rooms after the shooting they found letters which revealed that a number of well-known people had been the successful target for this type of blackmail.

In London May became involved with another crook, Eddie Guerin, but crime (including a £60,000 American Express robbery in Paris) brought imprisonments that led to separations. While parted from Eddie she took up with another accomplice, Charles Smith, and it was this involvement that brought about the Bernard Street shooting.

Eddie Guerin, unexpectedly released from prison and intent on revenge, made his way to Bloomsbury in search of the faithless May. But, by chance, it was May who spotted him first as she and Charlie were passing the underground station in a taxi. Charlie leapt out, started firing and hit Eddie in the foot. As May cowered in a doorway the wounded Eddie stumbled towards her cursing. A police chase followed in which May was arrested and Charles turned his gun on a constable – to find that he had used up all his bullets.

Both stood trial at the Old Bailey for attempted murder. The defence plea that they had only made the attack to prevent Eddie throwing vitriol over his former mistress was not convincing and Mr Justice Darling sentenced May to fifteen years; Charles Smith was given life.

May Churchill was released from Aylesbury gaol twelve years later and immediately deported to the States. There the 'Queen of the Underworld' wrote her memoirs. She died in a Philadelphia hospital in 1929.

No. 107 Gower Street is little changed but the front door is now blocked up. It is part of the Catholic Chaplaincy of the University of London.

There is nothing about 99 GOWER STREET, four doors away, to suggest that it was ever a 'Temple of the Occult'. The dignified Regency façade gives no hint that here in 1901 a man calling himself 'Theo Horos' and his wife, 'The Swami Bride of the Lord', systematically debauched young girls. Behind the three tall windows on the first floor was the 'Hall of the Neophytes' where initiations were carried out by Theo, dressed as a Chinese mandarin, and by the Swami in flowing, highly coloured robes.

Subdued lighting from exotic lamps shone on an altar and round the walls hung occult emblems when a girl of sixteen from Birkenhead – a typical neophyte – was called on to recite 'I, Daisy Adams, in the presence of the Lord of the Universe . . . of the Order of the Golden Dawn . . . do of my own free will . . . most solemnly pledge myself to keep secret this Order, its Name, the Name of its members . . .'

Further on in the complicated rigmarole the bewildered child accepted that, if she broke her oath, she would submit herself 'to a deadly and hostile current of will set in motion by the Chiefs of the Order . . .'

Daisy was only one of several girls lured to the Gower Street 'Temple' by advertisements in newspapers. Vera Croysdale, aged 23 from Hull, was later to testify how special clothes were ordered for her 'marriage' to Theo. Accepting him as divine, she went to bed with him and the Swami. Olga Rowson, a domestic servant of 26 from Bayswater, also said that she fell under their spell and could not resist sharing their bed.

Daisy Adams was told by Theo that he was Christ and that she was destined to give birth to a divine child. The sixteen-year-old girl was then pinned down on the bed by the Swami while he pursued this objective.

The solemn-looking Gower
Street house which was
'The Temple of Love'
and, right, the accolyte
'Bride of the Lord',
Editha Jackson.

When Daisy queried why, as well as herself, he should have Laura Faulkner, aged 20 from Camden Town, and other girls as his wives, Theo replied, 'Did not Solomon have 300 legal wives and 600 others?'

Divested of his mystical apparel and quasi-occult names, 'Theo Horos' was FRANK DUTTON JACKSON, a bearded sallow-faced man of 35, born in California, and the Swami was a fat ponderous woman called EDITHA LOLETA JACKSON, twelve years his senior.

Surprisingly for a woman calling herself the 'Bride of the Lord', Mrs Jackson claimed to be the illegitimate daughter of King Ludwig I of Bavaria and Lola Montez (p. 115).

Both had been involved in religious rackets in the States before they met, married and opened a series of 'Temples' in which religion and the occult were covers for getting money from women and procuring young girls. In 1900 they came to England and set up their Gower Street 'Temple'.

Theft of some jewellery owned by Vera Croysdale, the girl from Hull, and traced through a Strand pawnbroker, led to their unmasking. Restive at not becoming the formal as well as the divine wife of Theo, and unwilling for her jewellery to be 'gifts laid on the altar of God', Vera informed the police.

Charges of fraud at Marylebone Police Court in September 1901 were followed by more serious charges of rape and procuring for immoral purposes.

Entering the dock at the Old Bailey like a queen, her hair piled high in Grecian fashion, the Swami remained arrogant and defiant throughout the trial. She fought, point by point, the accusations of Sir Edward Carson as he outlined how Daisy had 'been submitted to treatment which would have shocked and repelled a woman hardened to vice, let alone a young girl of sixteen'.

The jury brought in a verdict of guilty in five minutes. Theo was sentenced to fifteen years and sent to Dartmoor. During her seven years in Aylesbury, the Swami found a book in the prison library about the Jezreelites, and on her release carried her corrupt interpretation of their message to Canada, where she was again imprisoned and where she died during the First World War.

Near Brunswick Square (and less than a hundred yards from the spot where Eddie Guerin was shot – p. 123) are three Georgian terrace houses which look very much today as they did in 1928 when a ground floor room with a double bed was let to the REVD HAROLD DAVIDSON. Mr Davidson took so many girls back to

28 BERNARD STREET that his landlady, Mrs Flora Osborne, gave him notice to leave on several occasions.

Mrs Osborne was only one of a great many landladies in London who had trouble with the Rector of Stiffkey either as a tenant or because he visited their female occupants at irregular hours. When the whole story blew wide open in 1932 private investigators had much else to testify: of girls whom the rector had been seen cuddling in Lyons or ABC tearooms; of a girl kissed in a Chinese restaurant in Bloomsbury; of a waitress in Walworth to whom he had made improper suggestions; of girls being given drinks in public houses; and of girls being taken to the theatre. The Revd Mr Davidson was very fond of girls.

When his alleged immoral conduct was brought before the Diocese of Norwich Consistory Court sitting at Church House, Westminster, between March and June 1932, it soon became clear that, to put it mildly, the rector's behaviour over the previous twenty years had been injudicious. On Monday mornings it was Mr Davidson's custom to abandon his pastoral duties in the little Norfolk village of Stiffkey and hurry by train to undertake metropolitan responsibilities which he found more pressing. The 5.05 a.m. train on Sunday generally got him back to his parish in time for Matins, but once he missed the Armistice Day Service.

Among the girls whom Davidson considered in especial need of spiritual guidance was Barbara Harris, aged 16, whom he approached at Marble Arch and on whom he made his first call at two in the morning. As she sat up in bed with her Indian lover, he assured her that God did not mind the sins of the body, only those of the soul. During the many years that he knew her, he grew to call her the 'Queen of my Heart' and she referred to him as her 'guardian'. He treated her to a visit to the Piccadilly Theatre to see a musical, *Folly to be Wise*. He was, she said, kind to her, and when asked if she usually remained friendly with people who tried to rape her, Barbara said frankly that she did if they came in useful.

Barbara was not alone. There were many others on the rector's visiting list, and several for whom he rented rooms from Bloomsbury to Shepherd's Bush. In West End pubs he was accustomed to being greeted with 'Hello, you old thief. How are all the girls?'

It was Rose Ellis, a rather amateurish young prostitute he first met in Leicester Square, who brought about his undoing. He had tried to get her various jobs and had even taken her to Paris, ostensibly to find her a position in a French family. Rose was one of the girls questioned by private detectives acting on behalf of the Bishop of Norwich who decided he must investigate whether the rector had transgressed the Clergy Discipline Act. As a result Church House heard the most sensational ecclesiastical court case in modern history.

The Revd Harold Davidson was 56 at the time of the hearing. Born into a clerical family, he was brought up by an aunt at Croydon and went to the Whitgift School. He had a natural stage talent and earned his fees at Oxford by solo theatrical bookings. His first curacy was at Windsor and he was at St Martin-in-the-Fields before going to Stiffkey in 1906. He served as a Naval chaplain during the Great War.

The Rector of Stiffkey. More in London than in his Norfolk pulpit.

The court was constantly mystified as to how the rector, married with five children, a bankrupt with a small clerical income, kept his family and was able to come to London, take bed-sitting rooms and treat so many girls to meals, theatres and cinemas. His ambivalence bewildered the presiding Chancellor. While insisting on his moral probity, the rector allowed himself to be photographed with a naked girl of fifteen. He declared himself pleased to be known as the 'Prostitutes' Padre' – 'to me the proudest title that a true priest of Christ can hold' – and when asked about his incessant, much recorded kissing of girls, his reply was: 'Time after time in the New Testament kissing has been enjoined upon the Church'.

On 8 July 1932 the rector was found guilty on five charges. He immediately wrote to the Privy Council, but his appeal was dismissed, and he was denied the right to hold services at Stiffkey. To raise £2,000 for further appeals Mr Davidson appeared in a barrel on Blackpool front, stared at by three thousand people until fined for obstruction. In October, having learnt that his final appeal would not be allowed, he was 'removed, deposed and degraded' by the Bishop at a solemn ceremony in Norwich Cathedral.

During the next five years, the unfrocked Rector of Stiffkey sustained himself by bizarre sideshow appearances culminating at Skegness Amusement Park during the summer of 1937 where it was announced he would lecture in a lion's cage. When he arrived he found there were two lions but he went in, seemingly undeterred, to play his role of 'Daniel in the Lion's Den'. He was killed before a horrified crowd. The lion-tamer's assistant who bravely pulled his mauled body from the cage was a girl of sixteen.

When Sarah Woodcock, an attractive milliner who ran a shop near Tower Hill, was asked to visit a house in Southampton Row she was given the impression that she was to meet a lady who might put some business her way. That was what she was told by Mrs Harvey who accompanied her late one December evening in 1767. She found herself at a magnificent house on the south corner of what is now Southampton Row and Guilford Street. Bow windows overlooked open fields, for Russell Square was not to be created for another thirty years. This was Baltimore House, site of today's PRESIDENT HOTEL.

The wondering girl was led through several fine rooms and was kept waiting for some time before a man appeared informally dressed in a linen nightgown saying he was a servant. He was, in fact, FREDERICK CALVERT, sixth LORD BALTIMORE. Although she did not know his real identity, Sarah recognised him as the .man who had come to her shop earlier in the month. He had bought some trifles and invited her to go with him to a play but, as a strictly brought up woman of twenty-nine, engaged to be married, she had declined.

Now tricked into visiting him, she reluctantly accepted tea, after which Lord Baltimore, still keeping up the pretence of being a servant, showed her round the house. He did not hurry. He played to her on the harpsichord, insisted she stay for supper and, moving with her to a window, suddenly wrapped himself around her in the folds of the heavy curtains.

From this moment his true intentions were unmistakable, and the events of the next twelve days, though reliably documented, suggest nothing so much as a melodrama in which the virtue of the innocent heroine is sullied by the wicked nobleman.

Sarah Woodcock was held prisoner at Baltimore House over Christmas and the scene of her seductions varies between Southampton Row and his lordship's country house at Epsom. The First Act curtain descends on the night of her arrival, with Baltimore saying: 'Don't worry. I shall not meddle with you.' Sarah (courageously): 'No more you shall!'

Act II opens with a dramatic scene in which Sarah goes to the window and tries to throw down a note to a passer-by but is dragged back by Lord Baltimore's servants. Her virtue is still intact and remains so for three nights. But we can almost hear hissing as the wicked peer writes a letter to her father in which he encloses £200.

In the Third Act the scene changes to Woodcote, the house on Epsom Downs to which Sarah is taken by carriage. On going to bed that night she parts the curtains to find Lord Baltimore waiting for her. Lowered lights indicate the passing of time and shroud two sexual assaults.

Throughout the drama, the villain of the piece, Lord Baltimore, a widower of thirty-six, appears to have behaved in a practised, world-weary, almost casual manner. 'One of those worn out Englishmen who have lost all moral and physical taste' someone described him. He was reputed to keep a harem at Epsom, and as a rich man – his family owned most of the state of Maryland – he obviously thought this was another willing recruit.

He seems to have been quite astonished when Sarah, who came from a family of Protestant dissenters, raised objections. Irritated, he threatened to 'tie her petticoats over her head and send her home in a wheelbarrow'. Why was she making all this fuss?

Lord Baltimore was further surprised when Sarah's father informed Sir John Fielding, the Bow Street magistrate, and was outraged at being beset by Fielding's 'scoundrels' as he referred to the Bow Street Runners who waylaid his coach. At his trial for rape at Kingston Assizes he insisted that the girl had been quite compliant and that had she wanted to escape she could easily have done so. According to the procurer, Mrs Harvey, Sarah 'went to bed with my lord with all the ease and freedom in the world, as freely as any woman went to a man'.

It came down to a question of consent, and Baltimore, who could produce all the witnesses he wanted, was acquitted. However, the verdict was unpopular with the public, who saw Sarah as the ravished victim of the wicked lord.

When Lord Baltimore died in Naples four years later, and was brought back to Epsom to be buried, there were demonstrations at his funeral.

We now leave Bloomsbury and cross Tottenham Court Road to the area which since the beginning of World War II has come to be known as Fitzrovia because of its relation to Fitzroy Square. In recent times a shop at 64 CHARLOTTE STREET has offered 'Great Bargains' and 'Special Offers', but it is supplying goods somewhat different from those which MRS THERESA BERKLEY had for her customers in the eight years when she did such excellent business after 1828.

Instead of modern office equipment, Mrs Berkley's stock in trade (at what was then No. 28 Charlotte Street) included whips with a dozen thongs, cats-o'-nine-tails studded with sharp points, flexible switches and straps decorated with tin-tacks. These instruments of chastisement showed the proprietor to be a very specialised brothel keeper indeed.

Specialised but not unique. At this date there were no less than twenty establishments in London providing flagellation. But it was generally conceded that Mrs Berkley was the governess whose severity outmatched such rivals as Mrs James of 7 Carlisle Street, Soho, Emma Lee of Margaret Street, and Mrs Phillips of Upper Belgrave Place.

Assistant governesses at Charlotte Street offered the customer the opportunity of being 'birched, whipped, fustigated [cudgelled], scourged, needle-pricked, half-hung, curry-combed, phleboto-mized [incisions into the veins], stinging-nettled, holly-brushed and firse-mized [scratched with gorse].

But the *spécialité de la maison* was the 'Berkley Horse', a flogging machine invented by the owner. Provided only for 'commensurate remuneration', this instrument, sometimes called the *chevalet*, may have had a rotary action with birches attached to a wheel ensuring that the person splayed out on a gymnasium-type horse received precision chastisement at a fixed or steadily increasing tempo. But this is guesswork. Although an etching of the machine in action is said to have been found among Mrs Berkley's effects at her death in 1836, the picture has apparently disappeared. All that can be said with certainty is that the horse's popularity during her eight years at Charlotte Street helped to make Theresa Berkley £10,000.

A few hundred yards to the west of Charlotte Street, another highly specialised establishment existed at 19 CLEVELAND STREET. This was a male brothel which stood in the shadow of the Middlesex Hospital (on the site today of the private wing). Its proximity to the hospital was to be an added cause for public outrage when the 'indescribably loathsome scandal', as one newspaper called it, broke in the late summer of 1889.

The brothel's existence became known to the police rather deviously. A fifteen-year-old messenger boy working at the General Post Office in St Martin's-le-Grand was accused of stealing. The boy told the police that the money wasn't stolen; he had received it for services to gentlemen at the Cleveland Street address. He and several other telegraph boys were paid four shillings a time, the other sixteen shillings of the sovereign paid by the customer going to the owner, Charles Hammond. Hammond was supplied with boys by George Veck, who worked at the post office.

Scotland Yard ordered a watch on the premises and a constable reported that 'a number of men of superior bearing and apparently good position' had been seen to call there, accompanied by boys in some instances, and on two occasions by a soldier.

Famous names were involved. The scandal which followed tainted the reputation of the Earl of Euston, eldest son of the Duke of Grafton, and of a Colonel Jervoise from Winchester. Prince Eddy, the eldest son of the Prince of Wales, was suspected of being a visitor. The Public Prosecutor was privately warned of this awkward possibility and it was openly mentioned in the American press. Deeply implicated, and with no chance of rebuttal, was LORD ARTHUR SOMERSET, the Old Etonian son of the Duke of Beaufort.

Various boys provided statements and gave detailed accounts of what took place when they went to bed in the brothel. Lord Arthur was identified as having called twice at Cleveland Street with a Guards corporal, and a seventeen-year-old telegraph boy named Thickbroom said he had acted indecently with him.

Three highly-charged trials followed, dealing with gross indecency (homosexual intercourse), criminal libel (against a radical journalist who took his exposé too far) and conspiracy (because witnesses were sent abroad before they could give damaging evidence). The wider issues of a cover-up were raised in Parliament.

It was a very tangled affair with more conflicting and suspect evidence than can be examined here. Only the outcome – not the various probabilities of guilt and innocence – can be recorded.

Charles Hammond, male prostitute and blackmailer, who ran the brothel for four years, was tipped off in time to make a getaway before the police raided the house. He went to France and finally to America. George Veck, who procured for him, and escaped from

'*A Den of Infamy*' – Illustrated Police News' *sketch of the Cleveland Street male brothel which brought about the downfall of Lord Arthur Somerset.*

Lord Arthur, 'Podge', as seen by 'Spy'.

the house in clerical clothes, was not so lucky; he was arrested and served nine months.

The Earl of Euston went into court where he confronted a male prostitute who alleged that the Earl had picked him up in Piccadilly and gone with him to Cleveland Street. Lord Euston insisted that he had visited the house to see *poses plastiques*, the Victorian equivalent of striptease. The excuse of heterosexual enticement was also seized on as a reason why the heir to the throne might also have gone there. Prince Eddy, then aged 24, was spirited off to India on a long tour just before the scandal took grip.

Lord Arthur Somerset escaped from the country but there was no escape from disgrace. Though illicit sex was widespread in Victorian London, there was no sympathy or mercy for homosexuals. His father, the eighth Duke of Beaufort, urged him to stay and fight, but he decided not to. He probably realised that he was doomed because the Criminal Law Amendment Act (the so-called 'Blackmailer's Charter'), passed three years earlier, made private as well as public homosexual acts a crime.

To avoid arrest Lord Arthur fled to Vienna and resigned his commission as a major in the Guards and as a member of the Royal Household. He never came back to England and after a life of exile he died in France in 1926.

That Somerset could have escaped, that arrests were not made as soon as they should have been, and that there was a Government cover-up was the constant accusation of Henry Labouchère, editor of *Truth* and moral campaigner, who had introduced the 1886 homosexual amendment bill. He raised the matter in a heated debate in Parliament and indicted Lord Salisbury. 'What is this case' he demanded 'but a criminal conspiracy by the very guardians of morality and law, with the Prime Minister at their head, to defeat the ends of justice?'

For something like forty years Charles Coburn in top hat and tails enjoyed his greatest success round the music halls, singing 'The Man Who Broke the Bank at Monte Carlo'.

> As I walk along the *Bois Boo-Long*
> With an independent air,
> You can hear the girls declare:
> 'He must be a millionaire!'
> You can hear them sigh and wish to die

You can see them wink the other eye
At the Man Who Broke the Bank at Monte Carlo!

The song was inspired by the great publicity given in the newspapers in February 1892 to an Englishman's winnings in Monte Carlo. After a run of success reported daily in the papers he finally broke the bank at £16,000.

Though for once in his life he had come by money honestly, the successful gambler wasn't at all pleased to find himself suddenly in the limelight. For a year CHARLES WELLS had been absent from his London home at 162 GREAT PORTLAND STREET (today the offices of the Agricultural and Food Research Council) and living on his yacht on the Côte d'Azur. He had escaped from a great many duped investors back in England who wanted to trace him. With his roulette winnings Wells quickly put to sea.

A slight bearded man of fifty-one from Broxbourne in Hertfordshire, Wells called himself an engineer and naval architect. He had worked abroad – in Russia (making sugar), Spain (mining) and France (manufacturing paper) – before returning to England in 1885 when he had started a career as an inventor. He took out patents on hot-air-engines for motor cars, an automatic foghorn, a torpedo and an olive oil purifier. The most prolific inventor known to the Patent Office, Wells succeeded with only one brainchild – a musical skipping rope which he sold for £50.

To finance these impracticable inventions he advertised from a small office in Fenchurch Street for investors, promising yields of £40,000 on £5 stakes. He was extremely plausible. Maiden ladies, doctors and clergymen rushed to make their fortunes. A member of the aristocracy put up £10,000, and the sister of a famous judge – Lord Phillimore – parted with £19,000.

Wells acquired so much money that he was able to move from the City to a luxurious apartment and office in Great Portland Street and to buy a yacht, *Palais Royal*, with a sixty-foot ballroom and a music room with a church organ. The ship's engines were very ancient but enabled Wells to demonstrate a fuel-saving apparatus (another invention) with which he tried to involve investors at various ports on his way to Monte Carlo.

Ten months of flitting from port to port after his Monte Carlo bonanza ended with his arrest at Le Havre. Twenty-four warrants had been taken out on behalf of duped investors. He was charged with obtaining £29,000 by false pretences and sentenced to eight years hard labour.

By 1906 Wells was again in the public eye. On the stand of the South and North West Coast Steam Trawling and Fishing syndicate at a trade exhibition in London he was offering the public a chance to invest in a life-saving invention which, bobbing up and down in the sea, would, he claimed, revive a drowning man. This was demonstrated in a tank by a defrocked clergyman; people came forward with money; within a few months Wells and the clergyman were in the dock and Wells was again on his way to Dartmoor.

On his release Wells disappeared to France with Jeanette Burns, a housewife – presumably somebody else's housewife – from Fulham. Somehow he managed to open a bank in Paris and went missing with two million francs. He and the lady from Fulham were apprehended – yet again he was on a yacht – in Falmouth harbour but this time he escaped on an extradition wrangle. The couple went abroad never to return. The Man Who Broke the Bank at Monte Carlo died in 1926 at the age of 85.

North of Trafalgar Square

A T 11 a.m. on 10 March 1914 an attendant on duty at the NATIONAL GALLERY noticed a small woman dressed in a grey coat and skirt contemplating *Venus with the Mirror* by Velasquez. Minutes later he heard the sound of breaking glass and his first reaction was to think that a skylight had fallen in. Then he turned round and saw the woman hacking furiously at the painting with a small chopper. He grabbed her by the arm but by then she had shattered the thick plate glass and inflicted six clean cuts and one ragged one on the back of the famous nude.

It was not the action of a mad woman or an ordinary vandal. MARY RICHARDSON, a thirty-one-year-old journalist, was a Suffragette, and as she was led away she told the gathering crowd: 'You can get another picture, but you cannot get a life, as they are killing Mrs Pankhurst.' Emmeline Pankhurst was then on hunger strike in prison.

The attack on the 'Rokeby Venus', so called because it had come to the National Gallery from Lord Rokeby in 1906, was the fourth mutilation of a painting by Suffragettes in ten months. A Romney was slashed in 1913, followed by two pictures in Burlington House – Sargent's portrait of Henry James and Herkomer's Duke of Wellington. The quickly assembled trustees decided to close the gallery until further notice and the Wallace Collection and the Tate were also closed.

Mary Richardson was charged with maliciously causing £40,000 worth of damage, pleaded guilty and was given the maximum sentence of six months. She appeared in court looking unwell – she had refused all food since her arrest four days earlier – and said that it was her tenth appearance before the magistrate in a year.

The incensed public, two of whom had angrily thrown guide books at her as police escorted her from the gallery, could see no logical relation between the cause of women's suffrage and

After slashing 'The Rokeby Venus' Mary Richardson leaves for the Bow Street Police Court under arrest.

destruction of a work of art. This led Miss Richardson to hand the Press a signed statement when she was sentenced: 'I have tried to destroy the picture of the most beautiful woman in mythological history as a protest against the government for destroying Mrs Pankhurst, who is the most beautiful character in modern history . . .'

Mary Richardson had told Emmeline Pankhurst of her intention and Mrs Pankhurst had assented. The axe, bought for a shilling in Theobald's Road, was hidden up the sleeve of her jacket during the hour or so she spent in the gallery waiting for the right moment. Her personal dislike of the picture, she said, made damaging it easier.

The painting was so well restored that only the slightest marks are now discernible in the back of the 'Venus', which usually hangs in room 41 of the Gallery. Mary Richardson died, unmarried, at a flat in Hastings on 7 November 1961 aged 72.

Lucy's Bagnio in Leicester Fields (on the site of the LEICESTER SQUARE THEATRE) saw the climax of an extraordinary medical investigation in December 1726. An illiterate woman, MARY TOFTS, arrived there from Godalming in Surrey following the news that in the previous April she had given birth to a litter of fifteen rabbits. She said her reproductive system had been disturbed as a result of being frightened by a rabbit when working in the fields.

A local apothecary, John Howard, who had acted as a midwife for thirty years, said he had felt the rabbits leaping in her womb and was sufficiently convinced to write to Nathaniel St André, a surgeon at the newly opened Westminster Hospital. The surgeon went down to Godalming accompanied by the secretary to the Prince of Wales and reported that soon after his arrival she had shown signs of impending childbirth and that he himself had helped deliver the forepart of a rabbit, stripped of its skin and 'of about four months' growth'. His account appeared in *A Short Narrative of the Extraordinary Delivery of Rabbits* . . . 'published by Mr St Andre, Surgeon and Anatomist to His Majesty.'

The sensational story spread rapidly. Sir Hans Sloane, President of the Royal Society, was asked his opinion. Alexander Pope wrote to a friend: 'I want to know what faith you have in the miracle at Guildford. All London is divided into factions about it.' George I sent his German surgeon, Cyriacus Ahlers, to Surrey to investigate (he reported removing portions of another rabbit) and Mary was examined by Sir Richard Manningham, chief accoucheur of his day.

Brought to London for observation, Mary Tofts was denounced by Manningham who attested that the woman was a fraud and had skilfully concealed the rabbits about her person. She tried to sustain her remarkable imposture, feigning labour pains, but four days after her arrival in Leicester Fields she was caught trying to obtain her future children – some rabbits. A justice of the peace warned her about the consequences of fraud and within a week she made a full confession in front of two eminent doctors and two peers.

Mary Tofts was briefly committed to the Bridewell in Tothill Fields and was threatened with prosecution under a statute of Edward III as 'a vile cheat and impostor'. But the charge was never pressed. Those who had been hoaxed probably realised that to bring down the full weight of the law on an illiterate woman would make them look foolish. As it was, the imposture led to St André being disgraced and ridiculed by Hogarth, while Voltaire was among many writers who produced pamphlets and squibs on human credulity.

The 'rabbit-breeder' (actually the mother of three children by her husband, an artisan clothier) returned to Godalming. She served a term of imprisonment as a receiver of stolen goods some years later, and died there in 1763 aged about 62.

By modern standards KATE MEYRICK, the 'Nightclub Queen', is not a very outrageous character. But in the 1920s she achieved notoriety by opening clubs for Bright Young Things hell-bent on the wicked pleasure of drinking after hours. She was continually sent to prison for assisting them.

For several years after the Great War you could not buy alcohol after 10 p.m. but Mrs Meyrick turned a blind eye on this restriction. In defiance of the puritanical Home Secretary, Sir William Joynson-Hicks, she

Nightclub Queen of the Twenties – Mrs Meyrick.

opened Brett's Club in the Charing Cross Road and then in 1920 bought the premises that made her famous – the '43' at 43 GERRARD

STREET. Magistrates called the place a sink of iniquity, but with its tiny dance floor and tables with white cloths and vases of flowers, we would consider it prim.

When interrogated and asked at one of her many trials why her members – among them the King of Rumania, Tallulah Bankhead and Steve Donoghue – wanted a nightclub, Mrs Meyrick said people found it useful for early breakfasts. 'What time did breakfast begin?' came the puzzled question. 'Ten p.m.' she answered cheerfully. Her first imprisonment followed a raid in 1924 when she was taken to Vine Street and sentenced to six months in Holloway.

This was a serious blow for a woman whose private image was very much that of a lady. The daughter of an Irish doctor, Mrs Meyrick had been presented to royalty, lived in style at Brighton and her children were at Harrow and Roedean. On the break-up of her marriage the problem of school fees was one reason for her inappropriate pursuits in Gerrard Street.

But her disgrace was brief. When she came out of prison for the first time Mrs Meyrick was treated by her friends and customers as a martyr. She was given a heroine's triumph on her return to the '43'. In the month after she left Holloway she defiantly opened another nightclub in Golden Square, quickly followed by the Manhattan in Denman Street and the Silver Slipper in Regent Street. By the time the next blow fell Mrs Meyrick had fully earned her title of the 'Nightclub Queen'.

She went back to Holloway again in 1928 and ten days after her release was arrested on a charge that was rather more serious than selling alcohol after hours. An anonymous letter was received by Scotland Yard asking how it came about that on his pay of £6 a week Sergeant Goddard of the Metropolitan Police was able to afford a freehold house in Streatham and a Chrysler car, and why he had two safe deposit accounts? There was an investigation, and £12,000 was found in one private safe. Four of the notes were traced back to Mrs Meyrick. The corruption charge against her carried a sentence of fifteen months' hard labour.

More raids. Further sentences. Mrs Meyrick began to tot up the imprisonments. Five in all by 1930. She still loved nightclub life but disillusion was setting in. When the '43' was subjected to a raid – its last – in February 1932 Kate Meyrick announced her retirement and gave the court an undertaking that she would not transgress liquor laws for three years.

On the occasions she went back to her club, before her death in 1933, she did so as a guest. Today she would not recognise the scene of all that tinkling Twenties' gaiety. The '43' is a Chinese supermarket.

Across Shaftesbury Avenue, and hardly more than three minutes' walk from Gerrard Street, is Brewer Street where the outrageous CHEVALIER D'EON lived for 33 years. This French army officer, diplomat and secret agent is principally remembered from the now-famous contemporary print which shows him in eighteenth-century costume divided down the middle, half man, half woman. D'Eon began dressing as a woman in the 1770s and for forty years all London speculated about his true sex.

The house which the Chevalier made notorious some years earlier was No. 38, demolished in 1934. Rebuilt and renumbered, it is now 71 BREWER STREET. The site is next door to Slater and Cooke, butchers, near the corner of Sher-wood Street.

In 1763 when Charles d'Eon from Tonnerre in Lower Burgun-dy was the chargé d'affaires at the French Embassy in London, he quarrelled with the ambassador and was ordered home on the instruction of Louis XV. D'Eon refused to accept the validity of the order; he declined to return.

To deal with this unusual situation the high-ranking Comte de Guerchy was dispatched from Paris to carry out the recall. Faced with a point-blank refusal by d'Eon to accept forcible extradition, the Comte attempted to kidnap him. This failed, and when the British Government declined to interfere in what it regarded as a matter of French concern, a party of more than two dozen French police officers assembled in London with orders to seize d'Eon and put him aboard ship.

This was d'Eon's cue to leave

Contemporary impression of a sexual enigma – Chevalier d'Eon.

Dover Street where he had lodgings and move into the Brewer Street house which he transformed into a virtual fortress. His garrison was manned by a number of friends – dragoons from his old regiment – and a few expatriate French deserters.

Fortified for a siege, the Chevalier had a small arsenal of pistols, guns and sabres and he himself appeared brandishing a red-hot poker. His assailants were invited to enter – but warned that all the downstairs rooms and the staircase were mined. The threat was enough. The French police retired. The Chevalier defused the house and with a library of 8,000 books, wines and furniture settled more or less happily in London.

Soon, however, questions were being asked about his sex. Was the Chevalier really a man or, as his blue eyes, small features and soft voice suggested, a woman? He deliberately encouraged speculation by openly denying he was a man; but he still dressed like one. Wagers were laid, and in 1775 the *Morning Post* announced that odds were seven to four – on his being a man. Before long some £120,000 was riding on the outcome and rewards were offered to anyone who could conclusively solve the mystery.

After two further years of doubt and just when there seemed a danger of interest flagging, d'Eon created a sensation by appearing publicly in London as a woman. For this first outing as a female he wore an elegant gown and a headdress adorned with diamonds. 'I am trying to walk in pointed shoes with high heels, but have nearly broken my neck more than once,' he confided in his journal. He enjoyed the curiosity he aroused and for the last part of his long life d'Eon consistently appeared as a woman. When he went to France and was presented at court he was officially accepted as such. The housekeeper who looked after him for fourteen years always called him 'Mademoiselle d'Eon'.

People in Milman Street, Bloomsbury, where he moved from Brewer Street, never saw him dressed in any other way. By the time he died, aged 82, in 1810 he had become a woman to the whole world. So when a posthumous medical investigation declared him 'a very man' the revelation came as a total surprise. After forty years of successful masquerade Chevalier d'Eon was buried in Old St Pancras Churchyard.

If Winston Churchill had been asked to unveil a Black Plaque he would have done so with enormous relish at 21 GOLDEN SQUARE. In the large, still surviving house in the south-west corner of the then fashionable square lived LORD BOLINGBROKE, and Churchill was almost hysterically opposed to this contemporary of his ancestor, the Duke of Marlborough.

An 'unprincipled miscreant adventurer' was his description of Queen Anne's Secretary of State. In his Marlborough biography Churchill said that by his 'personal vices of heart and mind, by deeds of basest treachery, by violation of law and public faith' Henry St John, first Viscount Bolingbroke, brought the country to 'the edge of an abyss'.

This is slapping on the colours with very broad strokes. Most historians suggest that Bolingbroke – in youth dissolute and all his life ambitious – backed the wrong horse at a critical stage in his career. On Queen Anne's death in 1714 he threw in his lot with Jacobites and plotted to bring James Stuart to the throne. This was treachery in the guise of high-principled beliefs, and his double-dealing cannot be denied. No bonfire burnt more brightly than the one he lit in Golden Square to mark George I's accession. No one bowed lower at the Hanoverian king's coronation. Yet by then he must already have been conspiring to bring the Old Pretender out of French exile.

Sir Robert Walpole and his Whig adversaries smelt out the plot, and, fearing arrest, Bolingbroke fled to France. He took devious precautions. He booked a box at Drury Lane Theatre on one night and told everyone that he would occupy it the next, but instead he was on the Dover Road disguised as a valet. He is believed to have carried £13,000 across the Channel.

His flight gave his enemies all the excuses they needed. Bolingbroke was impeached, attainted, and his name removed from the roll of the House of Lords. When he arrived at the exiled court of the Old Pretender at St Germain-en-Laye, near Paris, James appointed him his Secretary of State and – somewhat prematurely – made him an earl.

The failure of the '15 rebellion after James's brief landing in Scotland left Bolingbroke with his cause frustrated and his English enemies more firmly in power than ever. At 37 he faced eight years of exile, which came to an end thanks to the intervention of Marie Claire Deschamps, the widowed Marquise de Villette, whom he fell in love with and later married. The Marquise came to England and bribed George I's mistress, the Duchess of Kendal, with £11,000 to smooth the way to his repatriation (p. 104) in 1723.

Neither given back his seat in the Lords, nor any chance to return to political life, Bolingbroke had to make do with rural retirement. With the death of his father in 1742 he inherited the family manor house at Battersea, where he died nine years later. The epitaph on his tomb in the church between his house and the river defiantly describes him as 'The enemy of no national party, the friend of no faction' whose 'attachment to Queen Anne exposed him to long and severe persecution'.

In the same year as Chevalier d'Eon's affray in Brewer Street, CASANOVA came to London and immediately made his way to Soho. Now aged 38, the legendary libertine was an agile man, 5 ft. 9 in. tall, with pointed features, large nostrils and a wild, magnetic – and roving – eye. He arrived in London with £12,000 which he hoped to increase by organising lotteries, with which he had done well in France.

On his first evening in London (Monday 11 June 1763) Giacomo Casanova went straight to the house in Soho Square of an old-time friend and former mistress, Theresa Cornëlys. He had first met Theresa in Venice when she was a pretty coquette of seventeen, and ten years before this English reunion they had enjoyed a brief affair. In the intervening decade she had come to London and successfully established a fashionable resort for masquerades and concerts at Carlisle House. At the corner of Sutton Row, on the east side of the square, her 'Temple of Festivity' was on the present site of St Patrick's Roman Catholic Church.

Casanova was excited not so much at the prospect of once again seeing Theresa, now a stout 40, but because he was to meet for the first time a ten-year-old girl, Sophie, whom he believed to be his daughter, conceived in their short Venetian affair. Theresa's greeting was friendly, but he was piqued that she was not warmer; sexual indifference was something with which Casanova was unfamiliar. When she offered him only one small room, he took himself off to Pall Mall.

The Pall Mall house which Casanova leased for most of the nine months he was in London cannot be identified. But during the last part of his stay he moved to Soho to lodgings rented to him by a landlady, Suzanne Mercier, for a guinea a week. This has not previously been located but the rate books indicate that a Black Plaque for Casanova may confidently be assigned to 47 GREEK STREET, a building between the Prince Edward Theatre and L'Escargot restaurant.

Even if we believe only a fraction of the accounts in his *Mémoires*, Casanova does not seem to have been inhibited by the coolness of his old mistress; he quickly plunged into romantic activities in

Casanova about the time of his London visit. The great lover's first call was on his former Italian mistress who ran the fashionable Carlisle House assembly rooms (above). The rooms were on the site of the present St Patrick's Roman Catholic Church seen on the east side of Soho Square.

London. While he was finding his way round the town he used the services of girls recommended to him by the Earl of Pembroke, a decadent Colonel of Hussars to whom he had an introduction. He paid for his pleasures at rates of between four and six guineas, though a Miss Kennedy in Covent Garden accommodated him for three. But dissatisfied by roving in restless pursuit of pleasure he hit on the idea of advertising for a young woman to come to live with him. She had to be 'respectable', single and able to speak French. If she were also prepared not to receive any visitors she could occupy a floor of his house. There were many applications and from among them he chose Pauline, a Portuguese woman of 22 – married but parted from her husband. He delayed her seduction for several days for fear of alarming her. Then, following a riding accident – outside Kingston House, Knightsbridge, where he was rescued by Elizabeth Chudleigh (p. 195) – he returned to Pall Mall, and took to his bed. 'Divine creature,' he whispered to Pauline when, pale and anxious, she came to his room. 'It is nothing . . . a mere sprain.' His heroic acceptance of pain she found so affecting that during the night she slipped into his bed by moonlight.

After a passionate three weeks, Pauline had to return to Lisbon and Casanova sought solace with Anna Binetti, an old flame dancing in London with the Italian opera. Then he set up Marianne de Charpillon in a house in Chelsea (after the titillation of surprising her niece in the bath).

However, the great climax of Casanova's London sojourn came when he started a virtual harem in Pall Mall consisting of five sisters, the daughters of a woman from Hanover – an attractive arrangement but so expensive that he was forced to move quickly to Greek Street. During his last week in Soho he spent part of each day with the mistress of Baron Stenau, a Livonian nobleman.

Casavona's inability to speak English was apparently the cause of his one notable failure as an amorist in London. This was with Kitty Fisher (p. 113) whom he visited at her Mayfair flat in Carrington Street. Attracted by her notoriety, his opening gambit of 'I love you!' (said to be the only three English words he knew) was too much for Kitty who burst out laughing. She tried to make amends by reducing her much higher normal fee to ten guineas but the affronted Casanova retired, declaring himself unable to make love to any woman who was unable to understand what he was saying.

The Livonian Baron, whose mistress Casanova visited so persistently while in Soho, had his revenge by passing him a bill of exchange which he cashed not knowing it to be a forgery.

Threatened with arrest, Casanova fled from London on 11 March 1764, never to return during the remaining thirty-four years before his death in 1798 aged 73.

Confession may be good for the soul but FREDERICK FIELD overdid it. In October 1931 Field, who fixed up signs outside buildings for estate agents, went to a lock-up shop at 173 SHAFTESBURY AVENUE (a more recent office block has now swallowed it up). With him was the manager of his firm who helped him remove a board. When they let themselves in they found the dead body of a prostitute, Nora Upchurch. She had been strangled and her handbag was missing. Field had been there two days earlier but there was nothing to link him with the murder – until he decided to confess.

Two years later he went to a newspaper and claimed he was the murderer. He said he had killed Nora Upchurch, whom he had picked up near Leicester Square and taken back to the empty shop. She had bitten him and he had grabbed her round the throat.

Newspapers are not unfamiliar with cranks who arrive to pour out stories of their supposed crimes, and it was only following nine hours of questioning and after a photographer had accompanied him to Sutton to take a picture of the ditch in which he said he had disposed of the handbag, that the paper decided to publish and pay Field for his story. Then a reporter took him to Marlborough Street where he made a statement.

At Field's trial Mr Justice Swift made it clear that he disliked what has come to be called cheque book journalism; newspapers should not postpone informing the police until their story was on the streets. But, anyway, since he thought Field was lying, he advised the jury to bring in a verdict of Not Guilty, which they did.

But this was not the end of the story. Having confessed to one murder, Field went on to confess to another. Three years after his acquittal he declared that he had killed a woman, Beatrice Sutton, in her flat in Clapham. She had been smothered with two pillows.

It appears that Field again went to Fleet Street before informing the police, but he told a girl friend 'I thought I would get what dough I could'. This suggests that he tried to repeat his previous stratagem. But as crime reporters have good memories, and newspapers keep cuttings libraries, he would have been unlikely to succeed. Though he later retracted his account to the police that he had killed Beatrice Sutton, it was one confession too many. For the second crime he was hanged.

—— *8* ——

Marylebone

IN Marylebone and beyond, London has acquired a more than faintly scandalous reputation. We have a picture of high-stepping ladies comfortably installed not far from Regent's Park where they are discreetly visited by Victorian husbands weary of dull Belgravia marriages.

Probably all a bit exaggerated and, surprisingly, there are fewer scandals than we might expect in St John's Wood where tradition insists that ladies dispensed afternoon comfort on *chaises-longues* in charming little bijou villas. They and their protectors must have been very circumspect.

But only a little research is necessary between Portland Place and the Edgware Road to discover that since Regency times there has been a good deal of sin around. A delectable example is provided at 33 HARLEY STREET, (then No. 73), where JANE DIGBY kicked over the traces a few years after her marriage to Lord Ellenborough. This was before she embarked on an amorous career in which she captivated three kings (including a father and son), two princes, a German baron, an Albanian brigand and a brace of bedouin sheikhs.

The woman nicknamed Aurora (from Byron's *Don Juan*) was favoured from the cradle. Her father was an admiral; her mother one of the Cokes of Norfolk; she was brought up at Holkham. She was 'very fair, very young and very pretty' (Mrs Arbuthnot), spoke nine languages and was a talented painter.

At seventeen this tall, well-built girl with luxuriant brown hair and crescent eyebrows married Lord Ellenborough. He was a widower twenty years her senior but a title was useful. Jane had several affairs during the next two years, gave birth to a son (rumoured to be fathered by her cousin) and then, aged 21, met the grand passion of her life. He was Prince Felix Ludwig Johann von Nepomuk Frederich zu Schwarzenburg, attaché to the Austrian

Jane Digby, aged 20, about the time of the affair which led to her divorce.

Newspapers enjoyed a field-day with cartoons like this – 'Innocent employment for Foreign Princes' – showing what the servant saw from the house on the other side of Harley Street.

ambassador Prince Esterhazy.

The fateful meeting was at Almack's. Jane was immediately in love. They met every day, went to the races together, toured the new National Gallery. In the afternoons Jane left her Roehampton home for Harley Street where Prince Felix had lodgings. Her green phaeton highflyer, drawn by two sleek black ponies, would stop in Chandos Street, Wimpole Street or Cavendish Square and Jane would then walk to the house where her ardent lover watching from the first floor drawing-room ran down to open the door.

The flagrant affair became the talk of London – and Brighton, too. When Jane went down to visit her son on the south coast Prince Felix came to the Norfolk Hotel where she was staying, discreetly concealing his arrival by bowling up in a bright yellow coach with a carpet bag emblazoned with the Schwarzenburg crown and monogram.

The inevitable divorce followed and witnesses provided the newspapers with unsurpassed tittle-tattle during 1829. A servant in the house opposite testified seeing Prince Felix lacing up Jane's stays at the end of an afternoon's meeting in Harley Street. A broadside report of the case was an instant bestseller on the streets.

After the divorce and the birth of a daughter by Prince Felix, Europe and the further shores of the Mediterranean replaced London as the scene of Jane's adventures. Another child by the Prince – a son – died within weeks and when the great affair began to wane Jane went to Munich where (thirty years ahead of Lola Montez) she and King Ludwig were inseparable for seven months. Next came Ludwig's son Otho, King of Greece, and (rumour suggests) the future Emperor Napoleon III. After them there was a Bavarian nobleman, Baron Carl-Theodore von Venningen (one son by him), the passionate Count Theothoky of Corfu (another son) and a faithless brigand commander Hadji-Petros of Albania. Each was a successive husband or lover; the precise formalities seem irrelevant.

The final exotic touch, however, came when Jane, fulfilling our expectations of a romantic heroine, disappeared into the arms of desert lovers. She was 46 but her charm and ardour were timeless. From 1856 she lived a nomadic life in Syria, first with Sheikh Barrak who was cruel to camels and criticised her watercolours and then as the adoring wife of Sheikh Madjuel el Mesrab.

She died in 1881 and was buried in the Protestant cemetery in Damascus. But Jane Digby was not forgotten; her Middle Eastern exploits were to fire the imaginations of such queens of the lending libraries as Ouida and Elinor Glyn, to say nothing of E.M. Hull, the forgotten author of *The Sheikh*, which as a film made Valentino famous.

Jane Digby is a hard act to follow. But in her own way, LADY FLORENCE PAGET also showed daring and romantic impetuosity. She, too, created a scandal.

Far the best place to witness the drama she precipitated is from the pavement outside a rather unexpected address. It is the side entrance of Debenham's store (then Marshall and Snelgrove) in VERE STREET, a turning off Oxford Street on the north. Out of this doorway on a Saturday morning in July, 1864, Lady Florence,

Scene of the elopement. The Oxford Street entrance of Marshall and Snelgrove is to the left, the Vere Street exit to the right. The 'Pocket Venus' hurried through the store to a carriage, probably not unlike the one in the print, waiting to take her to Hanover Square.

The 'Pocket Venus' – Lady Flora Paget.

daughter of the Marquis of Anglesey, made a hurried exit.

Aged 21, with dove-like eyes and so petite that she was known as the 'Pocket Venus', Lady Florence had become engaged a week or so earlier to Henry Chaplin. The son of a clergyman, the wealthy squire of Blankney Hall, Lincolnshire, and a close friend of the Prince of Wales, Chaplin was a great catch and her engagement came as a relief to her father, who was none too well off and had the responsibility of eleven children. The couple went on several shopping expeditions and planned to marry in the month following Goodwood.

According to one version of the story (about which there are several legends) Florence's monocled fiancé came to the shop with her that morning and remained outside in the carriage when she went into the store by the Oxford Street entrance shortly after ten o'clock. If so, he must have become increasingly restless as time went by and she did not reappear.

Lady Florence walked through the haberdashery department and left the store most probably by the side door into Vere Street. A closed cab was waiting for her. The driver immediately flicked his horse and they made their fugitive way to Hanover Square where Florence alighted on the steps of St George's Church. She was hurried inside, and before midday was the wife of the Marquis of Hastings.

When the news became known, the impetuous change of heart by the 'Pocket Venus' created a sensation in Society, where she and both Chaplin and Hastings had often been seen together during the previous season. Until this totally unpredictable volte-face Hastings had been the rival – and seemingly the heroic loser – for her hand. There was a sense of outrage because on the night before the elopement they had, all three of them, shared a box at Covent Garden.

Lady Florence's fickleness is not hard to fathom. Common sense had influenced her acceptance of the dependable, upright Henry Chaplin; her emotions demanded otherwise. Harry Hastings was everything her fiancé was not – a hard-drinking, dissolute rake who wore his top hat 'on the Kildare side of his head' and was, in the slang of the day, 'a perfect Cocker'. She found him irresistible.

Memories of the elopement were revived three years later when the Derby was won by Hermit, a chestnut colt owned by the jilted Henry Chaplin. At auction, some time before, Chaplin had outbid Harry Hastings for the horse. Hastings who was now in a bad way financially might have been saved by Hermit but as if fate were against him he had backed a different horse which came in third. Lady Florence's husband never recovered from the loss, and eighteen months later he died of drink at the age of 26. It would have made a suitable curtain for a Victorian melodrama.

Inevitably the epilogue is an anticlimax. The virtuous Henry Chaplin – unlucky in love as lucky in horses – seems to have felt little resentment. He attended his former friend's funeral and, though he sometimes met Florence socially, they never resumed a close relationship. He married twelve years later and died in 1923. The widowed Florence, Marchioness of Hastings, married again six years later and, until her death in 1907 at the age of 64, settled for a withdrawn life very much in contrast to the dramatic bid she made for love when she was the 'Pocket Venus'.

Going deeper into Marylebone we come to 38 MANCHESTER STREET (today an English language school), a pleasant enough Georgian terrace house but hardly palatial enough for the birth of a Messiah. This event, devoutly expected by the followers of JOANNA SOUTHCOTT, was due to take place on 19 October 1814. In preparation for the Second Coming gifts began to arrive at the door. They included a £200 satinwood crib, a gold font, a silver cup and salver and large sums of money.

Nationwide anticipation was intense. Shops were filled with Joanna Southcott cradles containing dolls representing Shiloh, the expected Saviour. Among callers at No. 38 were the Russian ambassador and the Tsar's aide-de-camp. Twenty-two doctors were summoned, seventeen of whom declared that the prophetess, then in her sixty-fourth year, was pregnant. 'Excitement could not have been more intense if the dome of St Paul's had collapsed', declared one newspaper.

Autumn approached winter. Joanna Southcott took to her bed. The eagerly awaited 19 October came and passed. The faithful kept vigil by her bedside over Christmas but no Christ Child arrived. When she died at 3 a.m. on 28 December an autopsy revealed that internal flatulence and glandular enlargement of the breasts had given the appearance of pregnancy.

So died (and was buried in a cemetery in St John's Wood) one of the most extraordinary religious imposters. During her life she had thousands of devoted believers and she left behind a sect, some of whose members vowed never to shave their beards until her resurrection. Strange offshoots of her movement have survived into modern times.

The daughter of a Devon farmer, Joanna Southcott was born near Ottery St Mary in 1750. With a strict Biblical upbringing but little formal education, she carried out her prodigious deception without being able to write literately. After a period as a

Prophet of the Second Coming: Joanna Southcott.

shopgirl in Honiton she went into domestic service.

In 1791 Joanna became a Wesleyan Methodist and in the following year said she heard 'voices' that told her she had been chosen to be the Bride of Christ and, indeed, the Mother of Christ as well. She had always rejected sex but was happy to aver that she shared her bed with a 'most beautiful and heavenly figure'.

When her Wesleyan brethren proved sceptical, she turned to the Calvinists and, after interviews with seven men including three Church of England clergymen who visited her in Exeter, she agreed to come to London. A round-faced, rosy-cheeked woman in a poke-bonnet, she lived first in Paddington and then off Jamaica Road in Bermondsey. She quickly acquired followers among the credulous. Prophesying that a large proportion of the population would perish in the threatened Napoleonic invasion, she did a thriving trade selling signed letters bearing a red Celestial Seal that promised immunity and a life-span of a thousand years. Some 144,000 of these letters were sold. Byron thought them cheap at half a guinea.

Joanna Southcott published 65 books and pamphlets, but nothing so excited her followers as her announcement that she was pregnant by a divine spouse. Even when that promise was not fulfilled she managed to retain a posthumous interest by leaving behind her a sealed box which was to be opened when the country was in peril to reveal contents that would save the nation. There were intermittent calls for it to be opened, but Joanna Southcott had insisted that this had to be done in the presence of twenty-four bishops. Bishops showed a marked reluctance to co-operate.

Between the two World Wars the Panacea Society, in the frenetic figure of Mrs Mabel Baltrop of Bedford, carried out a sustained campaign to open the box. Sandwichmen paraded London with boards proclaiming: 'The Bishops must open Joanna's Box to save England from Ruin'.

All efforts were frustrated, and secrecy concerning the box's whereabouts led to a number of rival boxes appearing. One of them, unsealed at Church House, Westminster, in 1927, was found to contain a horse pistol, a woman's nightcap, a lottery ticket and a dubious novelette entitled *An Adventure in Greenwich Park*. Hardly items to avert Ruin. But then, Joanna Southcott's wishes had been disregarded: only one bishop was present.

Except that it is next door but one to a house which has a Blue Plaque to the historian Edward Gibbon, there is nothing very special about 5 BENTINCK STREET, off Marylebone Lane, now occupied by the Longman Group. But during the Second World War a luxurious flat in the house was let to GUY BURGESS, who shared it with ANTHONY BLUNT.

Their landlord was a mutual Cambridge friend, Victor, the future Lord Rothschild. They worked here with seemingly patriotic zeal for their country during the Blitz. This was some ten years before Burgess defected to Moscow and nearly thirty years before an astonished Britain learned that the Surveyor of the Queen's Pictures, by then Sir Anthony Blunt, had also been a spy.

Both were at Trinity College, Cambridge, in the 1930s. Blunt, the elder by five years, was a Fellow and they were members of a secret society, the Apostles, a number of whom were homosexuals and active in the Communist Party. It was probably the undergraduate Burgess who recruited Blunt into the international Communist organisation, the Comintern.

After Cambridge their paths briefly divided; Blunt, the art historian, to go to the Courtauld Institute, Burgess to the BBC. Soon after the outbreak of war Burgess joined Section D of MI6 and Blunt (though briskly removed from the Intelligence Corps because he had been a Communist) found a post without apparent difficulty in MI5. Blunt had access to important documents which he passed to the Russians, while Burgess was supplying them if not with names of British agents then with a great deal of valuable information picked up from his wide circle of influential friends.

Linked in personal and political conspiracy and probably abetted by Kim Philby (p. 210), they lived an extraordinary double life. With the excuse of pressure of work it was, for instance, Blunt's custom to take back secret papers at night from Whitehall either to Bentinck Street or Portman Square (where he had a room as the deputy director of the Courtauld Institute). These documents were passed on to the Russians for copying and when the two men found them too numerous to deal with, they were supplied by the Soviet Embassy with cameras. Blunt's most damaging information was supplying regular reports on all kinds of intelligence available to him in MI5.

Off duty the lives of the two men seem to have been uninhibited by worries about their duplicity, and despite wartime restrictions drink flowed at Bentinck Street parties. Two girls, Whitehall secretaries, were also living there, and one astonished visitor noted: 'this odd assorted collection of tenants sometimes gave the flat the air of a rather high-class disorderly house in which one could not distinguish between the staff, the management and the clients . . . All appeared to be employed in jobs of varying importance, some of the highest, at various ministries; some were communists and ex-communists; all were a fount of gossip about the progress of war . . .'

The same visitor, Goronwy Rees, author, academic and friend of Burgess, observed that Guy brought home a series of boys, young men, soldiers, sailors and airmen whom he had picked up among the thousands who were thronging the streets of wartime London. 'To spend an evening at Guy's flat', he recalled, 'was rather like watching a French farce . . .'

Malcolm Muggeridge, a wartime recruit to MI6, sourly contem-plated the presence of what he termed 'displaced intellectuals' like John Strachey and J.D. Bernal. Writing with hindsight, he saw Burgess ('Etonian mudlark and sick toast of a sick society') and these friends as figures not so much of conspiracy as of decay and dissipation.

Peace took Blunt back to the more rarefied activities of an art historian at the Courtauld and adviser on pictures to the Queen, for which he received a knighthood. From then on he had no direct access to secret intelligence but his position would have meant that he had plenty to keep the Russians interested. From 1951 until 1964 he was frequently questioned by MI5 until, seemingly, he admitted his past guilt and was given immunity in exchange for information provided.

For the more volatile Burgess, who had left Bentinck Street by the end of 1945, peace meant an extension of the charmed life he had enjoyed during the war. He does not seem to have been a covert member of any of the intelligence services though he may sometimes have acted as an outside informant for MI5. In the Foreign Service abroad he was a thorn in the flesh of ambassadors, infuriating them by his outrageous behaviour.

Not until his flight with Donald Maclean in May 1951, it seems, did Burgess ever arouse suspicion and it was some years after that before evidence came out that he had been a Russian agent. Though he was interrogated, he never gave away the old Cambridge and Bentinck Street companion whom he had loved – anyway until safely in Russia.

After a lonely life in Moscow, alleviated by a Russian boyfriend and gramophone records of old musicals, Burgess died in 1963. His ashes were brought back to be buried by his father's grave at West Meon in Hampshire.

Blunt's confession delayed his public denouncement until 1979, when he was stripped of his knighthood and renounced his many honours. He died at his flat, No. 45 Portsea Hall, Bayswater, in 1983 aged 76.

Three minutes away from Bentinck Street a small side turning links Weymouth Street and New Cavendish Street. It is lined with flats over garages, one of which – 17 WIMPOLE MEWS – blazed into notoriety in 1963. This was the home of DR STEPHEN WARD, a fashionable osteopath whose profitable sideline was to introduce famous men to pretty girls. He was the son of a vicar, went to a minor public school, and was an army captain during the war; above all, he enjoyed being in the social swim.

Ward's relationships with dubious women and his involvement with some thumping crooks led to his suicide at the end of a trial which the prosecution described as reaching 'the depths of lechery and depravity'. One of the women on whose immoral earnings he was accused of living (and who must share his Black Plaque) was CHRISTINE KEELER.

Christine had affairs with a great many men, and because her bedroom in Wimpole Mews was visited in far too rapid succession by a Cabinet Minister and a Russian diplomat, Britain was treated to the 'Profumo Affair', so prominent a feature of the Swinging Sixties legend.

Christine Keeler declares that Ward 'was never any kind of sex maniac' and that she was 'a scapegoat, a pawn in a political struggle'. As far as the Profumo case is concerned, she may well be right. This uncommonly good-looking girl who grew up in a converted railway carriage at Wraysbury, Buckinghamshire, came to London in the late 1950s to search for the bright lights. After a short spell as a Baker Street waitress, she found them at Murray's Club in Regent Street where she was a showgirl. It was here at the age of 17 that she met Stephen Ward and moved into Wimpole Mews. They spent three years together, on and off, during which time, she says, there was never any sexual relationship; her role was to attract people whom Ward found useful.

Among them was Eugene Ivanov, a Russian diplomat whom Christine met during a weekend in July 1961, while staying in a cottage which Ward rented on Lord Astor's Cliveden estate. That same hot weekend she was in some state of undress by the swimming pool when she was introduced to John Profumo, the War Minister. Christine says that she slept with Ivanov only once and that her affair with Profumo petered out within a couple of months. 'I didn't like him that much.'

It is ironical that a relationship which fell far short of a grand passion brought about so large a catastrophe. The affair might never have been heard of but for George Wigg, a Labour MP concerned with Security, who at the time of the Cuba crisis revealed the link between Profumo and Ivanov. Following allegations about the part he had played Profumo told the House of Commons: 'Miss Keeler and I were on friendly terms. There was no impropriety whatever in my relationship with Miss Keeler.'

Nineteen months after the end of their brief affair Profumo probably felt that something he considered transitory and unimportant could be slurred over. It was 'of minor importance only' he later wrote to the Prime Minister, Harold Macmillan, but when the lie was uncovered it was fatal.

Profumo resigned four months later, left public life and has spent the last two decades in social work: model self-effacement for a man in 'disgrace'. Captain Ivanov, who never discovered anything about Cuba from pillow-talk in Wimpole Mews, was recalled to Moscow. Christine Keeler went to prison for giving false evidence at Stephen Ward's trial. Now in her early forties and after two failed marriages, she lives with her son in the World's End part of Chelsea.

Stephen Ward's fate provides the affair with a climax of high drama, retribution and tragedy. In the month after Profumo's resignation Ward was charged at the Old Bailey on five counts of immorality: that he 'knowingly lived wholly or in part on the earnings of prostitution' and that he procured girls under the age of 21. Without important witnesses who might have come to his defence, and seeing his life in ruins, Ward took an overdose of Nembutal early on the last day of the trial and was in St Stephen's Hospital, Fulham, when the jury returned a verdict of guilty. He died on 3 August 1963, before the judge could deliver sentence. He was 50.

Half a mile away from Wimpole Mews, across Baker Street, is 1 BRYANSTON MEWS WEST which served almost as an annex for Ward's activities. MANDY RICE DAVIES, close friend of Christine Keeler, moved into the flat with its green and gold décor and a two-way mirror in 1961. There was also a Welsh harp though it is not clear who played it.

The rent at Bryanston Mews was paid by Peter Rachman (p. 312) who gave Mandy a mink coat, a 3.2 litre Jaguar and £80 a week spending money. On most days he visited around lunchtime; in the evenings they would go round the West End clubs; he invariably went home to Hampstead in the early hours of the morning.

Mandy, born in Solihull in 1944, came to London from Birmingham where she briefly worked in a store. When she was about 16 she was a model and hostess at Murray's Club, where she met Christine. They became friends, had lovers in common and when they were not sharing living quarters were in and out of each other's flats. Mandy was far more involved than Christine with Ivanov but as she never met Profumo she played no significant part in the scandal.

In October 1962 when Christine moved out of Wimpole Mews, Mandy moved in, paying Ward £6 a week for a room and, in what seems very like a shuttle service, Ward went to Bryanston Mews when the Wimpole Mews landlords, 20th Century Fox, wanted the flat back. Around the time of the scandal Mandy was involved with Emil Savundra (p. 315) who appeared in Ward's trials as the mysterious, unnamed 'Indian doctor'. He used to leave £25 a week at Wimpole Mews to help her pay for 'drama lessons' – a euphemism that in no way helped Ward when he was accused of, living on the girls' immoral earnings.

In the years since the hectic 1960s Mandy has married twice and made a successful career for herself, first as a nightclub owner in Tel Aviv, then as a film actress and writer of a novel. She appears to have come through her experiences cheerfully unscathed, and looking back on what she calls her 'affairs of the heart' says they have been enduring and that she is pleased that her lovers have remained friends.

Her one unexpected claim to immortality is her now famous remark in court when Ward's counsel said that Lord Astor had categorically denied her allegation that she had sex with him. 'Well, he would, wouldn't he?' said Mandy Rice Davies in a phrase now enshrined in the *Concise Oxford Dictionary of Quotations*.

Built in the early 1930s on the corner of George Street and Seymour Place, BRYANSTON COURT is a large block of luxury flats, comfortable, anonymous and typical of this part of London. We reach it after a short walk from Bryanston Mews. MRS WALLIS SIMPSON moved into No. 5 on the first floor soon after her second marriage. Here she entertained the Prince of Wales, and so began the relationship which led to the Abdication.

Previously she and her husband, Ernest Simpson, had been in Upper Berkeley Street but as she was starting to collect antique furniture they needed somewhere bigger. With its large drawing-room, three bedrooms and a dining room where they could give parties for ten, Bryanston Court was ideal.

It was in July 1933 that the Prince of Wales, then nearly 40, and spoken of as the world's most eligible bachelor, came to dine for the first time. He had been introduced to Mrs Simpson by Thelma, Lady Furness, with whom he had a close relationship. This was the start of many evening visits. It became the routine for the future Duke of Windsor to drop in for drinks about six, remain after any other guests had left, and then if Wallis's husband was absent he invariably stayed for a meal. His patient chauffeur became accustomed to long waits.

By the summer of 1934 the affair with Lady Furness had been broken off and Mrs Simpson became a permanent part of the Prince's life. When Ernest Simpson went to America on business he and Wallis travelled, sketchily chaperoned, to Biarritz, Cannes and Lake Como. The following February they went skiing at Kitzbühel.

Somewhat tired of bowing himself out of his own flat on transparently thin pretexts, Simpson decided to move into the Guards Club while his wife stayed on at Bryanston Court through most of 1936. When her divorce was pending, and just before the affair became public knowledge, she moved to 16 Cumberland Terrace in Regent's Park.

The country, which had largely been kept in ignorance of what was brewing, could hardly believe the headlines when the great Constitutional crisis arose. In the weeks leading up to the Abdication in December 1936 shock turned to anger and there were rumours that Mrs Simpson's Nash house had been threatened with a bomb. Ugly letters came through her front door. These violent reactions were the outcome of moral outrage and a feeling that somehow the monarchy had been sullied. Unforgivably an American divorcée had stolen away the nation's Prince Charming.

The Duke, who was King Edward VIII for only ten months, married Mrs Simpson in 1937. He died in 1972 aged 78. The Duchess, too ill to receive visitors in her final years, died aged 89 on 24 April 1986 in her dark, gloomy mansion, a former home of the Bourbon kings, in the Bois de Boulogne.

As a rough and ready rule it is probably true to say that rural bishops should not come to London in search of sin. Emphatically, they should not misbehave with guardsmen in West End public houses. Unwisely the BISHOP OF CLOGHER ignored both these precepts.

We do not know if the Bishop had an official reason for leaving his diocese (which stretches across the borders of County Tyrone and County Monaghan in Ireland), or why he was absent from the Protestant Cathedral of St MacCarten's. Perhaps he was on holiday; certainly he was the guest of John Fay and was staying with him at 21 MONTAGU STREET, off Portman Square; and unfortunately he was in clerical garb when he went into the White Lion in St Alban's Place on the evening of 19 July 1822. The public house was at the bottom of present-day Lower Regent Street.

The next thing we know about the Honourable and Right Reverend Percy Jocelyn is, to put it mildly, regrettable. It would have been disastrous even if the Bishop, a man in his mid-fifties, had not also been the son of the first Earl of Roden and in holy orders for well over twenty years. He should not have been discovered in a compromising position with Private John Moverly of the 1st Regiment of Guards in the back room of the inn. That he was observed by not one but seven witnesses suggests indiscretion verging on exhibitionism.

The Bishop was arrested and taken to Vine Street where he refused to give his name to the police and tried to tear up an envelope from his pocket before they could read the address. He then wrote a pitiful note to Fay, his host in Montagu Street: 'John, come to me directly. Don't say who I am, but I am undone. Come instantly and inquire for "a gentleman below stairs". Twelve o'clock. I am totally undone. P.C.' He spent most of the night praying in his cell.

Both Percy Jocelyn and the soldier were charged the next day at Marlborough Street and the Bishop was granted bail on sureties of £1,000. When the case next came up, at Clerkenwell Sessions, Private Moverly was there to face the music – conviction and imprisonment. The Hon. and Revd Percy was not: he had fled.

Back in Ireland he was called, but failed to appear, before the Metropolitan Court of Armagh where evidence was produced of a similar offence some years earlier in Dublin. At the end of the hearing by the assembled clergymen, he was defrocked by the Lord Primate. We can almost hear the outraged tones in which he was reproached in his absence, not so much for his act of immorality but because he, a prelate of the church, had associated with a private 'wholly beneath him in rank and station' and because the place he had chosen for this act of depravity was 'a common alehouse'.

His ignominy complete, the Cathedral of St MacCarten did not see its bishop again. Percy Jocelyn went abroad where he died in 1843.

By rights MARY ANNE CLARKE should be among the avaricious royal mistresses of Mayfair – she did live in Park Lane for a while – but it was at 62 GLOUCESTER PLACE (formerly No. 18) that she carried on a conspiracy with her lover the Duke of York, Commander-in-Chief of the British Army.

This relationship was exposed at a hearing in the House of Commons in 1809, when Parliament and public learned in fascinating detail how this woman with a lowly background had acquired the spacious terrace house along with a retinue of twenty servants that included three cooks and a dozen liveried footmen. How had she owned so many fine horses and carriages? How did she afford to dine off gold and silver plate? The answer was simple: with the connivance of her royal lover she had trafficked in Army commissions.

Born in 1775, probably the daughter of a Scottish butcher with a shop off Fleet Street, Mary Anne Clarke was taught to read and write by her mother's second husband, a printer. She married young, but deserted, and with three children to bring up, she decided she needed a rich lover. With a quick wit, slight figure and appealing blue eyes, she did not lack protectors. Three of them found her too expensive, but she was more fortunate with her next conquest – Frederick Duke of York, George III's second son.

The Duke leased the Gloucester Place house for Mrs Clarke and for three years this became his second London home, a luxuriously run alternative to his town house in nearby Portman Square and a welcome escape from his matrimonial establishment in Weybridge. He made his mistress an allowance of £1,000 but her extravagance so ran away with money that she was soon badly in debt. An added complication arose in the form of her husband, who came back into her life with threats of suing her royal lover for adultery. The Duke decided the time had come to break off the relationship.

He gave Mrs Clarke the Gloucester Place house as a settlement, but this did not end his entanglement. A far greater scandal broke when a Welshman, Colonel Gwyllym Lloyd Wardle, MP for Okehampton, began ferreting into her affairs. He strongly suspected that the huge sums of money spent by Mrs Clarke were

Mary Anne Clarke.

Outside her house in Gloucester Place Mrs. Clarke is dismissed as a royal mistress by William Adam, the Duke's legal adviser. A caricature published at the time.

somehow interrelated with irregularities in Army promotions.

Col. Wardle played a devious opening gambit. He suggested to Mrs Clarke that she might enjoy going with him to the Kent coast where he said he had to carry out a four-day inspection of Martello towers. She fell in with this improbable plan and over leisurely dinners at Hythe when Wardle did not stint on the wine, Mrs Clarke was indiscreet. She divulged that she and the Duke had influenced the creation of peers and baronets and the promotion of generals.

This was all Wardle needed to persuade Parliament to appoint a Select Committee, and in 1809 the House was packed when the chief witness, wearing a long powder-blue silk dress and carrying a white swansdown muff, made a theatrical entrance. She looked, someone remarked, as if she were entering a ballroom.

During her twelve appearances Mrs Clarke explained how she and the Duke of York had operated. At this time all commissions were obtained by purchase (a majority cost some £2,600 and a captaincy £1,500) but she had offered cut prices – as much as two-thirds below the normal figures. The applicant approached her and she spoke to the Duke. As Commander-in-Chief, he signed the papers. The applicant got his Army commission: she reaped the financial one.

This profitable arrangement went on for three years, and at a critical time when officers were needed to fight the French many of them never left civilian life: they stayed on perpetual leave drawing pay and allowances. These revelations gave the Duke of York no option but to resign as Commander-in-Chief. Mrs Clarke on the other hand was cheered in the streets. Her confessions made her the heroine of the day.

Cheering did not pay bills and Mrs Clarke told the Duke that if he did not give her an annuity she would publish her memoirs, his love letters and all the secrets of their affair. To prevent further scandal she was given a lump sum of £10,000 and £400 a year. The manuscript and 18,000 already printed copies of her memoirs were burnt in Salisbury Square.

After a further attempt at blackmail which landed her in the Marshalsea for nine months, Mrs Clarke went to live in France where she devoted herself to her three children. One daughter, Ellen, married an unsuccessful French inventor called Du Maurier, and it is Mary Anne Clarke's interesting memorial that her grandson was George Du Maurier, the *Punch* artist and author of *Trilby*, and her later descendants the actor-manager Sir Gerald and his daughter Daphne du Maurier. She herself died at Boulogne in 1852 aged about 74.

On 1 April 1898 a gaunt, grey-bearded man nearing 70 died at 21 SHOULDHAM STREET. April Fool's Day somehow seems appropriate, for ARTHUR ORTON had devoted half his life to the attempted perpetration of a gigantic hoax.

In his last years Orton was almost destitute, a discredited, pathetic figure. When they carried his body down from the upper floor of the small terrace house opposite Marylebone Baths it was for burial in a pauper's grave. Yet he carried on his preposterous claim to the end: in Paddington Cemetery the inscription on his coffin defiantly proclaimed: 'Sir Roger Charles Doughty Tichborne'.

This was the final gesture of the boy from Wapping who went to Australia to become a sheep slaughterer and whom Disraeli called 'the most infamous impostor since Titus Oates'. It was the last throw of the man who nearly twenty-five years earlier had been convicted of perjury and sent to prison. His sentence followed what were then the longest trials in the history of our civil and criminal courts. By the time of his death the 'Tichborne Claimant' had become a legend and 5,000 people lined the Edgware Road to watch his funeral go by.

As we have seen from the career of that other Marylebone impostor, Joanna Southcott, the world relishes a tall story, and Orton's assertion that he was the long-lost Roger Tichborne, wealthy landowner and heir to a baronetcy, was a very tall story indeed.

The real Roger Tichborne, member of a rich Hampshire family, had sailed for South America in the middle of the century. His ship went down on a voyage from Brazil to Jamaica and he was presumed drowned until, in the 1860s, his mother, Lady Tichborne, offered a reward in Australian newspapers for news of her lost son. She had a touching belief that he was still alive and had been picked up by a passing ship. In response came a letter from Wagga Wagga in New South Wales in which the writer addressed Lady Tichborne as 'My Dear Mother' and spoke of days in an open boat. He asked her for £200 passage money so he could come home to take up his position and title.

The overjoyed mother met him in Paris on his return from Australia in 1866 and immediately accepted him as Roger. Orton, emigrant son of a poor Wapping butcher, was roughly the same age as Tichborne, but that was about all. He was barely literate; his accent was far from that of Stonyhurst and the Guards; corpulent and rather gross, he bore not the slightest resemblance to the slim, missing Roger. But Lady Tichborne happily paid his debts and gave him an annual allowance of £1,000 during the five years in which he steeped himself in family history and assembled a hundred witnesses prepared to confirm his assertion that he was Tichborne.

Orton in convict uniform (below), walking behind a warder in Portsmouth prison. After his release, the Tichborne Claimant, (left) cadged drinks round Marylebone public houses.

Two trials followed his claim to the title and inheritance. The first – a civil action lasting 103 days – heard a mass of contradictory evidence. As a former public schoolboy educated by Jesuits he might have been expected to know the difference between Latin and Greek. Unlike Tichborne, he spoke no French. Tichborne had a tattoo on his arm; Orton had not. After his taking too frequent refuge in the phrase 'I can't remember', the jury decided he was an impostor. He was then arrested and indicted for perjury.

Arthur Orton's criminal trial at Westminster Hall was even more drawn out, and at the end of 188 days (following a summing up by the Lord Chief Justice which lasted a month) he was convicted and sentenced to fourteen years' imprisonment. Newspapers which he had provided with daily instalments of an engrossing serial rewarded him with a chorus of invective. *The Times* branded him as 'a lowborn, illiterate, vulgar scoundrel'; the *Standard* regarded him as 'the most daring swindler of our times . . . the most audacious rascal . . . the most consummate perjurer and hypocrite'; and the *Daily Telegraph* saw in his imposture 'the measure of the possible wickedness of man'.

But a bad press was far from bad publicity. After ten years, Orton emerged from Pentonville to attempt the revival of his cause in more unorthodox courts: at public meetings, in the ring at Sanger's Circus and on the stage of an Edinburgh music hall which paid him £200 a week. Within two months he had addressed 40,000 people. So potent was his fame that a young comedian playing the same circuit decided to call himself Little Tich in tribute to 'Big Tich'.

As time went on, interest declined in Orton's increasingly unconvincing story; his stage and lecture bookings dwindled. During his last few months in Shouldham Street Orton was so poor that he had to apply for medical relief from the parish. In the end the man who still maintained that he was Sir Roger Tichborne, Bt, could only raise a few coppers by displaying himself in Kilburn pubs.

Off the Edgware Road and two streets away from where Orton died is an insignificant alley called CATO STREET. There is already a Blue Plaque on 1A, a building which has not greatly changed over the years. But a black one would seem more suitable for the scene of what the *Morning Chronicle* was to headline as 'DREADFUL RIOT AND MURDER'.

In an upper room over a stable ARTHUR THISTLEWOOD, a political extremist and malcontent, ran his sword through a Bow Street constable. This occurred during a raid on 23 February 1820. 'Yesterday evening,' reported the newspaper,'the West End of town was thrown into the utmost confusion, the streets were lined with soldiers and spectators, and the greatest alarm prevailed . . .'

The alarm was caused not only by the raid in which the Bow Street Runners broke into a room where there was a meeting of about twenty men armed with guns, swords and daggers. More worrying to the Government were the rumblings of social and political unrest in Europe which found ominous expression in the Cato Street Conspiracy.

The actual incident was short and sharp. Bursting through the doorway Constable George Ruthven shouted: 'We are officers! Seize their arms!' As they forced their way in, Thistlewood, the

Remarkably little changed to this day, the stable in Cato Street where Thistlewood planned the assassinations is only a few yards off the Edgware Road.

ringleader, picked up a long sword which he ran through one of the officers, Richard Smithers. With a cry of, 'Oh, my God, I am donè!' Smithers fell back dead. Nine men were captured by the police and, accompanied by a detachment of Guards, taken to Bow Street. Thistlewood got away that night but was arrested next day at Moorfields.

The Cato Street affair was over almost before it began, but the country had reason for apprehension as the more wide-ranging plot was uncovered. Thistlewood and his group of fanatics had planned to assassinate the whole British Cabinet later that night, and there were enough gunpowder and hand-made grenades in the loft to confirm the story. The Cabinet was known to be dining at a house in Grosvenor Square and Thistlewood was to have gone to the front door as if to deliver a note. When the door was opened he and his companions were to force their way into the hall and overcome the servants.

The climax of the attack was to be the murder of the assembled ministers, among whom was the Duke of Wellington. 'I will cut off every head in that room,' Thistlewood had promised his men, 'and

Lord Castlereagh's head and Lord Sidmouth's I shall bring away in a bag.'

All this was inflammatory and alarming enough. But the trial revealed this was to have been only the prelude to a *coup d'état* in the City. A fireball was to be thrown into King Street Barracks, cannons captured and brought down Cornhill to the Royal Exchange. If the Mansion House did not surrender it was to be burnt down. The Bank of England was to be attacked and plundered.

No one hearing these threats was surprised to learn that Thistlewood had been in France during the French Revolution or that, in a career of inciting disaffection, he had previously been arrested and imprisoned. He and four of the Cato Street conspirators were hanged at Newgate and – as convicted traitors – they were also decapitated. Thistlewood died calmly sucking an orange on the scaffold, having defiantly declared: 'Albion is still in the chains of slavery. I quit it without regret.'

— 9 —

Belgravia and Pimlico

ELGRAVIA immediately suggests impressive squares and long straight terraces – stuccoed memorials to the enterprise of the Cubitt brothers. Their columned porticoes, wrought-iron balconies and steps leading down to the servants' areas are redolent of Victorian prosperity.

These houses in SW1 carry, too, more than a whiff of upper-class decadence for, as we shall see, many scandals and titled divorces have originated behind their ponderous façades. Normally, heavy front doors stand closed against prying eyes, but from time to time an official knock comes from men in raincoats who ask to be admitted, make searches and leave with evidence subsequently aired in courts of law.

One such raid on one such very typical Belgravia house occurred either in the late autumn of 1914 or (accounts vary) in April 1916 at 50 EBURY STREET when police and security officers searched the rooms of SIR ROGER CASEMENT. They took away a Letts' diary for 1903, a Dollard's diary for 1910 and a cash ledger, all of which were to gain notoriety as the 'Black Diaries'.

Casement, a distinguished British Consular Agent, was hanged at Pentonville, but before a plaque to match the colour of the diaries is even contemplated for the house where he lodged when in London, we must weigh up some conflicting opinions. Though he was convicted of high treason, and though the diaries brought him into disrepute, Casement is venerated by a great many people, especially in Ireland, as a martyr and patriot. They contend that the British Cabinet secretly exposed his private life for political ends in an atmosphere of wartime hysteria and in the climate of prejudice that then existed against homosexuality. The *News of the World* echoed public sentiment when it said that no one who read the diaries 'would ever mention Casement's name again without loathing and contempt'.

Roger Casement, born at Sandycove, near Dun Laoghaire in Co. Dublin in 1864, devoted nineteen years of his life to the investigation and exposure of the ill-treatment of natives in the Congo and Brazil. His integrity as a public servant won him great respect and he was knighted in 1911. But this esteem was swept away after the outbreak of the Great War when he went to America and Germany to seek support for Irish independence. In Germany he tried to raise a brigade from among the ranks of captured Irish soldiers in prisoner-of-war camps; they were to be

Sir Roger Casement.

shipped back to Ireland to fight the British.

As an Irish nationalist, Casement may have considered this justifiable but as a British subject (as indeed were all the Irish before 1922) his actions clearly constituted high treason. He was arrested on the south-west coast of Ireland where he was landed by a German submarine just before the Easter Rising of 1916. He had shaved off his beard, but his story that he was an English author out for a stroll did not convince the constable who challenged him. When he was found to be carrying a German railway ticket and a code book he was sent to London, charged at Bow Street and brought to trial at the Old Bailey.

The trial appeared straightforward, but behind the scenes there was furious discussion about what use, if any, could be made of the documents discovered in Ebury Street. The diaries showed Casement's private life to have been very different from his public image. Entry after entry revealed him as a homosexual and told of his encounters with men and boys in London and with natives in West Africa and South America. Their measurements, the pleasure they gave and the payments he made them were carefully recorded. A horrified Foreign Office man described the diaries as '200 pages of concentrated erotica'.

Even if this was an exaggeration, the Black Diaries were potential dynamite. The Government's only problem was how to detonate them to best advantage. The revelations could not be used at the trial unless – and this was suggested to Casement – he would be prepared to put them in as evidence and plead 'guilty but insane'. This he refused to do, knowing that a jury would never equate homosexuality with insanity and that this was just a device of the Government to lose him public sympathy.

After a three-day trial Casement was found guilty and sentenced to be hanged. But the Government were worried about executing a man whose crime could be ascribed to an excess of Irish patriotism; even more importantly, he was highly regarded in neutral America, from which country wartime support was desperately needed. The Home Office resorted to what now seems despicable behaviour. The diaries were photographed and selected passages secretly distributed round the House of Commons and in London clubs. They were 'leaked' to newspapers, especially in America. One was shown to King George V.

Influential public opinion was thus covertly built up against Casement with the result that many of his supporters – they included the Archbishop of Canterbury – withdrew their pleas for clemency. The Home Office could now safely reckon that the diaries would prevent his execution becoming a martyrdom.

The scandal of the diaries has tended to obscure the obvious truth that, whatever his private life, Casement was a man of unquestionable political integrity. His adherents like to believe that the diaries were forged, but examination of them at the Public Record Office (permitted in 1959 following their publication from transcripts) confirms that they are genuine. The homosexual entries could not have been interpolated.

A body, officially said to be that of Roger Casement, was exhumed at Pentonville and reburied at Glasnevin Cemetery in Dublin in 1965.

Down the road, and just round the corner from the house where the Black Diaries were found, is a slightly smaller house, 46 LOWER BELGRAVE STREET, also built very much to the Cubitt formula. But at No. 46 murder not treachery detains us and we are confronted with an unsolved mystery.

Here on the cold, wet night of 7 November 1974 a children's nanny was battered to death and the estranged wife of LORD LUCAN was wounded before he disappeared without trace. A coroner's jury found Richard John Bingham, seventh Earl of Lucan, guilty of murder, but he has never been brought to trial. He has simply vanished.

The alarm was raised when his wife Veronica stumbled into the Plumber's Arms, a public house across the street. Drenched, without shoes and bleeding from a gash in the head, she sobbed incoherently: 'Help me, help me! I have just escaped from a murderer. He's in the house . . .'

There were other disjointed phrases – 'My children, my children . . . he's murdered the nanny . . .' while the landlord bathed her wound and the police were called. Later that night, the next day, and for weeks that have now stretched into years, detectives unsuccessfully tried to establish exactly what happened and have failed to find the missing peer.

Cutting through a great deal of unproved suspicion, what may fairly be said is that Lord Lucan, who was living apart from his wife, let himself into the house sometime after nine o'clock intending to kill her. In the half dark he struck the nanny, Sandra Rivett, with a short piece of lead piping. She was much the same build as Lady Lucan. When he discovered his mistake he carried the girl down to the basement where he put her body in a large canvas bag. Lady Lucan, who was upstairs watching television with her children, went down to find out why the nanny was taking so long to make a cup of tea, and was herself attacked.

Still missing, still briefly in Who's Who: *Lord Lucan (wanted for murder, whereabouts unknown) photographed at St Moritz.*

Her story is that her husband told her he had killed the nanny in mistake for her, but strangely enough forty minutes appear to have elapsed before she ran out for help. In a telephone call – and to a friend he visited in Sussex later that night – Lucan said he had surprised 'an intruder' whom he had seen attacking his wife. Then the Earl had driven away in his car, never to be seen again. Did he kill himself? Leap into the Channel from the Newhaven ferry? Take refuge with a new name and different appearance in some country from which there is no extradition? These are among many unanswered questions.

Lucan's motives for wanting to kill his wife are almost equally mysterious. This good-looking Old Etonian of forty, gambler, man-about-town, and very much the old fashioned aristocrat, had been living apart from Veronica Lucan for a year. Their separation had been stormy. He had lost custody of the children; he contended his wife was mad and had her watched; though nicknamed 'Lucky Lucan' he had run up serious gambling debts. He is said to have had an illogical, persistent idea that Veronica was responsible for all these problems. But despite these factors, something as extreme as murder was very much out of character.

Lord Lucan's other arrangements that night – booking dinner for four friends at the Clermont Club – were social and they were as carefully pre-arranged as his clothes, which the police found laid out on the bed of his nearby house in Elizabeth Street. His passport was in a drawer.

Since he disappeared over a decade ago Lucan has never been officially declared dead. He still has a small entry in *Who's Who*. About a dozen reports that he has been seen – in South Africa, Australia, Holland, Ireland and the Caribbean – come in each year. All have proved false. Doggedly Scotland Yard keeps the file open.

If adultery were reason enough for a house to have a Black Plaque, few in Belgravia, we feel, would be without one. As LADY MORDAUNT remarked, 'Everybody does it', and she certainly suited her actions to her words. Her husband's absences from London – as MP for Warwick and on fishing trips to Norway – were her cue to entertain a great many visitors at 16 CHESHAM STREET, the house they took during the Season.

Among her afternoon callers was the Prince of Wales who would arrive about 4 p.m. and stay for a couple of hours during which time the butler had strict instructions not to disturb them. Bertie, then 29 and six years married, was only one of the 'Marlborough House Set' to beat a path to the door of Harriet, wife of Sir Charles Mordaunt and daughter of a Balmoral neighbour, Sir Thomas Moncreiffe.

During the 1868 Season Harriet Mordaunt's engagement book was exceptionally full. Chesham Street, the Alexander Hotel, Knightsbridge, even the Mordaunt family home – Walton Hall, Warwickshire – saw visits from Lord Cole, who was an officer in the Rifle Brigade, Lord Newport, a Guards officer, Arthur Farquhar, Lord Lucan (p. 95) of Crimea fame and ancestor of the missing modern peer) and Sir Frederick Johnstone.

She admitted these indiscretions to her husband. 'Charlie, I have been very wicked,' she told him. 'I have done very wrong.' Her confessions followed the birth of a daughter, sickly and weighing only 3½ lbs. She declared the child wasn't his but Lord Cole's, adding hysterically: 'I am the cause of its blindness.'

This wild talk of transmitting an imaginary affliction has a suspicious ring. If she were insane, her counsel could claim that she was legally unfit to plead; and while Mordaunt's counsel saw this as her device to prevent the divorce, doctors produced enough evidence of incipient madness. It was enough to prevent Mordaunt from getting his divorce in the sensational *cause célèbre* of 1870 during which the Prince of Wales went into the witness box and denied that he had behaved improperly with Harriet.

Five years later Sir Charles Mordaunt was granted a divorce – then only Lord Cole was cited – and for a while Harriet was in the custody of her father. She died on 9 May 1906. Her daughter Violet, the child who was small at birth and whose 'blindness' was no more than a passing ophthalmic complaint, grew up to marry the Marquis of Bath in 1890 and was the mother of the sixth Marquis, who installed the lions at Longleat.

Until 1926, after which date reported evidence has been restricted to the judge's summing up, every scabrous detail in a divorce case could be made public. Newspapers ran columns of lurid information. No sheet was left unturned. This is how we know the long list of Lady Mordaunt's lovers. As we shall see, the reporting of scandalous and quite probably invented accusations brought Sir Charles Dilke into disrepute. And in the case of Campbell versus Campbell in 1888, it is from the newspapers that we learn how the jury went round to the matrimonial home, 79 CADOGAN PLACE, and one by one knelt to peer through the drawing-room keyhole.

This conscientious investigation was to help them decide what, if any, impropriety could have been witnessed from this vantage point. They found that almost nothing was visible. Stories of the intimacy of LORD COLIN CAMPBELL with a servant girl had to be discarded as untrustworthy. Equally, there was no evidence for the supposed adulteries of LADY COLIN CAMPBELL. It was all very disappointing.

The case, however, did not lack indelicate incident or famous names. This murky divorce held prurient promise from the moment that Lord Colin, son of the eighth Duke of Argyll, rushed to his lawyers to file his divorce petition only to find that he had

Lady Colin Campbell, portrait by Giovanni Boldini in 1897, a decade after the scandalous divorce hearing.

been beaten to it by his wife Gertrude. She was a dark, strikingly beautiful woman whom Whistler had painted in the nude (*Harmony in Black and Ivory*) and referred to as his 'lovely leopard'.

The Campbells' archetypal Belgravia terrace house appears to have been heaving with unseemly activities. Lord Colin named four of his wife's lovers: the future Duke of Marlborough; Captain Shaw, the redoubtable amateur chief of the London Fire Brigade; her doctor, the society physician Dr Thomas Bird; and a military man, General Sir William Butler, who to avoid the trial made a tactical withdrawal to France. Lady Colin countered by citing their former housemaid Mary Watson, whom a witness said she had seen being dangled on Campbell's knee. She also alleged that he was suffering from 'a specific complaint' (syphilis) which he had transmitted to her on their honeymoon, and that women were not his only interest (implications of this were clear but left unspecified in *The Times* as 'unfit' to appear on its pages).

Medically examined, the housemaid proved to be a virgin. This more or less exonerated Campbell. On the other hand the girl did rather betray her mistress by telling the court that whenever the future Duke of Marlborough arrived to see Lady Colin (by way of the area steps) she would go up to the drawing-room and, employing a prepared code, say, 'Please, my lady, cook wants to see you.'

For her part, Lady Colin had a ready answer to all accusations. In the witness box she blandly explained that she could not possibly have committed adultery: she was always far too busy. Her days were completely taken up with the Cadogan Place house, entertaining for her MP husband, teaching at a night school for factory girls and dispensing soup at the Stepney Mission.

The allegations and refutations went on for nineteen days and ran the Campbells into the then huge expenses of £20,000. At the end the jury, fresh from the keyhole, found adultery unproved on either side. Alone, and with her reputation tarnished, Lady Colin discarded good works among the poor in favour of journalism. She became a travel writer for the *World* and columnist on etiquette for *Queen*.

In a house across the gardens of Cadogan Place a third Belgravia divorce case involved SIR CHARLES DILKE. He was ruined by allegations of what occurred at 76 SLOANE STREET. Quite rightly the LCC commemorated him as 'statesman and author' by putting a Blue Plaque on his house. Our Black Plaque is designed to recall the great Victorian scandal which subjected him to enormous publicity.

It would be ingenuous to assume Dilke's complete innocence, but as far as the main accusation is concerned he was unquestionably the victim of corrupt testimony by a wicked woman, Virginia Crawford, who claimed she had highly irregular sexual relations with him. As a result, the MP for Chelsea and a Cabinet minister expected to succeed Gladstone as Prime Minister, was disgraced. A horrified Queen Victoria tried to have him expelled from the Privy Council.

Mrs Crawford bluntly alleged that she and a servant girl named Fanny Gray had a threesome with Dilke at his Sloane Street house. She said he told her that he wanted to see her and the maid 'together' and that when the two of them were in bed Fanny came into the room naked and joined them. She asserted this happened several times during an affair that continued intermittently for two and a half years.

Dilke denied everything, but it was his rather woolly and unconvincing word against Mrs Crawford's assured, forthright one. A Victorian jury also seems to have been swayed by the curiously illogical argument that it was far more likely that a man

Dilke as shown on the cover of a contemporary song sheet.

would indulge in perversion than that a woman from a good family would invent such a story.

The revelations came in 1886 when Donald Crawford, a lawyer and Fellow of Lincoln College, Oxford, sued his wife Virginia, aged 23, for divorce. During the previous three years he had been receiving anonymous letters telling of his wife's misconduct: one naming a Captain Forster, and another, which said that she had been carrying on with medical students at St George's Hospital, added: 'Beware the Member for Chelsea.'

When her husband confronted her, Mrs Crawford told him: 'It is not Captain Forster. The man who ruined me was Charles Dilke.' This deliberate lie (to shield Forster, her real lover) made it imperative for Dilke to go into court to deny the accusation. At this time the politician was 43 and had recently become engaged following the death of his first wife. His new fiancée can hardly have been pleased by Mrs Crawford's allegations. Mrs Crawford said that Dilke had told her about a number of affairs and – the first major sensation – that he had admitted that when he was a young man her mother had been his mistress. It was her resemblance to her mother, she suggested, that had first attracted him to her.

In a photograph Virginia Crawford looks innocently young in a straw hat and sailor collar. But her evidence contradicts this impression. She related how, when she was 18, Dilke had first propositioned her at Bailey's Hotel, Gloucester Road, had taken her to an 'afternoon house' (payment by the hour) in Warren Street, and had made love to her in a rented house in Young Street, Kensington. But her most sensational charge of all came when she described the troilism at his Sloane Street house. 'He taught me every French vice,' she asserted.

Dilke's Sloane Street staff denied the story. So did the maid Fanny though she did not give evidence at the trial. It was established that Captain Forster was Mrs Crawford's lover. Despite all this, and though the judge dismissed him from the case, nothing could save Dilke. The mud stuck. W.T. Stead (p. 31), the moralising editor of the *Pall Mall Gazette*, campaigned against him. So did other political enemies. He lost his Chelsea seat, and though he was exonerated and returned to Parliament eight years later, he never achieved anticipated high office before his death at Sloane Street in 1911.

Latterly some unexpected information came to light about Mrs Crawford's past. It seemed that she and her sister Helen (both wives of men nearly twice their ages) had started living promiscuously soon after their marriages. Hunting as a pair, they had involved a number of men in tri-partite sex, generally at a house of assignation in Knightsbridge – liaisons which could easily have given her the idea of inventing a similar relationship with Dilke, herself and Fanny Gray.

A reformed sinner rather like Laura Bell (p. 108), Mrs Crawford never remarried after her divorce, and in later years turned to the Church. She became a Roman Catholic, did social work among fallen girls, and was the first Labour councillor for Marylebone. She moved to Campden Hill in 1931 and, the author of an impressive number of social and religious books, died in Kensington in 1948 aged 85.

Next door to Dilke's house in Sloane Street is the CADOGAN HOTEL where a Black Plaque would sadly proclaim that here the arrest took place which preceded the trial and downfall of OSCAR WILDE. For Wilde it was a moment only to be compared to the agony he experienced later when he was exposed to public gaze in convict clothes on the platform at Clapham Junction.

Oscar Wilde. The playwright was arrested in Room 120 (now 118) at the Cadogan Hotel, through the door on the right of the picture.

On the evening of 5 April 1895 the playwright was at the hotel awaiting the inevitable. His friend 'Bosie' – the young Lord Alfred Douglas – had gone to the House of Commons to find out from a relative what was likely to happen.

Despite growing apprehension Wilde could at least reflect that even while the clouds gathered two of his plays, *The Importance of Being Earnest* and *An Ideal Husband*, were triumphantly being presented in London. As he sat in the Cadogan, smoking incessantly and drinking a great deal of whisky, he knew the curtains would be going up in a couple of hours. Since he had lost the case in which he had sued Lord Alfred's father, the Marquis of Queensberry, for calling him a sodomite, his own tragedy was about to start with the Director of Public Prosecutions in the role of antagonist.

At six o'clock the police knocked on the door of Room 120 (now 118) on the first floor. Wilde unsteadily got into the waiting carriage for Bow Street. Ahead lay the Old Bailey, Reading Gaol, *De Profundis*, exile and death in Paris in 1900.

When Lord Alfred got back to the Cadogan he found only a brief note: 'Come and see me. Ever yours, Oscar.'

A classic Victorian murder complete with a rich husband of odd sexual inclinations, his adulterous wife with a mysterious background, and her impecunious young lover who, for good measure, is a clergyman . . . these people take us out of Belgravia south into Pimlico not far from Vauxhall Bridge. Unfortunately the actual house, 85 CLAVERTON STREET, was demolished, so we have to conjure up the events standing in front of a modern low block of flats called Whiteley House.

To Claverton Street in October 1885 came ADELAIDE BARTLETT who, always restlessly moving about, was in search of rooms for her husband and herself. She asked the landlady if the double bed could be replaced by two singles but when she said no, Mrs Bartlett told her it didn't matter; her husband could have a folding cot. They moved in next day.

Adelaide was a good-looking woman of thirty who for eleven years had been married to Edwin Bartlett, an enterprising grocer with a growing chain of suburban shops. Born in France, her exotic maiden name had been Adelaide Blanche de Tremouille and considerable doubt surrounds her background. She is variously described as being the daughter of Comte de Thouars d'Escury or 'the unacknowledged daughter of an Englishman of good social position.'

This is the first mystery about her. The second is how, aged 19, she came to make what was clearly an arranged marriage with a grocer at Croydon and, immediately after the ceremony, went to a finishing school at Stoke Newington and then to one in Belgium. When she left school she and Bartlett lived in Herne Hill, but they had an agreement that their relationship should be platonic. This was broken only once in eleven years – when she wanted (and apparently conceived) a child. The baby was stillborn.

Edwin Bartlett didn't appear to find this arrangement upsetting. As for Adelaide, she had an affair with his brother, Frederick,

Adelaide Bartlett. Acquitted of poisoning, she completely disappeared.

and (after moving house from East Dulwich to Merton) she met and fell deeply in love with a Wesleyan clergyman of twenty-six, the Revd George Dyson, whose chapel she and her husband attended. Each day when Bartlett went to work Dyson came round to teach her Latin and history. He was never seen carrying any books.

During the summer of 1885 the three of them were often together, even sharing a holiday at Dover. Adelaide claimed that far from objecting to her obvious affection for the young clergyman, her husband encouraged it. He enjoyed watching them kiss and eventually had 'given her' to Dyson. The only disadvantage to this cosy arrangement from her point of view was that it had awakened her husband's long-dormant sexual interest in her.

Two days after Christmas that year Adelaide asked Dyson to obtain some chloroform (needed, she said, to get Edwin off to sleep) and the clergyman visited three chemists in Putney and Wimbledon whom he told he wanted it to remove stains. As he was a man of the cloth they took his word.

For several months before this Edwin had been ill. A doctor thought he was suffering from some form of mercury poisoning but his various diagnoses of what was actually wrong were, at best, haphazard. Then with dramatic suddenness, on New Year's Day

1886, the doctor was summoned to Claverton Street at 4 a.m. He found Edwin Bartlett dead.

According to Adelaide, during the night her husband had taken some of the liquid chloroform which was in a bottle on the mantelpiece and mixed it with some brandy which he then drank.

Murder has seldom seemed more evident. That was the verdict of the coroner's jury against Adelaide Bartlett, and her lover was named as an accessory before the fact. But the charge against Dyson was dropped, and at the trial Adelaide was brilliantly defended by Edward Clarke, who in a six-hour speech claimed that it would have been impossible for Bartlett to be forced to take the drink without protest. Why had he not cried out? Why had he not choked if the liquid were forced down his throat, and why were there no traces of chloroform in his lungs?

Clarke suggested it was more likely that, sexually rebuffed, he had taken the fatal mixture and passed into a coma which deepened into death. Probably modern scientific analysis would have shown that Adelaide had been administering lead acetate to her husband ever since their arrival at Claverton Street.

Clearly Adelaide and her lover wanted Bartlett out of the way, but because evidence against her was only circumstantial she was acquitted. After a trial in which she seemed to have limitless resources to pay for the best solicitor and one of the leading barristers of the day, she completely disappeared. It may well be that she emigrated to America with her former lover and brother-in-law, Frederick Bartlett, who returned from the United States to support her during the trial. No one heard of her again, and even the most persistent journalists and writers concerned with the case have never traced her. It is known, however, that Dyson went completely to pieces and that the young clergyman's affair with Adelaide did not survive the scandal and ordeal of the trial.

As for Adelaide's guilt, Sir James Paget, Queen Victoria's surgeon, expressed what everyone felt when he cynically observed: 'No doubt the lady was quite properly acquitted, but in the interests of science she should tell us how she did it.'

Knightsbridge and Kensington

THE first houses of any importance west of Hyde Park Corner stand like twin sentinels to the park at Albert Gate. Large stuccoed mansions, they were built by Thomas Cubitt in 1844 on the site of the bridge over the Westbourne river where two medieval knights are said to have fought a duel, giving us the name Knightsbridge. The houses, not considered Cubitt's best speculation, were nicknamed 'The Two Gibraltars' – because it was said they would never be taken.

In fact, one of them, 58 KNIGHTSBRIDGE, (now the French Embassy) was bought within a year by a gross, burly Yorkshireman, GEORGE HUDSON, a former linen-draper who had become a millionaire during the great railway boom of the previous decade. The 'Railway King', as Sydney Smith dubbed him, controlled more than one-fifth of the country's network. He became Lord Mayor of York and MP for Sunderland. Despite his uncouth manner, his lavish parties at one of London's largest private houses attracted the leaders of Society.

No one realised at the time – and it is something which has largely been forgotten by railway enthusiasts – that Hudson was a swindler on a massive scale. He turned a huge income into a gigantic fortune by dishonest financial manipulation. He misappropriated shareholders' money to buy stock for himself; floated companies and used the capital to prop up failing ones; falsified dividend payments; and he spirited away into his own account money that should have been paid to landowners for railway rights.

Hudson's trick of issuing more than the authorised number of shares in rail companies netted him probably as much as £145,000 and his habit of quickly selling new issues at an inflated price gave the Stock Exchange the word 'stag' – after the statues still standing on the gate piers outside his front door. Because companies at this time were not obliged to publish audited accounts, his swindles

George Hudson's extravagant house in Knightsbridge is the large building on the right. The portrait and cartoon of the 'Railway King' show him before his downfall.

The Hudson Testimonial.

were undetected for several years. But when angry shareholders demanded investigations, it was discovered that he had diverted a total of nearly £600,000 from proper channels.

During the great boom that developed into 'Railway Mania' the self-made plutocrat rode high. People were too busy making money to worry where it came from. But a fall in the value of railway property coincided with Hudson's move to London and the vast expenses of Albert Gate undoubtedly tempted him to desperate measures.

Hudson's wife Elizabeth lavished £14,000 – a huge sum in 1846 – on furnishing and decorating 58 Knightsbridge. She spent extravagantly on herself. When she went riding in Hyde Park her carriage was painted in such gaudy hues that one newspaper said it could 'be *heard* from Knightsbridge to Notting Hill'. The parties she gave to break into London society might be ridiculed but were sufficiently opulent to attract Wellington and the Marquess of Westminster.

When disaster came, many people who had enjoyed Hudson's hospitality (and his financial tips) quickly dropped him. As he sank deeper into disgrace, few voices were raised in his defence.

Most people echoed the vituperation of Macaulay, who described Hudson as 'a bloated, vulgar insolent purse-proud, greedy drunken blackguard' who 'when he swaggered up to the House . . . looked like Mammon and Belial rolled into one'.

During his decline and fall Hudson escaped arrest for debt only because he had immunity as an MP; during Parliamentary recesses he had to live abroad. A street named after him in York was renamed. His effigy was removed from Madame Tussaud's. He was forced to sell his Yorkshire estates. He and his wife moved from the grandeur of Albert Gate to lodgings in Churton Street, Pimlico.

When he lost his seat in 1859 he went to France where he lived in poor rooms in Calais and Boulogne; his clothes were shabby and he was sometimes short of food. In a brave attempt to rehabilitate himself, Hudson came back in 1865 to stand for Parliament at Whitby, but he was confronted by debtors and imprisoned in York Castle. When he was released three months later the election had gone by and his chances with it. His last years were eked out on a small annuity bought by friends. It was said that the man who had been intolerable when he was a success was far more lovable in defeat. George Hudson died at his Pimlico lodgings in 1871 aged 71.

In the early 1930s there was a most unlikely resident for Knightsbridge at WASHINGTON HOUSE, 20 BASIL STREET. He was – or rather had been – a farm boy from the American Middle West. But by the time he came to live at Flat 14 in the Renaissance-style block near Harrods he had long since said goodbye to Madison County, Iowa, and had handed in his badge as deputy sheriff of Polk County. OSCAR MERRIL HARTZELL had found a more profitable and less arduous occupation than following the plough.

Hartzell came to London in the 1920s, and soon a great many people in the States were fascinated to learn that he was engaged in an important undertaking. He informed them he was helping an heir of Sir Francis Drake to recover a fortune that had been sequestered by the British Government. This money was the haul of Spanish gold which the Elizabethan navigator had brought back from South America on the *Golden Hind*, and was now held in the Tower of London. According to Hartzell, Drake had a son by a hitherto unknown third wife (possibly Queen Elizabeth I, he hinted) and it was on behalf of his lineal descendant that Hartzell was proud to be doing battle.

Most of the people to whom he wrote announcing his campaign had the name Drake. This he explained was why they had been selected for a chance to help the great cause which would entitle them to a share of the ninety million pounds in the Tower. Hartzell regretted that he could not reveal the name or address of the heir because his life might be threatened.

Soon he extended the scheme from Drakes to all-comers. Some 70,000 people were contacted through eleven agents working in Iowa and several other states. They were promised at least $500 for every dollar they subscribed to the fighting fund. The response was a striking testimony of the concern of the New World to see justice done in the Old. One farmer wrote saying: 'I'm takin' my settin' hens right off the nest to put everything I've got into this thing'.

To avoid using the US Mail (which could prosecute for attempted fraud) Hartzell arranged for contributions to be forwarded to him in London through American Express. It was not unusual for him to collect $2,500 a week (some £600), a very tidy sum in 1923 when he initiated the scheme which was to continue profitably for ten years.

To avoid difficulties, Hartzell required all donors to sign an undertaking of 'Silence, Secrecy and Non-Disturbance' and any who broke the vow were told they would be blacklisted and lose their share in the payout. Despite this proviso, by 1933 the

American authorities had built up sufficient evidence against Hartzell to demand his extradition. On his arrival in New York in February 1933 he was arrested and taken to Sioux City, Iowa, to await trial.

In the next eight months Hartzell contacted the great family of Drake supporters. He told them that his extradition had only been granted because the British Government was terrified of the consequences: the interest on the confiscated fortune was so vast that the United Kingdom could easily be bankrupted. This was enough for the faithful to put up yet more money for his legal costs and a further $50,000 for his personal use.

The prosecution had some difficulty in finding witnesses who would testify against Hartzell, and the strength of his support was shown by one Englishwoman who wrote to inform the court that she had willingly given Hartzell her jewellery when he had told her that he had been created first Duke of Buckland. The Iowa jury were made to understand that this title (granted by the King at a secret investiture) was unlikely.

An English barrister summoned to Sioux City armed with copies of Drake's actual will explained that, whatever the circumstances, no money could possibly be forthcoming because there was a Statute of Limitations in British law and it did not extend to 300 years.

Hartzell was sentenced to ten years imprisonment, and eight of his collecting agents were subsequently gaoled. This, however, has not entirely discouraged some American Drakes who are still resolutely hanging on to receipts in the brave hope that one day glittering prizes will float back from the Spanish Main. Oscar Merril Hartzell died in the State Penitentiary at Leavenworth in 1943.

Has any autobiography got away to a better start than the one written by a woman who lived at 16 TREVOR SQUARE? 'I shall not say why or how I became, at the age of 15, the mistress of the Earl of Craven' was how HARRIETTE WILSON began her scandalous memoirs which sent a tidal wave of prurient excitement through late Georgian London.

It may have been that she couldn't think of much to recall about the Earl, whom she found a bore when she lived briefly with him in Brighton, and whom she rapidly exchanged for Frederick Lamb, the future third Viscount Melbourne. Other Regency notables were chronicled far more fully in her *Memoirs* published in 1825.

*Corner house in Trevor Square.
Here Harriette Wilson (left)
wrote the second volume of her
scandalous memoirs.*

The most famous courtesan of the day was said to change her lovers as easily as her shoes. Among them were the 'amiable, thoughtless' sixth Duke of Argyll with whom she lived in Mayfair, Lord Ponsonby ('the handsomest man of his time' and her great love), the dandified Marquess of Worcester, Wellington's Peninsular War aide-de-camp, and – only naturally – Lord Byron, who first kissed her at a masked ball.

The *Memoirs* were written in Paris at a safe distance from her exposed and outraged lovers. The book went into thirty-one editions and from the royalties Harriette was able to take the small corner house in the pleasant Knightsbridge square when she returned to London at the age of 42 in 1829. She moved in with her brother, a French maid and a husband, Colonel Rochfort, who drove her to drink.

Harriette had rich pickings from the £10,000 made by the book. She also had a great many individual £200 payments demanded from those who wanted their names kept out. One of the few to resist her blackmail was the Duke of Wellington, who sent her the classic reply scrawled in red ink: 'Publish and be damned!' In consequence he found himself described not luridly, but, far worse, as boring. She called him an 'unentertaining visitor' resembling a ratcatcher. Of Wellington's departure from her house one day she noted: 'I am glad he is off, thought I, for this is indeed very uphill work. This is worse than Lord Craven.'

The autobiography, which bubbles with malicious humour, appeared in serial form. The names of the 'exhibits' – dukes, marquesses, down through earls and honourables to mere esquires – were advertised in advance. The date and exact hour of publication (two o'clock precisely) ensured that the publisher's office in Royal Opera Colonnade, off the Haymarket, was besieged.

On the Trevor Square house our Black Plaque could record that here Harriette wrote a second volume of memoirs in which she again recalled her brisk appetite for love. For some reason she cast it in the form of a novel called *Clara Gazul*. Perhaps she felt that now she was married, middle-aged and a little too plump, it would be wearisome to try to extract individual silence money from her old lovers; a single killing would be better. In this she succeeded. A number of people thinly disguised as fictional characters took fright and raised a lump sum between them. She suppressed most of the copies, and with this further nest-egg decided the moment had come to disappear.

In 1830 she left the trim little plaster and brick house in the south-east corner of the square and two years later faded into oblivion. Harriette Wilson simply vanished. Nothing more about her is known for certain.

Solid and imposing in a heavy Victorian way, 5 BEAUFORT GARDENS does not look at all as it did when a particularly grotesque and pointless murder took place there in 1946. In November of that year planks and cement bags littered the entrance to the house in the leafy cul-de-sac off Brompton Road; it was being renovated for occupation by the HON. THOMAS LEY, at one time Minister of Justice for New South Wales.

The murder was committed – or anyway started – in the front room of the house when a rug was thrown over the head of a quiet and inoffensive barman of 35 named John Mudie who had been lured to London from Reigate. A clothes-line was tied round his body and ankles. He was then pushed down into a swivel chair. A french polisher's rag was forced into his mouth as a gag. What exactly happened to Mudie after that is uncertain. The next thing recorded is that two days later his body was found in a rain-drenched chalkpit near Woldingham in Surrey.

As the circumstances of the 'Chalkpit Murder' became known, the more mindless and revolting it appeared. It was the crime of an insane man whose victim had done nothing to merit the jealousy that resulted in his being kidnapped, brought to Beaufort Gardens and killed by a contract murderer.

The insane man was Thomas Ley, the former Australian minister, an immensely fat solicitor of 70 who, as he was moving into his new address, conceived the idea that his housekeeper and former mistress, Mrs Byron Brook, had had an affair with Mudie. For ten years Ley had been impotent and in that time there had been no sexual relationship between Mrs Brook and himself, but apparently he still loved her and was subject to fits of violent jealousy. Although she was only four years short of 70, he accused her of affairs with three young men. One was her own son-in-law, another Mudie, the barman who had briefly occupied a room in the same house as her daughter.

Mrs Brook had once unwisely observed that she thought Mudie had beautiful eyes. She had met him only once but this casual remark was enough for Thomas Ley to see him as a rival and organise his murder. Working on the Beaufort Gardens restoration was a foreman joiner, John Smith, and Ley paid him to go down to Reigate, where Mudie had a job, and, on the pretext of asking him to act as a barman at a party, to bring him back to the Knightsbridge house. Another man was given £200 to hire a car and, after the murder, to get rid of the body.

Medical evidence was divided about the fate of the wretched Mudie after he reached No. 5 and the time he was dumped in the Surrey chalkpit is not known. The prosecution could not say how he had been strangled, and the jury were faced with a summing up by the Lord Chief Justice in which they were told that it was not precisely known *how* the murder was done, really *why* it was done, or *who* had actually done it. Lord Goddard said they must simply use their common sense.

The driver who dumped the body turned King's Evidence and was acquitted. Thomas Ley was found guilty but insane, and died of a brain seizure in Broadmoor within three months. John Smith, the foreman joiner who had received most money from Ley, was sentenced to death but this was commuted because of the unwritten practice that a subordinate should be shown mercy when the main culprit cannot be fully punished.

Interest in RUTH ELLIS, the last woman to be hanged in England, tends to focus on the Magdala public house at the bottom of South Hill Park, Hampstead. That is where she shot David Blakely on Easter Sunday, 10 April 1955. But the last place she lived – and where she and Blakely had made love after visiting the cinema only three nights before – was a bed-sitting room at 44 EGERTON GARDENS, off the Brompton Road.

The shooting was a violent end to a very unsatisfactory relationship, and, as in the Beaufort Gardens affair four streets away, murder was prompted by jealousy. It was a sad, sordid business involving Ruth, the blonde manageress of a drinking club nearby in the Brompton Road, and Blakely, her on-off boyfriend, an amateur racing driver. She was 28; he was 25.

Recently a theory has been advanced that Ruth Ellis shot her lover not as an act of vengeance on him as a person but out of her disgust with the class system – that she was a girl from the wrong side of the tracks visiting retribution on an upper-middle-class mummy's boy with a big house in Buckinghamshire. It is more convincingly explained as a *crime passionnel* which in France or America, or even Scotland, would probably have meant not more than a few years imprisonment for manslaughter. Her hanging had a direct influence on public opinion about the death penalty, which, never again repeated for a woman, was suspended in 1965.

Ruth Ellis, born in Rhyl, North Wales, in 1926, came to London at 14 during the Blitz. She took jobs as a waitress and in a factory, met a Canadian soldier, had a child by him, and then discovered he was married. After the war she posed in the nude at a 'camera club' and her slim good looks secured her a job in one of the drinking clubs which were a growing feature of post-war London. Marriage to a man named Ellis – whom she met at the club – ended in divorce for cruelty within two years.

This downhill story seemed to be halted when she met Blakely, the good-looking amateur racing driver. He was the first customer she served after she was made manageress of the Knightsbridge Little Club. She also acquired an alternative older lover, Desmond Cussen, an ex-bomber pilot, a successful business man whose devotion was doglike.

While the ex-pilot provided security of a sort for Ruth and her two growing children at a Devonshire Street flat, she carried on a love affair with Blakely, a relationship which he was too besotted to break off yet felt to be socially beneath him. The affair blew hot and cold until early in 1955, when Ruth left Cussen and moved into the bedsitter provided by Blakely at 44 Egerton Gardens.

A violent, passionate relationship was bedevilled by Blakely's casualness, his frequent disappearances and her suspicion that he was seeing other women. It reached a climax on Good Friday (when he failed to keep an appointment and she traced him to a Hampstead flat): on Saturday night (when hidden in a doorway, she saw him leave a party at the flat with his arm round a woman): and on Easter Sunday (when, after drinking a bottle of Pernod, she traced his car to the Hampstead public house). She had a pistol.

Ruth waited by Blakely's car outside the Magdala and when he came out with some beer to take away she shot him. FOUR BULLETS AS HE LAY DYING was the *Daily Mail* headline.

Her trial lasted only two days. The defence plea of manslaughter became hopeless when she was asked what her intention had been when she fired. She replied: 'It is obvious that when I shot him I intended to kill him.' She was sentenced to death and refused to appeal.

Still unsolved is how Ruth Ellis came to have a gun and whose gun it was. She maintained at the trial that she had kept it hidden away unused for three years. But it had recently been cleaned and oiled, and the day before her execution she told her solicitor that in fact she had been given it by Blakely's rival, Desmond Cussen. This possibly extenuating evidence came too late for a stay of execution.

Cussen, who now lives in Australia, has consistently denied any involvement.

A crowd of 1,000 stood outside the gates of Holloway when she was hanged at 9 a.m. on 13 July 1955 by Albert Pierrepoint, the public hangman. It was his last execution.

There is nothing at all romantic about the massive block of early 1930s flats in Prince's Gate where Knightsbridge meets Kensington Road. But KINGSTON HOUSE stands on the site of a mansion with the same name built about 1763 for an extremely romantic lady. Old Kingston House, demolished in 1929, was one of several fine residences facing Hyde Park – Gore House, Kent House, Stratheden House – which have been the victims of developers.

It was built by the second Duke of Kingston for ELIZABETH CHUDLEIGH who was his mistress for twenty years and bigamously married to him for four. She gave magnificent parties, staged firework displays and, with her great charm, attracted royalty and London Society to Kingston House. If we put up her Black Plaque over the modern east entrance we shall probably not be far from the original eighteenth-century portico through which she once helped the injured Casanova (p. 146).

The 'bigamous Duchess of Kingston' played for high stakes – and finally won them. Born in 1720, the daughter of the Lieutenant-Governor of Chelsea Hospital, Elizabeth was courted in her early twenties by the sixth Duke of Hamilton and never ran short of lovers. She was almost certainly the mistress of George II for a while and also of his brother, 'Butcher' Cumberland.

Throughout her life Elizabeth's behaviour was outrageous, as in 1749 when she caused a scandal by appearing apparently naked at a Somerset House ball. She went as Iphigenia, but, said Horace Walpole, 'she was so naked you would have taken her for Andromache'.

At the time when everyone was gossiping about this incident Elizabeth met the Duke of Kingston in the Pump Room at Tunbridge Wells. She was then not quite 30, pretty, with bold eyes, provocative mouth and (as a painting of her in transparent chiffon by Reynolds shows) a lovely figure. The Duke was 48, single, a millionaire and, Elizabeth noted, 'simple, gentle and retiring'. Perhaps she found something appealing in this considerable contrast to herself. Once she had disentangled him from a French mistress and an inconvenient milliner, they settled down to an affair said to have been conducted with decorum.

Notorious for appearing
naked in public – 'The
Bigamous Duchess of
Kingston' – Elizabeth
Chudleigh – at a masquerade
in Ranelagh Gardens in
1749 (below).

How the word decorum could be applied to an open liaison which lasted so many years is not clear. They were constantly seen together and, before they made their home in Knightsbridge, she entertained for the Duke in a house he built for her in Hill Street, Mayfair. It is also rather puzzling that their marriage was so long delayed. It may have been because Elizabeth was often preoccupied with other lovers here and abroad – Frederick II of Prussia among them – or because hanging over them was a difficulty which could no longer be ignored when after the twenty-year affair they at last decided on marriage in 1769.

There floated up out of the past an event which had occurred quarter of a century before. Elizabeth Chudleigh had taken part in a distinctly odd wedding ceremony. It was staged at the dead of night in a ruined church used as a summer house on a Hampshire estate; there were only four witnesses and no entry in the register. In these strange circumstances Elizabeth, then about 25, had married Augustus Hervey, grandson of the Earl of Bristol. The relationship so secretly embarked on was brief; they had a child who died; and they quickly parted.

Now nearing 50, and anxious to regularise her position with the Duke of Kingston, Elizabeth wanted this all-but-forgotten ceremony to be disallowed; so did Hervey who also wished to remarry. The evidence presented to the Ecclesiastical Court was collusive and incomplete. Elizabeth failed to mention, for instance, that some years earlier she had actually acquired a certificate of the old marriage when it had seemed that Hervey might shortly come into his title and that though they were separated she would become the Countess of Bristol.

The court, told none of this, declared her free to marry Kingston and the long-delayed wedding took place by special licence from the Archbishop of Canterbury. All embarrassments seemed laid to rest.

Unfortunately they were to be revived with alarming suddenness four years later when the Duke died. Elizabeth inherited all his personal assets and a life interest in his vast estates. This provoked a disinherited nephew to make enquiries about the old marriage and what Elizabeth and Hervey had told the Ecclesiastical Court. He produced enough evidence of suppressed information and of collusion with Hervey for an action to be brought against her for bigamy.

Elizabeth was in Calais but came home to stand trial in April 1775. As she was a peeress – if not the Duchess of Kingston then, as

Hervey's wife, the Countess of Bristol – this was heard before the House of Lords in Westminster Hall. Brought from Kingston House by sedan chair, she faced the court supported by a retinue of four ladies-in-waiting, three doctors and a parson. After a four-day hearing she was pronounced guilty and as a bigamist was faced with the statutory but never seriously threatened punishment of being branded on the hand.

On the last day of the trial lights shone in Kingston House in apparent anticipation of a celebration dinner, but this was a ruse to allow Elizabeth to escape across the Channel. She was now in her mid-fifties but travel and more amours lay ahead. She bought an estate near Calais and another at Munich; she was granted the title of Countess of Werth by the Electress of Saxony; spent time in Vienna, and with Prince Radziwill in Poland; and acquired yet another estate at St Petersburg where she had an affair with a cosmopolitan adventurer.

Finally she came to rest in France at a house near Fontainebleau where she died in 1788 aged 68. Horace Walpole supplied Elizabeth Chudleigh with a sardonic epitaph: 'I was weary of her folly and vanity long ago, and now look on her only as a big bubble that is burst.'

A few yards west of Kingston House the customary peace of Kensington was shattered in 1980 by the opening shots of a battle which led to what amounted to a six-day civil war. During the attack and the occupation of the Iranian Embassy seven people were killed and four wounded.

Just after 11.30 on the cold spring morning of Wednesday, 30 April, a spray of bullets hit the outer glass doors of the embassy at 16 PRINCE'S GATE, a five-storey Victorian terrace house set back from Kensington Road. Three Iranian gunmen stormed into the building and linked up with three other terrorists who had quietly entered earlier. After a few minutes of confusion they had taken complete control and made prisoners of twenty-six embassy staff and visitors including some foreign journalists and two BBC men waiting for visas.

The assailants were Khuzestanis dedicated to obtaining independence for their oil-rich territory in south-west Iran: their immediate purpose, to take hostages against the release of ninety-one of their fellow Khuzestanis held prisoner in Tehran. The six terrorists had been in London nearly a month planning their attack in Lexham Gardens, Earls Court. Their leader OAN (*nom de guerre*

'SALIM'), a stocky man in his late twenties, conducted the whole violent operation with an almost courtly calm and efficiency.

During the six days of this extraordinary foreign 'war' fought on British soil five hostages were released on various humanitarian grounds but the main contact from inside the embassy with the outside world was made not through the police or Foreign Office. Matters were arranged by the captive journalists and by a civilian 'neutral' – Tony Crabb, Editor of BBC Television News – who was let into the building and asked by the terrorists to arrange for their demands to be broadcast to Iran. The propriety of this was obviously questionable.

Tension grew over the Bank Holiday weekend. The building was under police surveillance. The SAS were standing by. Journalists from all over the world were keeping a round-the-clock watch from Hyde Park.

As the embassy was technically foreign territory, outside interference was a delicate diplomatic matter, but this state of affairs changed abruptly on Monday evening. The terrorists dumped the dead body of the embassy press officer outside the front door. Their demands had finally been broadcast to Iran but without avail; now they announced that they would kill one hostage every 45 minutes. The time for British intervention had come.

Half an hour later there was an explosion and black smoke poured out of the first floor windows. The SAS commandos had managed to blow their way into the embassy from the next door house. Simultaneously, millions watching on television saw eight black-clad members of the SAS descending by ropes from the roof on to a balcony at the back of the house and breaking into the room where the gunmen were guarding their hostages.

Within seventeen minutes the spectacular raid was over. In the final gun battle five terrorists and one hostage were killed. Two hostages were wounded and three SAS men received minor injuries.

The siege (which occurred two weeks after the abortive American attempt to free its hostages from the US Embassy in Tehran) was the first drawn-out incident of its kind to be televised. Ironically, in view of the role played by the BBC, ITN stole a march by smuggling an electronic camera round the back of the building to show the abseiling entry of the SAS; with a high-powered James Bond-style commentary this made a scheduled film, *Detour to Terror*, seem very small beer. On the BBC the final assault blacked out a John Wayne western and the World Snooker Championship.

Another writer of scandalous memoirs lived half a mile from the home of Harriette Wilson in Trevor Square. FRANK HARRIS occupied 23 KENSINGTON GORE during the 1880s and here he acquired material for his autobiography *My Life and Loves* in which he so robustly chronicled his misdeeds.

No. 23, an unusual Victorian survival with a pointed gable roof, stands like a dark tooth in an uneven denture of modern glass and old stuccoed buildings. It was a good deal more spacious than the flat in Field Court, Gray's Inn, where Harris lived during two years of feverish editorship of the *Evening News* (an appointment said to have been obtained by the seduction of Lady Folkestone, the proprietor's wife). Now he was ready to edit a literary magazine, *The Fortnightly Review*.

Frank Harris was then thirty, a flamboyant figure with fierce handlebar moustaches who wore elevators to increase his height, and in compensation for being only 5 ft 5 ins talked at the top of his voice. He was well on his way to acquiring the reputation of the blackguard, liar and lecher of whom Wilde wrote: 'Frank is invited to every house in London – once.'

He does not seem to have resorted to Harriette Wilson's device of demanding money to keep names out of his book, but he was not above blackmail – as when he persuaded Daisy, Lady Warwick to hand over compromising letters she had received from a member of the royal family, presumably the future Edward VII. 'You did not *give* them to him?' H.G. Wells asked her in horror, predicting rightly that Harris would not return them without a demand for money.

Even if we take some of the exploits of which Harris boasted with a pinch of salt, he seems to have packed an inordinate amount of experience and travel into his life since his birth in Galway in 1856. He claimed to have run away from school at 15, and crossed to America where he became a shoeblack, hotel clerk, cowboy and cattle rustler. He propagated Communism as a student at the University of Kansas, was admitted to the bar, became a correspondent in the Russo-Turkish war of 1877, a student at Heidelberg (reading philology) and a stockbroker's clerk. All this was before he embarked seriously on London journalism.

In his book his seductions are luridly described but his conquests generally given only their first names – Kate, Lorna, Lily and the

Frank Harris. Cartoon in Vanity Fair. *His Kensington Gore house saw seductions in the 1880s which feature in* My Life and Loves.

rest – though some, like Enid Bagnold, were not ashamed to admit their submission. Harris told Miss Bagnold, then a young assistant on one of his magazines, that sex was the gateway to life: and so, she wrote, 'I went through the gateway in an upper room of the Café Royal.'

His great love Laura C— deserted him, but after his marriage to a rich widow in 1886, she came back to visit him ('so splendid, so shameless') in Kensington Gore. Quickly they went upstairs to bed. When he lifted her chemise 'her superb form brought heat into my eyes', and, consolidating his re-conquest, Harris demanded: 'Come to me on our three holy days – Tuesday, Thursday and Saturday.'

For a few years after his marriage to the wealthy widow of Park Lane, Harris kept on No. 23, and by the end of the century had entered a dazzling literary firmament as editor of the *Saturday Review* with contributors like Wilde, Wells, Hardy, Kipling and Bernard Shaw, a friend for forty years who was amused rather than contemptuous of his loud-mouthed boasting. Max Beerbohm, another of his writers, called him the best talker in London.

Harris admitted to most vices except homosexuality saying (loudly before shocked diners in the Café Royal): 'You must ask my friend Oscar about that', but musing: 'If Shakespeare had asked me I would have had to submit.'

The first volume of *My Life and Loves* was written in America and the other three in Nice, where he went to live in 1923. They narrowly escaped French prosecution for corrupting public morals, and Harris was forced to keep stocks hidden in his apartment for surreptitious circulation. The book, banned by British and American customs for more than thirty years, was not published openly in this country until 1964.

Despite its appeal to the prurient as the 'senile and lip-wetting giggle of an old man' (Upton Sinclair), because of distribution problems and pirated editions the book was never the money-spinner which Harris hoped.

In his last years, however, he was able to live quietly on the Riviera, taking a daily apéritif at his favourite café while his second wife, Helen O'Hara, prepared lunch. After one last flamboyant gesture – he flung an emptied glass against his bedroom wall – he died on 25 April 1931 aged 76.

A book of a very different kind, also banned on publication, brought huge notoriety to the author who lived at 37 HOLLAND

STREET, off Kensington Church Street. Unlike Frank Harris's scurrilous name-dropping revelations, *The Well of Loneliness* was sincere, dignified – even a bit dull – but ran into trouble because it treated female homosexuality at a time when the subject was taboo. RADCLYFFE HALL used no obscene words and avoided intimate descriptions, but her novel caused an attack in the *Sunday Express* by the editor, James Douglas, who declared he would rather put a phial of prussic acid into the hands of a healthy boy or girl than let them read the book.

Such an inflammatory onslaught was enough to bring the world's press to the terrace house with Dutch-style gable in Holland Street. The author read the article as she was breakfasting in bed one August Sunday morning in 1928 with her close friend of many years, Una Lady Troubridge, and before long they were besieged by reporters and photographers. While at first they quite enjoyed the publicity and excitement, they decided the time had come to get out of London. A cottage in Rye would be more remote and private.

Born in 1880 near Bournemouth to a rich and indolent man of leisure, Marguerite Radclyffe-Hall (her real name) was his daughter by an American from whom he quickly became divorced. Marguerite was left financially independent, and even before going to King's College, London, and to Dresden, she was dressing as a man, smoking, and involving herself in lesbian adventures.

Poetry, of which she published four volumes, was her driving literary passion, but she wrote seven other novels besides *The Well of Loneliness*. Though fiction, the book, drawing on her wartime experiences, was partly autobiographical and charted the author's tangled relationships, especially with Lady Troubridge. It was 'soberly and carefully' published by Jonathan Cape who stated he did not want to appear to be doing something daring or heroic. When Douglas's article appeared, Cape immediately wrote to the Home Secretary offering to withdraw the book. A reprint of 3,000 copies (following an initial 1,500) was stopped. Even so, as the publisher, Cape was summoned to Bow Street. He did not appear, but Radclyffe Hall was in court in a leather coat with an astrakhan collar and wearing a black Spanish hat over close-cropped hair. She constantly interrupted the magistrate who threatened to remove her, and she was annoyed because Norman Birkett, defending, asserted that the relationship of the two main characters in the book was 'normal'. She always referred to herself as an 'invert'. The magistrate, Sir Chartres Biron, concluded that the book was an obscene libel tending to corrupt and he ordered it to be destroyed as an offence against decency.

At the appeal in the following month Sir Robert Wallace called it 'a disgusting book – that is an obscene book and a book prejudicial to the morals of the community'. He dismissed the appeal. The furious author and her lover locked the door of 37 Holland Street behind them a few days later. They were relieved that there had been no trouble in selling the lease: legal fees were pressing.

For Christmas 1928 they went to Rye and to Paris in the following February. There the Pegasus edition was on sale and the author received news that the American edition had topped 50,000 copies. This was despite (or perhaps because of) a New York court's declaration that the theme was anti-social and focused attention on 'perverted ideas and unnnatural vices'. A decade was to pass before the book could be sold freely in England.

In 1934 Radclyffe Hall fell in love with a young girl, Eugenia Souline, who came to nurse Una Troubridge during an illness in Paris. However, Una continued to live with her and, after a relationship that had lasted thirty years, was with her when she died in Dolphin Square in 1943. Radclyffe Hall is buried in Highgate cemetery in a mausoleum she had bought years before for an earlier love, Mabel Veronica Batten.

Gloucester Road to Chelsea

I N a journey which takes us through the decorous streets of South Kensington into the riverside utopia which is Chelsea we are in for some nasty shocks. We encounter three murderers, two traitors, a brothel-keeper and the wickedest man in the world.

People coming out of Gloucester Road Underground station are faced with a terrace of modern shops interposed by a dignified doorway with a classical portico. There is nothing to tell them that at 79 GLOUCESTER ROAD, between a pizza restaurant and a hamburger bar, the occupant solved one of the worst problems that confronts a murderer – how to get rid of bodies. JOHN HAIGH dissolved them in acid.

Haigh, a small, dapper man with a moustache, rented the basement for his rather unusual business which was making plastic fingernails. This apparently required a bath containing prussic acid. Here in 1944 this former choirboy, confidence man and convict shot a boy named Donald McSwann and dissolved him in the bath. Ten months later he invited McSwann's parents down into the basement, shot them and similarly disposed of their bodies. This enabled him to make £4,000 by selling their effects using a forged power of attorney.

Haigh lived not far away at the Onslow Court Hotel in the Old Brompton Road and in 1949 sitting in the comfortable lounge he told a wealthy widow of 69, Olivia Durand-Deacon, about his work. Would she like to see how artificial fingernails were manufactured? When she agreed he took her not to the scene of his previous crimes in Gloucester Road but to Crawley in Sussex where he had rented a workshop and also had a bath of acid. After shooting her and dissolving most of her remains, Haigh profitably got rid of her jewellery.

Mrs Durand-Deacon was missed and Haigh was quickly traced

John Haigh and, (right) 79 Gloucester Road, now much changed though the portico survives. Here he had the acid bath in the basement.

by the police. He confessed to her murder and to the killing of the McSwanns; and there were also, he said, a doctor and his wife whose bodies he had destroyed after drinking a glassful of their blood. How many people Haigh had killed is uncertain. The Vampire of Kensington, as the press called him, confessed to nine. In prison he went through an elaborate pantomime to suggest that he was insane, but his hopes of being sent to Broadmoor were unsuccessful. Haigh was hanged at Wandsworth in 1949.

At the bottom of Gloucester Road, South Kensington becomes a confusing labyrinth of squares, crescents and gardens lined with ponderous Victorian terraces. They were built to last, and most of them have. Numbering is so complicated that explanatory signs have had to be put on many corners. These enable us to find 83 ONSLOW GARDENS, with a front door under a heavy double portico. The house, converted into large flats, was the home in 1938 of WILLIAM JOYCE, better known as 'Lord Haw-Haw'.

During the Second World War, Joyce broadcast anti-British propaganda from Germany. His talks with the nasal introduction 'Jairmany calling! Jairmany calling!' were a source of half-believed, half-derided information about British disasters. It was part of the Haw-Haw legend that he had secret Fifth Column informants who gave him news suppressed in the British press.

The holder of a British passport which he obtained by saying he had been born in Ireland before Partition, Joyce was the most widely known traitor of the war. When he was arrested near the Danish frontier in 1945 and brought back for trial at the Old Bailey, the controversial issues created by the case caused enormous public interest. Was his nationality British?

Joyce was born in New York in 1906 with an Irish-American background. When he made his first application for a British passport (from Dulwich in 1933) he described himself as a private tutor born in Galway and 'a British subject by birth'. Until he quarrelled with Mosley (p. 55) he was an active member of the Blackshirts, and a scar on his right cheek was probably a memento of a razor wound in an East End battle.

In August 1939, about a week before the outbreak of war, Joyce left England for Germany and made his first broadcast from Berlin on 18 September, fifteen days after war began. His motives would seem to have been those of a man who sincerely believed the British would benefit from a totalitarian Nazi regime. He became a naturalised German in the next year.

His broadcast in September 1939 – the first of hundreds he made over the next five years – gave a completely fictitious account of Dover and Folkestone being destroyed by German bombing. The date was vital because, as was shown at his trial, it fell within the period that his British passport was valid.

Joyce was not without sardonic humour. His broadcasts with his imitations of Churchill were often very funny. A detective who brought him back to England for trial recalled him looking

'Lord Haw Haw' – *William Joyce.*

down from the Dakota and saying, 'The White Cliffs of Dover! God bless old England!' When discussing whether he could challenge any Jewish jurymen, he suggested that if more than six of them were selected perhaps he, too, should take the oath with his hat on.

He sat in court, a short impassive man with shaved scalp and scarred cheek, listening to three days of legalistic wrangle about whether he was, or was not, a British subject, whether he had 'enveloped himself in the Union Jack', and whether he was guilty of 'crime by estoppel' (denial of something previously affirmed).

When it was found impossible to prove that he was British by birth or naturalisation, the court fell back on a third count – that by the very act of applying for and holding a British passport (and making the early Dover-Folkestone broadcast while the passport was valid) he was guilty of treachery.

It was argued that during a time when he was deriving protection from the Crown (and so owed allegiance to it) he had 'given comfort to the King's enemies'.

The jury took only twenty-three minutes to find Joyce guilty on the third count; the Court of Appeal concurred; so (with one dissent) did the House of Lords. Many lawyers were uneasy about the outcome, but probably the general public, unconcerned about the hair-splitting legal arguments and still angry in the aftermath of the war, considered Lord Haw-Haw to be guilty. Joyce was hanged at Wandsworth gaol on 3 January 1946. He was 39.

Victorian vice had many guises. We are inclined to think of organised nineteenth-century prostitution in terms of the dozen or so night houses around Piccadilly, the dubious bagnios of Panton Street, low-class brothels in Shoreditch. We do not expect to find sin flourishing in terrace cottages in a respectable tree-lined district of Chelsea. Just south of the Fulham Road, 125 OLD CHURCH STREET, now rebuilt as Clock House on the corner of Elm Park Road, had an innocent enough look. But callers, who needed good introductions to be admitted, discovered that the owner, MARY JEFFRIES, was running a high-class brothel.

The cottages had intercommunicating doors and the girls for whom Mrs Jeffries charged the then considerable sum of £5 a time were young and attractive.

Suspicion that things were not as they should be in Church Street first occurred to a newly appointed Chelsea police chief when he observed the frequent arrivals of cabs and carriages – some as early as eleven o'clock in the morning, others as late as eleven at night. A few were still waiting outside at 5 a.m. Inspector Jeremiah Minahan called on Mrs Jeffries, a severe-looking woman of seventy, who told him, 'I keep my house in good order.' There were no complaints, she insisted, from the neighbours – in the 1880s the only possible grounds for charges against her.

Mrs Jeffries confided further. She told the inspector that she ran other equally exemplary houses in London, among them one in Thurloe Place, another in Fulham Road, a third in St James's Villa, a little further up Church Street. She boasted her girls were so popular that she sent many abroad to Paris, Berlin and Brussels. Her own cut, she added righteously, was only £2 out of the clients' payment of £5.

By April 1883 the inspector's dossier was sufficiently full for him to act. But to his surprise when he made his report to Scotland Yard he met with an icy reception and was reproved for describing Mrs Jeffries's houses as 'brothels for the nobility'. He went higher – and equally fruitlessly – to the Home Secretary, and was virtually forced to resign from the police when he got in touch with three newspapers. None of them was prepared to follow up his accusations of immorality.

The policeman-turned-ardent-crusader then started a closer investigation of Mrs Jeffries. He discovered that she had started her career in a Mayfair brothel called Berthe's where she had risen to second in charge. After a visit to Paris, she came back with extended horizons. Perversions, she had learned, paid well. She decided to open in Chelsea in opposition to Berthe. As part of a door-to-door service, she dispatched her own brougham to collect specially requested girls from their homes and to take messages about their availability to clients at such clubs as the Turf, the Bachelors and the Marlborough.

Having assembled all this information, as well as lurid details about a thirteen-year-old girl who had been deflowered on a payment of £15, Minahan and the London Committee for the Suppression of Traffic in English Girls thought they had enough evidence. 'The Empress of Vice', as Mrs Jeffries was described, was arrested and at the preliminary magistrate's hearing in 1884 her coachman, three servants, two prostitutes and a butler from across the road were called to give evidence.

When the case reached Middlesex Sessions the authorities began to behave very curiously. Certain people were refused admission to the court. The public gallery was kept empty. A whispered conference was held between the judge and opposing counsel. Mrs Jeffries was told by her barrister to plead guilty. To the Committee's frustration, the prosecution spoke in her favour; no breach of the peace, he seemed happy to admit, had been proved.

Before going into the box, policemen were warned that under no circumstances must they let slip any names of clients at No. 125. They dutifully complied. Not so, ex-Inspector Minahan; and very soon a great many things became clear. He named among others Lord Fife, soon to be married to Queen Victoria's granddaughter, and Lord Douglas Gordon, a Member of Parliament, formerly of the Coldstream Guards. For even better measure he added the Prince of Wales and the King of the Belgians.

As the Belgian King alone was stated to have paid Mrs Jeffries £800 a month, the punishment imposed on her could hardly be called excessive. She was fined £200.

Before we reach the King's Road, a turning in Old Church Street opposite the once notorious No. 125 leads into Carlyle Square. The lease of a white corner house, 18 CARLYLE SQUARE, was bought by KIM PHILBY in 1944 or early 1945, and he lived there with his future second wife Aileen during his most perilous year as a spy.

A comfortable family home which catches the afternoon sunshine, No. 18 is very much the kind of place you would associate with someone in the Foreign Service who in his early thirties was on his way to the top. There is no clue that the owner was – in the words of Alan Dulles, head of the CIA – 'the best spy the Russians ever had'.

Those who knew Philby find it hard to think of him in melodramatic terms. Everyone liked Kim. With his slight stammer, humour and easy-going manner he did not in the least fit the picture of a traitor leading a double life. He seemed a highly intelligent, effortless epitome of his background and education. Son of an Indian Civil Servant and Arabist, he had been educated at Westminster and Trinity College, Cambridge, where he had taken a Second in Economics.

Yet from Cambridge days in the early 1930s Philby was committed to Communism, seeing it as the better of two totalitarian ideologies. 'So many of my contemporaries made the same choice' he wrote; few, however, went as far as he did in 1934 when he became, as he admits, 'a straight penetration agent in the Soviet interest'. As a cover he diligently built up a convincing right-wing persona. He joined *The Times*, reported the Spanish

Civil War (from the Franco side) and was in a war correspondent's uniform in France in 1940. He then joined Section D of MI6, which had been set up to carry out special operations. This became Special Operations Executive (SOE) and no one queried his transfer in August 1941 to Section V (counter-espionage) of MI6. By 1942 he was responsible for counter-espionage in Spain and North Africa.

Kim Philby.

It was not until 1944, however, that Philby became really valuable to the country he most wanted to serve. After years of patient waiting the Russians achieved their greatest intelligence coup. By a supreme irony he was created head of a department – Section IX of MI6 – set up to *combat* Communism and the Soviet Union. It wasn't all plain sailing. Just after he started the Soviet section there occurred one of those crises which are a spy's continual nightmare. A KGB officer, the Russian Vice-Consul in Istanbul, asked Britain for asylum, and promised to trade the names of three British agents working for the Soviet Union in London. When, as a matter of course, the news reached Philby, as head of Section IX, he knew one name would be his. Fortunately for him it was also a matter of routine that he should be sent to Turkey to deal with the problem. Before packing his bags in Carlyle Square and flying to Istanbul, he warned the Russians of the danger he was in, and by the time he arrived the would-be defector had been spirited back to Moscow.

We can only guess at the dissimulating expressions Kim Philby needed to wear for so long to cover fears of detection. If any man had to smile and smile to be a villain it was Philby. How much damaging information he supplied is also something that can only be imagined. Though the Government finally admitted in 1963 that he was the 'third man' who tipped off Burgess and Maclean (p. 157) – this led to his downfall – the full extent of his duplicity has not been publicly revealed.

Philby is suspected of sabotaging the joint Anglo-American operation to overthrow the pro-Soviet regime in Albania which resulted in the death of friendly insurgents. On another venture twenty agents infiltrated into the Caucasus were never heard of again. But these are only the sensational highlights; what his colleagues find so appalling is that he not only betrayed agents but informed the Russians of *everything* important that came to his knowledge up to 1951.

On top of many smaller pieces of evidence, the final clue about Philby was probably given by a Soviet defector. By then he had left the Foreign Service and was the *Observer* correspondent in Beirut. When an official was sent there to interrogate him, Philby saw the net drawing in and in January 1962 disappeared to Moscow.

Now 75 (b. 1 January 1912) Philby is still in Moscow. He has Soviet citizenship and, in place of his British OBE, the high Russian honour of the Red Banner. His duties, which involve interpretation of British affairs, call for a daily copy of *The Times*, and the probably apocryphal story has it that Kim, once an enthusiastic follower of first-class cricket, still turns eagerly to see the scores.

Two murders were committed in Chelsea on one day – 9 May 1870 – in squares off the King's Road just over half a mile from each other. WALTER MILLER, a Scotsman in his early thirties, was responsible for both killings, the first of which took place in the morning, the second later in the day. They were brutal and inconsequential and a Black Plaque could go up either at 24 WELLINGTON SQUARE or 15 PAULTON SQUARE.

Around ten o'clock on that Monday morning an elderly clergyman arrived in Wellington Square to visit No. 24, which he owned. The Revd Elias Huelin, who had a good deal of property in Chelsea, had come from Paulton Square where he lived to see how some repairs were getting on. As he walked up the steps to the front door Miller, who was employed as a plasterer, was lying in wait for him inside the house.

Miller hit the clergyman over the head with a spade, removed all his money and valuables and hid the body in a cupboard. He then set off down the King's Road for Paulton Square and the house of the man he had just killed. Working at No. 15, a slightly smaller but similar house to the one in Wellington Square, was Ann Boss, a woman in her early forties, the Revd Mr Huelin's housekeeper. No sooner was he in the house than Miller strangled her with rope and dumped her body in a large wooden box.

Miller was now ready to enjoy himself. But before he started out on two days and nights of drinking he settled on a disguise. A neighbour calling at the house was confronted by an improbable figure with shaved side whiskers and a dyed beard who said he was the clergyman's nephew from Jersey, an impersonation supplemented by some incomprehensible French.

Miller spent most of Tuesday, the day following the murders, being driven by cab to pubs all over Chelsea. At one of them he bought drinks for a stoker whom he asked to find him a girl to take to the Alhambra. He ended up with Elizabeth Green, a matchseller from the Haymarket. This miserable, partly paralysed creature was treated to a great many drinks, and given some new clothes and a pair of boots before Miller took her back for the night to Paulton Square.

There was more heavy drinking on the Wednesday, when Miller did two very silly things. First he sent a plumber round to Wellington Square and this led to the discovery of the clergyman's body. Next he asked a removal man to come to Paulton Square to carry away some furniture to his house in Fulham.

Miller took the carter down to the basement kitchen and indicated the box in which he had put the strangled, injured body of the housekeeper Ann Boss. It was insecurely roped, and as the carter lifted it he found blood on his hands and a congealed pool on the floor. The horrified man hauled Miller into the square where he broke loose before being arrested. On his way to the police station Miller took some poison which he had bought from a chemist earlier in the day; it was as if he realised that his wild, meaningless escapade was bound to be short-lived.

While he was being revived in hospital, news of the two murders brought ghoulish crowds in their hundreds to the two squares to stare at the houses which were the scenes of the crimes. When he came to trial at the Old Bailey Miller pleaded not guilty but no credence at all was given to his story that the killings were the work of the nephew from Jersey – the character he had so theatrically impersonated in a dyed beard – and he was sentenced to death.

Had he known of the violent murder committed by Miller a few doors away, ALEISTER CROWLEY, who lived at 31 WELLINGTON SQUARE in the early 1920s, might well have celebrated the deed with a retrospective Black Mass. The killing which had taken place over half-a-century before would have been bound to appeal to the man whose proud boast was that of being the Wickedest Man in the World. This was not the only title claimed by Crowley, or bestowed

'*The Wickedest Man in the World*' – *Aleister Crowley. He coined the title.*

on him. Alternatives were the Beast 666 (pseudonym for the Devil), Cannibal at Large and the King of Depravity. Crowley is one of the few people who we can be sure would have positively welcomed a Black Plaque.

From early in life, Aleister Crowley seems to have been hell-bent in his determination to acquire a world title in evil. Perhaps it was rebellion against his decorous birthplace (Leamington Spa, on 12 October 1875), reaction to his pious upbringing (his family were Plymouth Brethren) and the embarrassment of a conventional education (Malvern, Tonbridge, Cambridge). More concerned with becoming a magus – adept in the secret arts – than obtaining a Moral Science tripos, he came down from Trinity without a degree.

With the stigma of puritanism in a Warwickshire spa hanging over him, Crowley decided that he needed to be a born again anti-Christian. For his rebirth he selected the Temple of Iris-Urania, and in 1898 he appeared there as a Neophyte of the Hermetic Order of the Golden Dawn. The temple was, in fact, in Great Queen Street, off Drury Lane, and sounds perilously close to the Freemasons' Hall. The Infant Beast was 23.

Deciding his real names, Edward Alexander, were unsuitable for a demonologist, he changed them to the more exotic alternative of Aleister. Names were among Crowley's less depraved fetishes. When he had a daughter by Rose Kelly, the first of his wives, he called her Nuit Ma Ahathoor Hecate Sappho Jezebel Lilith Crowley. She died young – people said of Acute Nomenclature.

Aleister Crowley devoted a great part of his lifetime trying to reach the Astral Plane on which he would achieve the Ultimate Orgasm. To this end he smoked opium, sniffed cocaine, ate hashish and did not stint on laudanum and veronal. These provided material for his book, *The Diary of a Drug Fiend*, written in 1922 at his home in Wellington Square.

This Chelsea backwater with an outlook on a sedate garden and small fountain hardly carries the full flavour of wickedness, and for a more compelling picture of the Beast at this time we need to visit him at the Abbey of Thelema at Cefalu in Sicily. In this shrine which he established for mystical orgies we find him, probably in Highland dress, with his face heavily painted and his ears hung with rings. The Beast is dabbing oils on to his painting *The Lesbians*. His dog Satan is at his feet; he is smoking opium and is attended by several violently jealous 'wives'. 'My house is going to be a Whore's Hell,' he intones, 'a secret place for the quenchless fires of lust and the eternal torment of love.'

Toiling Sicilian peasants observing the Beast with his ménage of 'wives' and young girls whispered darkly about a baby said to have disappeared and crossed themselves as they passed a goat being prepared for a Black Magic ritual. There were official complaints; Crowley was expelled from Sicily after three years.

These activities must be regarded as bourgeois compared to his more serious ambition: achievement of the Ultimate Orgasm which would produce a Monster Child. Seemingly the creation of an Anti-Christ required the mother to be a Scarlet Woman who had to be chosen from among a variety of prostitutes. The rites, involving sodomy and fellatio, were best conducted in a New York Turkish bath. This sounds a complicated performance but then sex for mere pleasure was something in which the Beast rarely indulged. Several bastards but never the longed for Monster Child were conceived. Readers inquisitive for more information are referred to Crowley's book – *Magical Record of the Beast 666*.

Some years later, still resentful at being kicked out of Sicily, Crowley brought an action against the artist Nina Hamnett for the description of his life at Cefalu in her memoirs *Laughing Torso*. She pleaded justification. After hearing some of Crowley's writing, the judge told the jury: 'I have never heard such dreadful, horrible, blasphemous stuff . . .' Not surprisingly the case went against him. It is to be hoped that the Beast cannot strike from beyond the grave and that Miss Hamnett's publishers and co-defendants, Constable and Company, are virtuous enough to ward off the Evil Eye.

This 1934 court action added to the debts with which Crowley was beset but, though he was nearly 60, there was life in the old Beast yet. In his unremitting pursuit of the unspeakable, he continued to bestow his Serpent's Kiss on women unwise enough to offer him their hand. He bit their wrists and drew blood with teeth said to be specially sharpened. This vampire habit only ended in 1937 when one of the pointed teeth broke off in a Jermyn Street Turkish bath near Paxton and Whitfield, cheesemongers, the shop over which he was then living.

As might be expected, Crowley did not stint on blasphemy. His favourite practice was to baptise a frog in the name of Jesus of Nazareth, 'arrest' the frog at night, accuse it of sedition and impale the creature on a crucifix. To make money, of which he was often short, he offered a course of sexual rejuvenation (£25 a week) consisting of Elixir of Life pills made partly from his own semen.

The Beast founded his last, and one would imagine hardly adequate, temple at a Hastings boarding-house where he went just after the Second World War. His daily consumption of heroin (said to be enough to kill a roomful of people) led to a bout of bronchitis from which he did not recover. Bent and shrunken, with a thin goatee beard and skull-like head, the Wickedest Man in the World died there on 1 December 1947.

Hopes he had once expressed that he would be embalmed in the ancient Egyptian manner and buried in Westminster Abbey ended in cremation at Brighton. But at least he went out shocking the world with a chapel service consisting of a heretical 'Gnostic' requiem. He was 72.

——— *12*———

The City

T HE City might be expected to have a long catalogue of dark deeds to match its great age and turbulent history. We are able to disinter a few evil exploits from the past and identify their perpetrators, but wicked people are surprisingly thin on the ground and records of their transgressions tantalisingly sparse.

There is an additional problem caused by the Great Fire and the Blitz. Many of the medieval alleys and courtyards which saw disorders have disappeared under faceless modern offices. To pinpoint the places where the wrongdoers lived and misbehaved has not always been easy. A good deal of topographical detective work has been needed to decide on sites for Black Plaques between Temple Bar and Aldgate Pump.

On the right-hand side of Fleet Street, just east of the bronze griffin which marks the entrance to the City, is Middle Temple Lane. Going through the Wren gateway we are in an area which lawyers with their cantankerous love of legal niceties claim is not really part of the City at all.

For centuries members of the Middle Temple and Inner Temple have maintained that they are outside the City's jurisdiction and have never given up the fight to preserve their independence. What might be called over-reaction led to a serious riot in 1668. It was followed ten years later by a disastrous fire which started in PUMP COURT, three staircases away from the alley leading into MIDDLE TEMPLE LANE.

On both occasions a Lord Mayor, proud in his regalia of office, precipitated the trouble. The first to come to blows with the Temple was SIR WILLIAM TURNER who rashly arrived for a banquet at the Inner Temple on 8 March 1668 preceded by his swordbearer carrying the ceremonial Sword of Justice. The Lord Mayor had already received a message from his host, the Reader of the Inner Temple, that this might lead to a demonstration. But choosing to ignore the warning about the symbol of the City's authority, Turner replied he would 'see who dares put it down'.

The students were waiting for him. The moment he crossed the boundary they shouted in protest, crowded in on him and forced the sword to be lowered. According to Pepys their aggressive behaviour made Turner 'go and stay all the day in a private counsellor's chambers'. He escaped later 'by stealth', but was spotted and mobbed in the cloisters, his retreat followed by derisive calls of '*Mr* Mayor'.

The City complained about the affray to Charles II and the principal offenders – eight students – were summoned before the Privy Council. The affair was smoothed over and might have been forgotten altogether had not another Lord Mayor, SIR JAMES EDWARDS, again incited the students ten years later by appearing in the Temple with the Sword of Justice carried upright before him.

The occasion should have been too serious for worries about protocol. A fire had broken out in the third floor chambers in Pump Court, below and next to those of the lawyer and antiquary, Elias Ashmole. Cloisters and courtyards were aflame and the great medieval Middle Temple Hall was threatened when the Lord Mayor arrived to see what assistance he could give. A north-east wind was increasing the danger. On that particular night – 28 January 1678 – the Thames was under thick ice, which prevented a supply of water to the pumps.

In this grave emergency it was Sir James Edwards's intention to bring whatever help he could to the Duke of Monmouth who was directing the fire-fighting operations of the militia. But his arrival with the sword had the opposite result. Students turned aside from the fire and set on him. At first astonished, and then furious, Sir James retreated into Fleet Street where, according to a rumour almost certainly put about by the students, he went into a tavern and proceeded to get drunk. Staggering out on his return to the Mansion House, the story continues, he met a City fire engine coming to the rescue and angrily turned it back.

These two official miscalculations and the lawyers' angry reaction to them have not been forgotten. In recent years one Lord Mayor wanted to make his way from the waterstairs on the Embankment up Middle Temple Lane to the Quit Rents ceremony at the Royal Courts of Justice. He was formally met by members of the Inns and required to accept a protest couched in half-serious legal language.

As recently as 1984 road widening at the south-east end of Fetter Lane destroyed all that remained of FLEUR DE LYS COURT. A Black Plaque must go up on the newly created brick wall on the corner of Fleet Street to mark the approximate spot where ELIZABETH BROWNRIGG opened a private lying-in hospital in 1765. Her sadistic treatment of young girls whom she employed was unprecedented even by the cruel standards of the times.

Mrs Brownrigg was in service until she married a Greenwich housepainter, and the first seven years of her marriage were

The appearance of Elizabeth Brownrigg deteriorated in the eyes of artists as her crime grew in notoriety. Right, she appears a normal middle-aged widow but, (below) in her prison cell, has developed into a gaunt malevolent figure. The girl Mary Clifford is seen being flogged and in the coal hole.

devoted to bringing up her own children. She eventually had sixteen, and to help with their upkeep she applied to the parish of St Dunstan-in-the-West, Fleet Street, to act as midwife to the local workhouse and was subsequently given permission to start the lying-in hospital.

To help at the hospital, Mrs Brownrigg recruited orphan girls who were supposed to be apprenticed in household duties. For a time the first of the girls she employed were treated well, but then inexplicably Mrs Brownrigg started to subject them to vicious punishments. One, Mary Jones, was laid across two chairs, stripped naked and flogged. This punishment was said to have continued until Mrs Brownrigg's arms gave out, when water was thrown over the girl and her head ducked in a bucket.

Another child, Mary Clifford, who was eventually to die, was even more brutally treated. She was stripped, beaten and kept in near-starvation in a freezing coal hole. A chain was put round her neck to attach her to a yard door and, hung by her hands which were tied together, the girl was suspended from a beam and then flogged until blood flowed.

On a later occasion a neighbouring baker who heard moans reported the noise to a constable who visited the house where he found a girl called Mary Mitchell covered in ulcerated sores. Warrants were issued for the arrest of Mrs Brownrigg and her son who tried to escape in disguise but were captured at Wandsworth. Her husband was also apprehended. They were charged with violent assault but this was changed to murder when the wretchedly ill-used Mary Clifford died in hospital. Mrs Brownrigg was sentenced to death; her husband and son given six months.

Pictures of the condemned woman in her cell show a gaunt sallow-faced person in late middle age wearing a huge platter-shaped hat. Her hands are clasped in prayer. Her latter penitence was mentioned in a contemporary account but the public demonstrated their sense of outrage by jeering and hissing Mrs Brownrigg on her way to Tyburn where she was hanged in 1767. So that 'the heinousness of her cruelty might make the more lasting impression on the minds of the spectators', her dissected body was exhibited at Surgeons' Hall.

On our way down Fleet Street we encounter adultery, but not a great deal is known about the incident, which is hardly surprising as it happened more than five hundred years ago. The antiquity of the deed makes it worth recording, and there is, anyway, something enticing about putting a Black Plaque on ST BRIDE'S CHURCH.

It was on 29 September 1414, during the Feast of St Michael and All Angels, that SIR WILLIAM NECHTONE found himself in serious trouble. He was the Chaplain of St Bride's – at this time a complimentary title was not unusual for a priest – and was arraigned before the Mayor of London, City Recorder and Court of Aldermen. He had been taken in adultery with a lady called Matilda de la Mare.

The scandalous details, if they exist, are too early to be preserved in the Diocesan records at Lambeth Palace and all the Guildhall Letter Book tells us is that the civil authorities were powerless to act. The liaison might be regrettable but such was the power of the Church, which resented secular interference, that his was not a crime for which the Court could impose a penalty. All the City Fathers were able to do was to decree that anyone who employed Nechtone in future would be liable to a fine of twice the sum he was paid.

The adulterous priest's punishment lay in the hands of his bishop; it is likely to have been exemplary and was probably not unduly proclaimed. This was a time when the Catholic Church was under attack from the Lollards and would not have wished to advertise the kind of clerical corruption which these fanatical reformers were railing against.

We are on firmer and certainly more detailed ground with MARY FRITH, known as 'Moll Cutpurse', who lived and died in Fleet Street 'within 2 doors of the Globe Tavern over against the Conduit'. The conduit is marked on the sixteenth-century 'Agas' map opposite Shoe Lane, and the Globe was on the corner, which makes her modern address 134 FLEET STREET, today a shop run by the *Daily Telegraph*.

Moll was one of the most colourful characters of the seventeenth-century underworld. Dressed as a man, carrying a sword, and smoking a long clay pipe, she flourished in an age of floggings, ear-croppings, public hangings, disembowellings and rampant venery. At various times she was a pickpocket, forger, receiver, highwaywoman and transvestite.

We know a good deal about her because her life and unsavoury times are described in a contemporary pamphlet and because she is the real-life prototype of *The Roaring Girl*, a play written by Middleton and Dekker when she was in her middle twenties. She is described as 'a very Tomrig and Rumple scuttle' – that is a tomboy

Mary Frith alias 'Moll Cutpurse'.

– whose 'rude inclinations' led her to challenge male gallants to duels. The playwrights noted that her sexual ambivalence meant 'that she might cuckold the husband and then do as much for the wife'.

Born probably in 1584, Mary Frith was the daughter of a shoemaker in Aldersgate Street, and lived near old St Paul's where she followed the trade which explains her nickname. Especially on rainy days the cathedral was used as a public thoroughfare, and was thronged with people who were easy prey for thieves.

Cutpurses worked in pairs. One trick was to pretend to mistake a woman victim as a relative and rush forward to embrace her while the confederate cut off the leather bag on her girdle. Moll's alternative stratagem would have been to come up behind the 'gull', put her hand over his eyes, and ask him flirtatiously to guess who she was while the accomplice wearing a horn-thumb – a sharpened sliver of horn attached to the thumb – dealt swiftly with the purse.

Moll went to prison several times. As a cutpurse she was sentenced to be burned on the hands, and when she was nearing 50 she came in from the cold to set up as a receiver of stolen goods and to run a school of thieves.

During the Civil War she turned highwayman and her most famous exploit was the waylaying of the Parliamentary General Fairfax on Hounslow Heath. Moll shot him through the arm and rode off with his gold. To prevent pursuit she shot two of the general's horses, but the military caught up with her at Turnham Green. She was taken to Newgate, tried and sentenced to be hanged. But Newgate could not hold her. Somehow Moll escaped; some said by bribing a prison official with the quite enormous sum of £2,000.

How much can we believe of all this? Like most notorieties, Moll probably attracted myths. We do not necessarily have to believe the story that she gave orders she was to be buried face downwards – so as to be as outrageous in death as she had been in life. Prone or supine, when she died on 26 July 1659 aged 78, Mary Frith was placed in the churchyard of St Bride's, across from her house in Fleet Street. Her marble headstone is said to have disappeared in the Great Fire.

A man who lived a dangerous triple life as an organiser of crime, receiver of stolen goods and informer on the thieves stealing on his behalf, made his headquarters near Newgate Prison. Deliberately so. JONATHAN WILD liked to be near his work. In 1719 he moved into a large, handsome house in Old Bailey. This was pulled down in the last century.

Even the site of Wild's home, which he used as the centre of his operations, has disappeared under a massive building which has gone up since the Blitz. To discover exactly where he lived we need

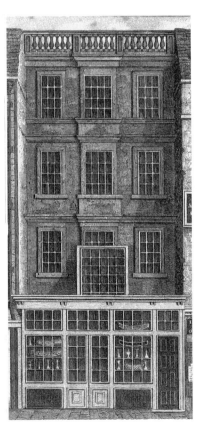

Wild, the elegant double-dealer, and the house he occupied in Old Bailey as it looked before its demolition in 1813. A small café is on the site today.

to pace out sixty yards from the corner of Ludgate Hill which brings us to 30 OLD BAILEY, now a café.

Outwardly Wild appeared an honest man; dressed in a lace-trimmed coat, he carried a silver staff – symbol of his authority as a thief-taker. But this was just a cover for his real activities. He employed thieves, whom he blackmailed and denounced. Openly advertising his house as a place to recover stolen property, he acted as a fence, trafficking in the goods brought to him and selling them back to the persons robbed. He found this the most profitable of all his dealings because those robbed paid better than ordinary dealers.

Wild was able to continue this double dealing until a law was passed – nicknamed the 'Jonathan Wild Act' (because it was aimed at him) – making it a felony to take a reward for returning stolen goods to their owner without arresting the thief or bringing evidence against him.

The man who advertised himself in the newspapers as 'Thief-Taker General' was born in Wolverhampton about 1682. The son of a wigmaker, he came to London when he was about 22, ran into debt and was sent to the Wood Street Comptor. Once out of prison, he opened a brothel in Drury Lane and a public house in Cripplegate before starting on the main activities of his double life.

Wild has been called the first modern gangster because of the 'Corporation of Thieves' he organised and also the 'father of the CID' in recognition of the posse of thief-catchers whom he led. In his Old Bailey house he assumed the role of a man of quality with a coach and six and liveried footmen. He invited the clients whose property he had returned to stay for dinner. If they were interested he showed them an eighteenth-century equivalent of the Black Museum filled with trophies of crime – jemmies, highwaymen's guns, fragments of bloodstained cloth and 'Engines for the forcing of Doors'.

In the best gangster tradition Wild had a succession of wives complemented by a seraglio of mistresses – never less than six at a time – and all regally maintained. Everything contributed to his luxurious standard of living. What may be called his Lost Property Office brought in some £10,000. His State rewards for 'Rogues brought to Justice' amounted to £2,400. Even deducting the bribes he had to pay to constables, court officials and judges, Wild's earnings must have been well over £500,000 in modern terms – all tax-free.

Retribution when it came was on a technicality. Wild, arrested early in 1725 on various charges, and still carrying on his business from a Newgate cell, was visited by a woman from whom he received ten guineas for his help in getting back some lace stolen from her. At his trial he was indicted for stealing the lace and when this could not be made to stick the prosecution brought a further charge against him under the 'Jonathan Wild Act'. For receiving a reward from her for goods which he knew to be stolen he died on the gallows at Tyburn on 24 May 1725, hanged on a slender thread of lace.

As we have seen at St Bride's, famous churches do not all have unsullied histories. The cheerful peel of Bow Bells was briefly drowned in an uproar when, in the last year of Richard I's reign, ST MARY LE BOW in Cheapside was seized and occupied by a bearded giant of a man whom John Stow calls 'a most seditious traitor'. In a running fight against the City authorities, WILLIAM FITZOSBERT climbed the steeple in 1196, 'fortified it with munitions and victualles' and, according to his vilifiers, took a pair of mistresses with him for company.

FitzOsbert's background is shadowy, but he was a member of an eminent London family, is known to have fought in the Crusades and to have been a man of strength and stature. He was nicknamed 'Longbeard' because he wore his beard at an excessive length – as a symbolic expression of his dislike for the Normans. More than a century after the Conquest, strong Anglo-Saxon sentiments were still proudly maintained.

FitzOsbert may have been an alderman, is sometimes described as a lawyer, and was apparently a demagogue of considerable eloquence. A hero of the people, with a following said to number 50,000, he was much feared by the authorities. This rabble-rousing agitator thundered daily against the Mayor and his fellow aldermen in St Paul's Churchyard on questions of taxation; he was in open conflict with the Church which branded him an 'instigator and contriver of trouble' when he attacked the clergy's privileges.

Fearing that Longbeard was about to provoke an uprising in a City which he had stirred into extreme unrest, Hubert Walter, the Archbishop of Canterbury, who was also civil administrator, ordered his arrest. Longbeard was surprised by a force of soldiers but, after killing one of them, he took refuge in St Mary le Bow. The church, he thought, would give him sanctuary. When the Archbishop ordered his removal Longbeard carried his resistance into the square belfry tower and prepared for a siege. To the horror of other clergy, the Archbishop's reaction was that he must be smoked out by fire. There was considerable damage to the fabric of the church before he staggered into Cheapside, severely wounded, to be seized and taken to the Tower.

FitzOsbert was sentenced to death, and dragged by the heels to Smithfield where he was hanged with nine of his followers. In the City split with dissension his defamers said that as he died he forsook Christ and appealed to the devil to deliver him.

History appears divided about whether Longbeard's defiant battle of St Mary le Bow was dastardly or heroic, whether he was a villain or a patriot. The priestly and valuable London historian Matthew Paris insists that he suffered 'a shameful death for upholding the cause of truth and the people'. But the normally amiable Stow (writing centuries after the event) is extremely intemperate. FitzOsbert's death, he wrote, brought about 'the ende of this deceyeur, a man of euill lives, a secrete murtherer, a filthy fornicator, a polluter of concubines ...'.

A narrow lane runs down from Smithfield into Snow Hill north of Holborn Viaduct. On what is called Pie Corner a small gilded statue of the Fat Boy marks the place where the Great Fire ended. But of even more interest a few yards away is 20 COCK LANE, scene of a most famous fraud.

Today No. 20 is a small neo-Georgian house used as an office and not greatly unlike the house to which curious Londoners including Dr Johnson and the Duke of York flocked during January and February 1762. They came to witness the manifestations of the 'Cock Lane Ghost'.

For the first recorded seances ever held in London, people packed themselves tightly into the candlelit room of Elizabeth Parsons, a twelve-year-old girl, who was alleged to be in touch with a dead woman. 'To have a proper idea of the scene,' Goldsmith wrote, 'the reader must conceive a very small room with a bed in the middle; the girl at the usual hour of going to bed is undressed and put in with proper solemnity ...' People then asked her questions, and answers were tapped out in the form of knockings which came from under the girl's bed.

The ghostly spirit was said to be that of a young gentlewoman called Fanny who had been poisoned by her husband in Norfolk. When her husband was away the child Elizabeth had been her bedfellow, which was why she became Fanny's 'familiar'. If any scepticism was shown, instead of knocking there was an abrasive sound which led to the ghost being called 'Scratching Fanny'.

The Cock Lane Ghost

An artist's imaginative impression of Elizabeth Parsons or else her 'familiar', the ghostly girl Fanny, poisoned by her husband. The house where the fraudulant seances took place was a few doors down on the right from Smithfield (below).

The vicar of St John's Clerkenwell persuaded the girl's father RICHARD PARSONS to allow the manifestations to be tested in the presence of Dr Johnson. The doctor published a report in the *Gentleman's Magazine* which stated that the knocking was not supernatural but counterfeited. Further investigations revealed that some kind of ventriloquism had been used and that the girl had hidden a board in her bedclothes to make the knocking noises.

Parsons and his accomplices, among whom was a clergyman, were tried for conspiracy. They were found guilty and the father sentenced to prison for two years. He was also ordered to appear three times in the pillory, but people seemed to have a sneaking admiration for the deception because he was pelted not with rotten vegetables but money, and they even raised a public subscription for him.

London has had its occasional outbreaks of mob violence. Although the Gordon Riots were not on a comparable scale to the Reign of Terror in Paris a decade later, they led to mass destruction, looting and an attack on Newgate Prison. Over 450 Londoners were killed or wounded by the militia during the troubles that began at a meeting in the City on 1 June 1780.

The meeting was held by the Protestant Association at Coachmakers' Hall (destroyed in the Blitz) which was on the site of the present Shelley House at 1 NOBLE STREET, just south of London Wall. Incited by a fanatical anti-Papist, the half-mad LORD GEORGE GORDON, members of the Association passed a resolution to march on the House of Commons and demand a repeal of the Catholic Relief Act. Soon the night sky was to be red from fires.

Provocation was only partly religious. The riots were kindled by dissatisfaction with the King and Parliament, and doubtless owed something to the inbred instinct of Londoners to demonstrate against anything they disliked. Lord George Gordon called for 20,000 fellow-citizens to rally the next day at St George's Fields, Southwark, and march with him to present a petition to Parliament.

The distinctly erratic Gordon arrived in Parliament Square at the head of something like 30,000 people crying 'No Popery!' and a deputation of the 'better sort of tradesmen' submitted their protest about such issues as the restoration of Catholics' rights to buy and inherit land. As it was a Friday, the Commons languidly decided to postpone consideration of the petition until after the weekend.

This started the rampage. Catholic chapels near St James's and in

Lincoln's Inn Fields were set on fire. The mob then moved on to the Catholic district of Moorfields, to Smithfield and Wapping. In a symbolic equivalent of the attack on the Bastille, Newgate Prison was besieged and fired. Five arrested rioters were released from their cells.

The worst day, called 'Black Wednesday', saw Catholic homes, shops and chapels attacked all over London. That night 120,000 gallons of spirits were ignited in a Holborn distillery and thirty-six individual fires started.

Lack of precise targets led to the riots fizzling out but not before George III had called out his Guards and the Lord Mayor had persuaded Alderman John Wilkes, formerly a stout defender of individual liberty (p. 64), to muster the volunteer militia to defend the Bank of England. Beside several hundred killed or wounded, the toll included over a hundred houses attacked and twelve public buildings damaged or destroyed. Of the 160 people arrested and tried, Lord George Gordon was acquitted, but 25 were sentenced to death, including four women and a boy of sixteen.

Whether Gordon approved fully of the riots which he instigated in Noble Street is uncertain. Though cleared of treason at the time, he ended up in Newgate where several years later, and increasingly demented, he died on 1 November 1793. Aged 42, he had taken to a strict adoption of Jewish customs, played the bagpipes, entertained six or eight people daily for dinner, and held a ball once a fortnight – all in the confines of the prison. He died singing '*Ça ira*', the great song of the French Revolution.

The St John Ambulance Brigade recorded sixty-three street casualties during the Lord Mayor's Show of 1902. The worst case can safely be said to have been Reginald Baker. He was stabbed to death.

At any other time, and in any other place, Baker's murder by his mistress KITTY BYRON would have been quickly forgotten – the action of an unhappy woman driven to extremes in an emotional crisis. But a stone's throw from the Mansion House, and in full view of the crowds waiting to cheer the Lord Mayor, the pretty, well-dressed young woman of 23 took out a knife on the pavement outside LOMBARD STREET POST OFFICE.

At Kitty Byron's trial, one of the last to be held at old Newgate, the jury heard a wretched little domestic story: the young girl and the married older man; the milliner and someone described as a stockbroker; the heavy drinker and his sober pleading mistress; she in love; he regarding her as below him socially; violent quarrels in which he knocked her about.

Baker was 44 and had left his wife to live with Kitty the previous July when they had taken rooms in Duke Street, off Manchester Square: Baker's wife and children were somewhere in the West Country. Whatever his exact work was on the Stock Exchange, he was constantly hard up and a cheque to their landlady, Mrs Liard, bounced. The cheque and the couple's frequent quarrels drove Mrs Liard to say they would have to go. She advised Kitty that she ought to break with Baker, but the girl told her she loved him too much. When Mrs Liard took Baker on one side, he confided that he considered Kitty beneath him. Tactlessly the landlady relayed this to Kitty. It proved the last straw.

Shortly after her conversation with Mrs Liard, Kitty went to a cutlery shop in Oxford Street and bought a sharp knife. No need to wrap it, she told the assistant; she would carry it in her muff. From Oxford Street she travelled straight to the City.

People were lining the streets by the Mansion House as she walked into the post office where she arranged for a telegraph boy to take Baker a message: would he come to see her at once? It was quite a short message and the Stock Exchange no distance away. Baker ignored the request. So she sent a second. This brought Baker across to the post office where he angrily reproved her for being extravagant. Replying that the telegram had cost only 3½d, she walked with him to the door.

As they stepped out into Lombard Street she plunged home the knife. Baker fell back against the wall and with a release of all her pent-up fury she knifed him twice more. Just as quickly anger turned into a tragic realisation of what she had done. People saw Kitty throw herself on top of the slumped body, crying 'Let me kiss my Reggie.'

When the body had been taken to the Cloak Lane mortuary, the police found a wallet in Baker's pocket, empty except for a divorce court citation from Mrs Baker which he had received only that morning. His wife had named the woman who had murdered him.

At Kitty Byron's short trial it became clear that Baker, who was known as a drunk, had few friends and many who had got to know Kitty deeply sympathised with her. Members of the Stock Exchange subscribed twice over for her expensive defence.

Kitty's plea was that she hadn't intended to kill her lover; just strike him. A verdict of murder was unavoidable but there was a plea for clemency and the Home Secretary commuted the death sentence. After less than six years Kitty Byron was released in 1908, changed her name and went to live in the country.

Who was responsible for the greatest disaster in London's history? Was the Great Fire of London an accident or dastardly design?

Although he never suffered the consequences, blame for the outbreak falls squarely on THOMAS FARRINOR, baker to the King, at whose premises in Pudding Lane the fire started.

Pudding Lane, between Eastcheap and Lower Thames Street, was a narrow thoroughfare of overhanging gabled buildings, and it was ten o'clock on a Saturday night when Farrinor went up to bed above the bakery, leaving 'his providence with his slippers'. He insisted that he had thoroughly 'drawn' the fire in his oven, but it seems the coals were not fully raked over and that a pile of faggots was left too close by.

Between 2 a.m. and 3 a.m. on the morning of 2 September 1666 the house was full of choking smoke and Farrinor, his wife, daughter and servant escaped from a garret window along a gutter. A maid left behind was the first casualty and among the comparatively few victims of the calamity which devastated practically the whole City.

By the time the fire had been extinguished four days later 13,200 houses had been destroyed and 100,000 people made homeless. Four hundred streets, alleyways and courtyards were reduced to a mass of smouldering rubble. Flames engulfed 84 parish churches, 44 halls of City livery companies and the Royal Exchange. St Paul's was left a gaunt ruin without roof or windows. The medieval City had gone for ever.

Farrinor's negligence seems unquestionable, but public fury turned on Papists and foreigners and found a better scapegoat in a mad French Huguenot who confessed to deliberate arson. At his trial he claimed to have put a fireball on a pole through the bakery window. The Lord Chief Justice and Farrinor, though he was eager to be exonerated, thought this far-fetched. But since he was found guilty by the jury and hanged at Tyburn, STEPHEN HUBERT goes down in history, however improbably, as the official culprit.

Pudding Lane was rebuilt after the fire and has been much altered subsequently. The now lost address – 25 PUDDING LANE – was where Lloyd's Bank stands today at No. 29, on the north-east intersection of Pudding Lane and Monument Street.

Our identification of this as the site of Farrinor's bakery is based on a stone tablet which reads:

HERE BY Yᴇ PERMISSION OF HEAVEN HELL BROKE LOOSE
UPON THIS PROTESTANT CITY FROM THE MALICIOUS
HEARTS OF BARBAROUS PAPISTS, BY Yᴇ HAND OF THEIR
AGENT HUBERT, WHO CONFESSED, AND ON Yᴇ RUINES
OF THIS PLACE DECLARED THE FACT, FOR WHICH HE
WAS HANGED, (VIZT.) THAT HERE BEGAN THAT DRED
-FULL FIRE, WHICH IS DESCRIBED AND PERPETUATED
ON AND BY THE NEIGHBOURING PILLAR.
ERECTED ANNO 168 [1, 1] N THE MAJORALTIE OF
Sʀ PATIENCE WARD Kᴛ.

This tablet was presented to Guildhall by the owners of the
building in 1876, at the time when No. 25 was demolished to
construct Monument Street. Guildhall Museum assumed that it
belonged to this address. The house was a cooper's in the early part
of the eighteenth century, was then rebuilt, and the site is now
incorporated in the modern bank. The Bakers' Company, doubtless with a sense of guilt (and anticipating us), put up a plaque here
in June 1986. This should settle the matter, but unfortunately
doesn't quite. On the Monument, erected in the 1670s, a Latin
inscription is precise in stating that the Fire broke out 'at a distance
eastward from this place of 202 feet which is the height of the
column'. The distance to the attributed site in Pudding Lane is 52
feet shorter.

── *13* ──

Whitechapel and the East End

LIKE the City, the East End of London has been greatly changed by bombing and the rebuilding of slums. Sordid courtyards and narrow streets have been replaced by council houses and shining office blocks. One effect of this has been to efface nearly all reminders of JACK THE RIPPER.

With the disappearance of Whitechapel's gas-lamps, cobbled alleyways and the foggy nights associated with the Ripper murders, it is difficult to understand the hysteria and terror aroused in this area in the autumn of 1888. Five women were found, one after another, all horribly mutilated, and on each occasion the unknown killer disappeared into the night eluding 600 policemen, detectives in plain clothes, bloodhounds and amateur vigilantes who patrolled the mean streets.

The first definite Ripper murder took place in Buck's Row (now DURWARD STREET) when Mary Anne Nicholls, a forty-two-year-old prostitute, was found with her throat cut on 31 August. Nearly all the houses in the street have gone, and our Black Plaque must go up on a wall next to a dilapidated wooden gate which from a contemporary artist's impression can be identified as the spot where a police constable came across her body. A week later another woman, Annie Chapman, was disembowelled half a mile away in the backyard of 29 Hanbury Street (now rebuilt as part of Truman's brewery). On the night of 30 September two women – one 45, the other 43 – were carved up within forty-five minutes of each other. The site of the first of these two murders, that of Elizabeth Stride, was a backyard in Berner Street, a courtyard near Commercial Road. This has completely gone, the name changed to Henriques Street.

Though not surrounded by tall dark buildings as it was then, Mitre Square still survives. In the south-west corner of the square some small cobblestones have been exposed, the size of a woman's body, which mark the exact spot where at 1.45 a.m. Catherine

Discovery of the first
'Ripper' murder and what
remains of the
Whitechapel site in
Durward Street today.

Eddowes, the fourth Ripper victim, was found with her throat cut and her stomach open. She was the mother of three children and a prostitute living apart from her husband. Her body was discovered just five hours after she had been released from Bishopsgate Police Station where she had been taken drunk and incapable.

The fifth and last Ripper murder was at Miller's Court, off Dorset Street, a bad area where Mary Kelly took the unknown killer back to her 4s. 6d. a week room. The site is now covered by part of Spitalfields Market but across Commercial Street is a public house called 'Jack the Ripper' which Mary knew as the Ten Bells when she used to call in for a drop of gin.

If Whitechapel has obliterated most associations with the Ripper, there is no lack of speculation about his identity. These vary from the absurd – a policeman gone mad, a Russian spy, a gorilla, even a woman, Jill the Ripper – to the ingenious but barely plausible. Of the latter the most beguiling involves the Duke of Clarence, Queen Victoria's grandson, who, according to the theory, had an illegitimate child by a Roman Catholic shopgirl who was also an artist's model. When the child was born, Mary Kelly, the last victim, acted as midwife and she and all the friends to whom she gossiped were silenced on direct orders from the Prime Minister, Lord Salisbury.

Because of his supposed surgical skill a favourite theory is that the Ripper was a doctor with a sexual abhorrence of immoral women. Probably the most convincing explanation is that he was a man with a split personality, outwardly respectable but periodically possessed: in the Jekyll and Hyde mould, he had an ungovernable desire to kill. This gives limited credence to the idea that he can be identified with an unsuccessful barrister who took to teaching and disappeared from a Blackheath school. Shortly after the last murder he drowned himself in the Thames. The inquest on the last victim, Mary Kelly, was summarily closed and further investigations called off, and this has led to the suspicion that Scotland Yard came into possession of some very special, highly sensitive information which consequently was never disclosed and has now been destroyed.

So much legendary glamour surrounds DICK TURPIN that we naturally want to find the place in London most closely associated with him; but it is not easy. The famous highwayman was born in Essex, went to the gallows in York, and his London activities are very hard to pin down. The most trustworthy address is the OLD

RED LION public house at the north end of LEMAN STREET, ALDGATE.

Richard Turpin was born at Hempstead, seven miles from Saffron Walden, in 1705 and, the son of a butcher, was apprenticed to a Whitechapel butcher before acquiring his own shop at Thaxted. Then he turned to crime. He was a sheep and cattle thief (to supply his own shop), then briefly a smuggler on Canvey Island before joining a gang operating from Epping Forest. For a while he lived in the marshy rural area of Millbank, but his life as a highwayman kept him constantly on the move.

Different inns were brief meeting places before nightly sorties. Among them were the Spaniards on Hampstead Heath, the George at Woolwich, the Green Man on Putney Heath, the Old Magpie on the Bath Road – places on the fringe of London from which attacks could be made on coaches rumbling towards the capital.

Our records are newspapers like the *Grub Street Journal* for 21 August 1735, which reports Turpin and his companions carrying out robberies on the Portsmouth Road between Putney and Kingston Hill. Two months later they were on Blackheath. Stories about 'Gentlemen of the Road' always made good reading. The special appeal of Turpin and his partner Robert King was that they could be quixotic; when they stopped a poor man on Hackney Marshes and found he had only eighteen pence in the world they sent him on his way half-a-crown the richer.

Romantic fiction feeds the legend. The ride to York on Black Bess has its origin in Harrison Ainsworth's 1834 novel *Rookwood*, while Bess's death of an exhausted heart belongs to the circus tent, Juvenile Toy Theatre and a number of films. But a heroic flourish by Turpin at his death in 1739 seems authentic: he flung himself from the cart under the York gallows to break his neck and prevent a lingering death on the rope.

Turpin's execution came exactly two years after the incident which takes us to Aldgate and the Old Red Lion. Felons can disguise themselves; camouflaging horses can be harder; and on Monday, 2 May 1737, a coachman driving into the yard of the inn recognised a bay mare stolen by Turpin the previous Saturday from the Green Man, Epping. He informed the horse's owner who came down to Aldgate and with constables kept a watch on the stable.

That evening Turpin and Robert King were in nearby Goodman's Fields and, not knowing that the stolen horse was under observation, they asked King's brother Matthew to fetch it from the inn. Matthew was followed: shots were fired as the constables tried to make an arrest. Turpin escaped but his partner King received a bullet wound from which he died.

The creation of a traffic roundabout fed by Commercial Road and Whitechapel Road has changed the face of Aldgate but we can reconstruct the story with the help of John Rocque's 1746 map. This shows Goodman's Fields (between modern Alie Street and Prescot Street) bordered on the east by Lemon (now Leman) Street with Red Lyon Street (now the north end of Leman Street) at the junction with White Chapel.

The Old Red Lion public house is closed, and the empty building, still displaying the name, is incorporated in the south entrance of Aldgate Underground Station. The Old Red Lion (built 1903) replaced the earlier inn of Turpin's day. Before it closed a key reputed to belong to the eighteenth-century stable was kept in the bar.

After pursuing shadows through the rebuilt streets of the East End it is a relief to reach 130 WHITECHAPEL ROAD. This was formerly No. 215, and although a factory-like building occupied by an importer and wholesaler named Pranks makes it impossible to locate precisely the warehouse and yard at the back, we have found the site of the Wainwright murder.

One Friday afternoon in September 1874 a pretty golden-haired girl named Harriet Lane arrived at the warehouse at four o'clock. Harriet was carrying a small parcel containing only her nightdress.

A year to the day later – 11 September 1875 – the same girl was carried out into the Whitechapel Road: she was much changed; Harriet was in ten separate pieces and wrapped in two parcels of American cloth.

The man who brought about this ugly transformation was HENRY WAINWRIGHT, a prosperous tradesman with a brushmaking business. In private life he was well regarded as a Conservative, churchwarden, social worker, model husband and father of four children. There was a maid to answer the front door of his comfortable home in Tredegar Square, just under a mile and a half from the warehouse, and morning visitors were invariably made welcome with wine and biscuits.

Almost exactly half-way between his home and business Wainwright, a tall, bearded man of thirty-six, had another address under another name. At 70 Peter's Street (now Cephas Avenue), which he occupied for four years, he was known to the neighbours as Percy King. Harriet, by whom he had two daughters, was called Mrs King.

This smoothly conducted double life came to an end after Wainwright ran into business difficulties. He moved Harriet into modest furnished rooms in Sidney Square and cut her allowance of £5 a week. When she began to create scenes he calmly and with some help from his brother set about plans to get rid of her. He dug a shallow grave at the back of his warehouse, loaded a pistol and arranged for her to make the four minutes' walk from the square to his premises on that Saturday afternoon. He shot her in the head three times, cut her throat and buried her in chloride of lime.

She might still be there if, a year after her murder, the mortgagee of the Whitechapel Road warehouse had not foreclosed and Wainwright been compelled to leave. With a body to move, he acted with his usual cool calculation. He exhumed Harriet, cut her up and summoned a former employee named Stokes to help him carry the two heavy parcels containing her body out to the front.

While Wainwright fetched a cab something prompted the young man to open one of the parcels. He was horrified to see a human hand. With remarkable composure he closed up the parcel, helped Wainwright load the body on to a four-wheeler and then, at a brisk trot, followed as the cab was driven to Commercial Road where Wainwright, smoking a large cigar, picked up a ballet dancer – doubtless Harriet's replacement. Stokes ran behind the cab over London Bridge to an address in the Borough owned by Wainwright's brother. Breathlessly he called a policeman.

There had not been a public execution in London for seven years but when Wainwright went to the execution shed at Newgate Prison on a cold December morning, it was hardly a private occasion. Eighty-seven guests were present at the invitation of the Lord Mayor and Sheriffs, drawn by curiosity following the sensational trial. Before the white cowl was put over his head Wainwright allowed his customary calm to be ruffled to the extent of regarding the spectators scornfully and saying: 'Come to see a man die, have you, you curs!'

Sidney Square where Harriet Lane lived at No. 3 for the last five months of her life, and which she left to make her last assignation with Wainwright, is only a few yards down the road from 100 SIDNEY STREET, scene of the immortal siege.

Here a small group of anarchists held out against 400 policemen, a platoon of Scots Guards, the Fire Brigade and a detachment of Royal Engineers in a building now replaced by WEXFORD HOUSE, between Lindley Street and Stepney Way. Legend, but no proof,

Rooftop view of Sidney Street seen from the Mile End Road direction. Cross marks the besieged house.

insists that the leader of the anarchists was PETER PIATKOW ('Peter the Painter').

The alliterative attraction of the names – 'Siege of Sidney Street' and 'Peter the Painter' – has fixed the six-hour battle more firmly in the mind and imagination of the public than it perhaps deserves. But what happened on the raw January morning in 1911 was certainly dramatic. It was the climax of a man-hunt which had started the previous month when three policemen had been killed while attempting to arrest a gang of foreigners who were burgling a jeweller's in Houndsditch. One man who escaped was Piatkow, described by the police as 'Peter the Painter', aged about 29, a Russian anarchist.

By dawn on 3 January the police had traced the fugitives to 100 Sidney Street, which they surrounded. When an officer knocked at 7.30 a.m. he was answered by a burst of fire from an open window and a sergeant was shot through the lungs and foot. The besieged men kept the attackers at bay with fast-firing automatics and the authorities responded by assembling a military force that included a battery of field guns from St John's Wood Barracks. The besiegers, it was sarcastically suggested later, were well equipped with everything except an airship. With a sense of occasion Winston Churchill, the Home Secretary, arrived in top hat and fur-collared overcoat.

During a morning of increasing tension roof-top seats were let at ten shillings a head; a reporter's overcoat was ripped by a bullet; a dog and a stray cat were shot dead; three civilians were slightly injured; an over-excited ex-policeman aged 74 died from a heart attack when reading of the battle in an evening paper.

The idea that Peter the Painter was present at all was a rumour inspired by the papers, but when in a Wagnerian crescendo the house caught fire at 1 p.m. he was not one of the two men found dead. Legend, however, cast him as a will-o'-the-wisp figure who somehow escaped from the house disguised as a red-haired woman. Subsequent stories were that he died on the *Lusitania*, or went to Russia to become a leader of the Bolshevik Revolution.

Strictly our Black Plaque should not mention Peter Piatkow; instead we should give the names of the men whose charred bodies were identified – FRITZ SVAARS, aged 27, and his companion, aged 25, who went to his unconsecrated grave in Ilford cemetery simply as JOSEF.

On the corner of Cambridge Heath Road, and facing Sidney Street is a distinctive late Victorian public house with a beer garden and a sign showing a girl helping a blind man. This is the BLIND BEGGAR in the MILE END ROAD, scene of a gangland shooting with a Chicago flavour. At 8.30 p.m. on 8 March 1966 RONNIE KRAY walked into the nearly empty saloon bar and gunned down George Cornell who was sitting on a stool drinking light ale with two other members of 'the Richardson Gang'. He then nonchalantly walked out to a waiting car.

The Blind Beggar killing was part of a bid by Ronnie Kray and his twin brother Reggie to take control of London's underworld. It was to be two years before the brothers were arrested following what can only be called an orgy of crime and violence.

Then in their early thirties, the most notorious pair of criminals in London history came from an East End family. One grandfather had run a stall in Petticoat Lane and their maternal grandfather was a boxer and music hall artiste. They were born on 17 October 1933 in Hoxton but for most of their lives they lived in Vallance Road, Bethnal Green.

Tough, aggressive, often involved in street fights, the twins were first in trouble and put on probation at the age of 12; they became professional boxers at 17; most of their National Service was spent AWOL or in military prisons, where they met other aspiring criminals. With Al Capone as their idol they were obsessed

The Blind Beggar public house where Ronnie Kray shot a rival gang member in cold blood as he was drinking in the saloon bar.

Ronnie is on the right of brother Reggie.

with the idea of becoming the most feared criminals in London.

From a modest start with a cinema in Bow, which they turned into a billiards hall, they branched out into protection rackets. Their technique for 'looking after' a second-hand car dealer was to put a bullet into the leg of a dissatisfied buyer unwise enough to make a complaint.

West End drinking clubs were their mark in the late 1950s and they opened a nightclub for illicit gambling and a bookmaker's business. Esmeralda's Barn, a nightclub in Knightsbridge, brought them their first big-time gambling profits and before long they were protecting other clubs in Mayfair and Chelsea.

From time to time the Krays went to prison; this was generally when they did not succeed in bribing a jury. On one occasion when Ronnie, a homosexual and the moodier and slower of the two, was declared insane, the sharp, clever Reggie 'sprang' him from Long Grove Hospital in Surrey by substituting himself. Being twins had its advantages. Later in another daring coup they sprang Frank Mitchell ('Mad Axe Mitch') from Dartmoor.

Their career of crime embraced every kind of racketeering – fraud, intimidation, trading in narcotics and pornography – on a scale unprecedented in this country, and in the early 1960s the twins, working in tenuous league with the Mafia, began to model their activities directly on American gangsters. Supremacy over rival criminals became their dominating concern.

Their principal rivals were another set of brothers, the Richardsons in South London, and 'the Firm', as the Krays styled themselves, was determined to end threats from them. After festering in the February of 1966, warfare against the Richardson gang broke out in the following month with the killing of a friend of the twins in Catford. The direct result was the crime Ronnie Kray had always dreamed of – the open gangster-style killing at the Blind Beggar.

The murder of George Cornell on the bar stool left no clues, and no witnesses would talk. Though the Krays were suspected of the shooting and were known to be involved in many other crimes, Scotland Yard took no urgent action against the country's greatest gangsters until early in 1967 when Chief Inspector Leonard ('Nipper') Read asked and was given three months to bring them in – as he put it, to 'go down into the sewers after the twins'. With twenty-seven men ('Nipper's Army') he set about collecting evidence and finally, after a world-wide investigation, the hunt was narrowed down to a Victorian mansion near Sudbury in Suffolk.

Hidden in the shrubbery, the police kept a watch on the Krays and observed with amused astonishment that the twins had turned 'county', with Ronnie playing squire in a checked cap.

The three months Nipper had asked for stretched to eight and then, with sufficient firm evidence for an arrest, his army pounced.

Once the Krays were safely behind bars, witnesses could at last be persuaded to talk. The man who had driven Ronnie to the Blind Beggar turned Queen's Evidence. The barmaid appeared as a witness. The long trial ended with life sentences – 'not less than thirty years' recommended the judge – which the Kray twins, now in their mid-fifties, are serving in maximum security wings of separate gaols.

When Thomas Briggs, an elderly chief clerk of a Lombard Street bank, reached Fenchurch Street station just before ten on the Saturday night of 9 July 1864 he caught a train consisting only of first-class carriages to Hackney. He had been dining with some relatives in Peckham and expected to make the last stage of his journey to his home in Clapton Square in under half-an-hour. He never arrived.

A bag and stick belonging to Briggs and a good deal of his blood were discovered by two men who got into his carriage, then empty, when the train pulled into Hackney. His body was found unconscious on the line a mile or so beyond Bow Station. He had been brutally assaulted, robbed of his gold watch and chain, and thrown from the train. Thomas Briggs died the following evening, the first man to be murdered on an English railway.

One curious clue was a top hat also found in the blood-spattered carriage. It did not belong to Briggs; it had been left by the murderer. The hat had an unusually low crown, and this feature was to help identify the murderer as a German named FRANZ MÜLLER. When Müller was arrested in New York six weeks later he was found to be in possession of the murdered man's top hat, which he had cut down to the same height as his own.

Müller, who was 25, had come to England from Saxe-Weimar two years before. He was a gunsmith's apprentice, but failing to get work he took employment with a tailor, and at the time of the crime was living in lodgings at 16 Park Terrace, now 216 OLD FORD ROAD, Bethnal Green, opposite Park View Estate.

From this modest house Müller went to the train where he carried out the robbery and prepared for his flight. After pawning

The first railway murderer –
Franz Müller.

various items, and following his long prearranged plan to go to the New World to better himself, he bought a ticket for New York and left London docks on a sailing ship six days later.

By then a number of clues had identified Müller as the murderer and two police officers accompanied by two witnesses went up to Liverpool where they boarded a steamship for New York. Because steam was able to overhaul sail, the police landed a fortnight ahead of Müller. The sensational murder and chase made headlines on both sides of the Atlantic and in America even challenged news of the Civil War, then at its height.

As the sailing ship with Müller aboard came into New York harbour crowds of sightseers in boats circled her shouting, 'How are you, Müller the murderer?' Anticipating by fifty years a similar chase across the Atlantic after Crippen (p. 251), Müller was arrested as he came down the gangway. He was adjudged guilty by the public long before his Old Bailey trial when he was sentenced to death and confessed before he was hanged.

Müller's fatal mistake had been to leave his hat in the carriage and then to doctor the one belonging to the murdered man by cutting down the crown in the same way as his own. For some years a 'Müller' became the nickname for this kind of squat top hat.

North-East London

MELANCHOLY hangs like a grey sky over London's northern outskirts. Mean suburbs are inclined to suggest blunted lives, and in the more ill-favoured parts of Hackney, Tottenham and Holloway this is accentuated by rows of drab terraces and semi-detached houses.

It may be illogical and quite unscientific to make a correlation between crime and the outward appearance of places where people live; yet in many north London neighbourhoods we seem to sense the frustration that might incite people to kill. The ugliness of many of these houses built some hundred years ago for lower middle-class residents would be enough to prompt murder if killing led to a way of escape.

It comes as no surprise to find that five out of the six houses in north-east London which are the strongest candidates for Black Plaques were the homes of murderers. Three of them – Crippen, Seddon, and Nilsen – had a huge notoriety which, analysed, turns out to be the reaction of a public surprised that outwardly ordinary people should have gone to such extreme lengths. They seem to have been consumed with a desperate desire to change their lives and also their environment.

Until its recent renovation when a great deal of paint was used to exorcise unpleasant memories, 23 CRANLEY GARDENS, MUSWELL HILL, was calculated to sadden the soul. With its pseudo-Tudor gabled front, this late Victorian house is a memorial to the mistaken zeal of some long-forgotten jobbing builder. By the time DENNIS NILSEN, a lonely bespectacled clerk of thirty-seven, went to live there in 1981, it was seedy and run down. He occupied the front top attic high up under the gable.

When early in the evening of 7 February 1983 the police drove Nilsen away from the house with its broken wooden paling, they were detaining, as they thought, a man who might possibly have murdered two people. They asked him whether he was responsible for one or two deaths. 'Fifteen or sixteen,' Nilsen replied.

The detectives were astonished, and in the charge room of Hornsey Police Station quite incredulous as they heard the first halting confessions of the man who worked at the Kentish Town Job Centre. Nilsen's victims – many of them sad creatures like himself – had been stowed under floorboards or sometimes left about the flat for days. Because he retained a vestigial affection for them he was loath to start on the sad last rites of dismembering them, burning their flesh in garden bonfires or rendering the flesh down on a stove.

Sometimes he put limbs out in bags for the dustmen or flushed them down the lavatory, and it was disposing of larger lumps of flesh that led to the drains being blocked at 23 Cranley Gardens. When other tenants complained to the landlord's agents, a Dyno-Rod engineer was called in and found suspicious remains under a manhole cover. Nilsen, at work at the time, was arrested when he got back that night just before six.

The murders are too recent to need detailed description. But the motives remain interesting because they can never be fully explained, despite attempts by psychiatrists who tried (but failed) to prove 'diminished responsibility'. The causes would seem to indicate a pathetic rather than a culpable killer, a product, if ever there was one, of the lonely, depressing suburbs.

From a Scottish boyhood and broken home, Nilsen (born 23 November 1945) spent his life after the death of his grandfather in a hopeless search for a loving relationship. After an eleven-year Army career and a number of frustrated homosexual affairs, he joined the police force on probation in 1972, but loneliness remained his continual affliction. 'Total social isolation and a desperate search for a sexual identity' was how he himself put it.

In 1978 Nilsen and his pet dog, a one-eyed mongrel called Bleep, went to live at Cricklewood. At 195 Melrose Avenue, near Gladstone Park (a rather less melancholy address than his later one at Muswell Hill) he had the first of the relationships that led to twelve killings.

After a solitary Christmas, he picked up an Irish youth in a local pub on New Year's Eve. He took him home, they had a lot to drink but no sex, and, Nilsen wrote: 'I was afraid to wake him up in case he left me.' Trembling with fear he then strangled him and brought his body back to the bed: this was a tragic pattern that was to be

*Repainted and
renovated, 23 Cranley
Gardens retains no
trace of the multiple
murders committed in
the attic room under
the gable by, (right)
Dennis Nilsen.*

repeated with variations so often at Cricklewood during the following two years.

Not all of the twelve men he picked up and murdered at Melrose Avenue have been identified: they were mostly drifters from out of London whom nobody missed. His last victim before he left Cricklewood was a twenty-four-year-old boy from a mental hospital, and the three he killed after he moved to Cranley Gardens were also drifters. 'I was desperate for company even if it was only a body,' he wrote.

In his journals Nilsen stated that he had limited sexual relations with six of his victims and none with nine. He also claimed the odd girlfriend. Alcohol and music helped him dispel his inhibitions and gave him stimulation. Afterwards he suffered horror and remorse. Arrest, he said, came as a relief.

The problem of Nilsen's mental state led to a protracted ten-day trial at the Old Bailey in October 1983, when after more than twelve hours a jury of eight men and two women finally reached a majority verdict that he was guilty of six murders and two attempted murders. His recommended term of imprisonment is a minimum of twenty-five years. Poor Bleep, who could not accompany his master, died in Battersea Dogs Home.

Part of a curved terrace of fidgety little houses, 14 WATERLOW ROAD, HIGHGATE, has a present-day anonymity which erases memories of its unfortunate past. The gate and woodwork have been painted a bright red and the street's name has been changed from Bismarck Road since the December evening in 1914 when GEORGE JOSEPH SMITH walked up the steps to ask about a furnished room which was to let. He gave his name as John Lloyd and was accompanied by his new bride, a clergyman's daughter aged 38, Margaret Lofty. It was intimated that they were on their way to a Scottish honeymoon.

The landlady, Louisa Blatch, told them she had a nice room on the top floor and, before Smith paid seven shillings deposit and went away to fetch the luggage, she was asked a question which only later was to seem particularly ominous. Miss Blatch replied, yes, there was a bath.

The next day, a Friday, 'Mr and Mrs Lloyd' visited a local solicitor where Margaret Lofty made a will leaving everything to her husband and went to Muswell Hill post office where she drew out the balance of her savings, some £19. The previous evening they had called on Dr Bates, an Archway Road doctor, to whom

Smith went to some lengths to explain that his wife was far from well. The doctor prescribed something to bring down her temperature.

Things moved quickly. At 8.15 on Friday night Margaret Lofty, apparently still running a temperature, asked for a hot bath. The landlady heard some splashing, but she thought nothing of it, especially when shortly afterwards Smith was heard playing the harmonium in the communal parlour and then went out to do some shopping. On his return he went upstairs and moments later he urgently called Miss Blatch to come up. At the bathroom door she saw Smith with his wife's body in his arms, her legs still in the bath. She felt the woman's wet arms. They were cold, and she was obviously dead.

So died the third woman in what became known as 'The Brides in the Bath' case because of Smith's deadly routine which was to marry and get money from unsuspecting women before he drowned them.

His first victim, whom he bigamously married, he had drowned at Herne Bay in 1912 after getting her to change her will in his favour. Several other women were married and escaped penniless before he drowned Alice Burnham in her bath at Blackpool and received her life insurance money.

The third murder was discovered because Alice Burnham's relatives read an account of the Highgate inquest on 'Mrs Lloyd' and, thinking her death suspiciously similar to that of their own Alice, informed the police.

Smith, who was born at 92 Roman Road, Bethnal Green, in 1872, was an inveterate criminal from the age of nine. Before he was 25 he had been in prison three times for theft. His one legal marriage in 1898 was the prelude to a succession of seductions, liaisons and bigamous marriages.

In the opinion of Marshall Hall, who defended him, his power over women amounted to the hypnotic. He was capable of passionate words and caresses precisely at the time he was planning murder. Minutes before he killed Margaret Lofty he was seen comfortably reading a newspaper while she knelt before a fire. Having watched her die struggling under the water in the bath he was able to walk calmly downstairs and start playing the harmonium. He was a murderer so callous that the judge at the trial said, in passing sentence: 'An exhortation to repentance would be wasted on you'. George Joseph Smith was hanged on 13 August 1915.

A mile from Waterlow Road, 63 TOLLINGTON PARK, UPPER HOLLOWAY is the kind of London house – semi-detached with steep steps leading up to a pilastered front door – that normally you would never give a second glance. Only the name Seddon stirs memories of a murder which shocked our grandparents.

It is a big house and you can see why FREDERICK HENRY SEDDON who lived there with his wife and five children decided to let the top floor. The woman who took it in July 1910, Elizabeth Barrow, a spinster of forty-nine, was grateful when her landlord outlined a plan by which she would receive an annuity if she transferred some of her property to him.

Seddon, who was 40 and district manager of an insurance company, was hard up. His money worries and his manipulation of Miss Barrow's finances went against him when he came under suspicion of murdering his upstairs tenant. He became her sole executor and her death occurred early one September morning seven weeks after she arrived at Tollington Park. This followed more than a fortnight's serious illness with symptoms of diarrhoea for which the doctor had been visiting her daily. Both Seddon and his wife were at her bedside throughout the night she died.

Two days later Miss Barrow was given a cheap funeral and a public grave in Islington Cemetery. It was five days before her family heard of her death though two of them lived quite near. They were suspicious and informed the authorities. Miss Barrow was dug up. The pathologist found that her body contained a lethal dose of arsenic.

How the poison was obtained and administered could not be proved, but it was known that during some hot weather early in the month one of the Seddon children had bought some fly papers containing arsenic and these had been put up in her sick room. The prosecution said that boiling just one of these papers would produce sufficient quantity of a tasteless liquid to provide a lethal dose.

At the trial Seddon was found guilty but his wife was acquitted. No proof was ever submitted to show that either of them had administered poison. Concerned about a conviction based on circumstantial evidence, 250,000 people signed a petition on Seddon's behalf and there was a protest meeting in Hyde Park. When he was hanged at Pentonville a crowd of 7,000 outside the prison uttered a gasping cry when the black flag was raised. Seddon, a freemason, went to the drop declaring his innocence before 'the Great Architect of the Universe'.

From Tollington Park it is another mile's journey to a street in Holloway which can claim to be one of the most famous in the history of London crime. Few addresses can compete with 39 HILLDROP CRESCENT. No murderer is ever likely to surpass the notoriety of DR HAWLEY HARVEY CRIPPEN.

Crippen, an American with a degree in homoeopathic medicine, came to London in 1900. He moved into Hilldrop Crescent three years later, but a disappointment faces those for whom the little doctor's poisoning of his wife holds so compelling a fascination. The actual house in the curving street off Camden Road where he buried his wife in the basement was destroyed by a bomb in the Second World War. It has been replaced by a small block of council flats, MARGARET BONDFIELD HOUSE.

The three-storey house to the right with its flight of identical stone steps is similar to No. 39 but ghouls demanding their full measure of blood may feel this insufficient. They are referred to Constantine Road, Hampstead, (p. 309), where we are able to put a Black Plaque on the house where Ethel le Neve was living after she became Crippen's mistress. Within six weeks of his administering five grains of hyoscine hydrobromide to his wife, Belle Elmore – this was after midnight on 31 January 1910 – Ethel le Neve moved into Hilldrop Crescent.

The Crippen story never tires with telling. It is the classic 'triangle' murder: mild little man; overbearing wife; and the young typist who enters his life. The wife disappears and the girl goes to live with the purveyor of patent medicines. Neighbours notice she is wearing the wife's jewellery and inform Scotland Yard. The couple panic and decide to bolt, which leads to the discovery of the wife's body buried in the cellar. With the girl disguised as a boy and the doctor as her father, they sail for Canada. Suspicious ship's captain sends a wireless telegram (the first to secure an arrest) and detectives leave for Quebec on a faster boat. Couple arrested and brought back for trial.

The excitement of the hue and cry was relived all over again at the Old Bailey when details were revealed of the murder which had caused so much speculation. The trial was crowded with sensation-seekers, society women and actors who, as if at a theatrical matinée, were studying counsel for striking gestures and novel expressions.

Crippen singularly failed to live up to the popular idea of a monster. With a sandy moustache, gold-rimmed spectacles and receding hair, the forty-seven-year-old doctor appeared to one court reporter to be marvellously cool and calm. He faced cross-examination imperturbably with a demeanour of innocence, even superficial geniality.

It fell to the Lord Chief Justice, Lord Alverstoke, to remind the court of the 'ghastly and wicked nature of the crime' before he pronounced the death sentence. Hawley Harvey Crippen was executed at Pentonville on 23 November 1910. Ethel le Neve was acquitted.

Between a bus station and a block of flats in ROOKWOOD ROAD, CLAPTON, is a church with a tall spire guarded by winged beasts. These fierce allegorical creatures from the Book of Revelations cast in bronze and carved in stone can hardly be called welcoming. But at least a visit to a church makes a change after a surfeit of murder.

Now called the Cathedral Church of the Good Shepherd, the church was named the Ark of the Covenant when built in 1896 and was also known (ambiguously as we shall see) as the Abode of Love. Mystical and forbidding, this was for sixty years the London headquarters of the Agapemonites and was created by their leader, Henry Prince.

Prince was a renegade Church of England curate who claimed to be the reincarnation of John the Baptist. This was extreme enough but it was his successor, the REVD JOHN HUGH SMYTH PIGOTT who, going one better, made this the most infamous church in London. There, on Sunday, 7 September 1902, the follower of John the Baptist informed a packed congregation that he was the Messiah: 'I am the Lord Jesus Christ who died and rose again and ascended into Heaven.'

This was a message that caused Smyth Pigott's believers – the Children of the Resurrection – to fall on their knees shouting for joy, but it had a less favourable reception from several thousand sceptics who converged on Rookwood Road the following Sunday. Hisses greeted the Messiah when he arrived by coach under the protection of the police and with a woman on his arm. The crowd broke through a bodyguard to force their way into the church where, without surplice or robes, Smyth Pigott reiterated his claim. He left smiling though he was being pelted with stones and attacked with sticks and umbrellas. Had it not been for the mounted police, wrote one reporter, he would have been thrown in the pond on Clapton Common.

So virulent were his assailants that Smyth Pigott decided to leave his house, the Cedars, on the Common, and retreat behind the high walls of the country abode of the Agapemonites in the Somerset

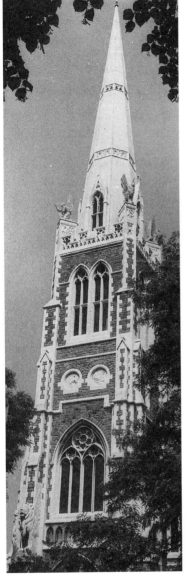

The eccentrically decorated Clapton church where the Revd John Smyth Pigott, seen here in later years, informed his congregation that he was the Risen Christ.

village of Spaxton. Here two years later his married life was augmented by the arrival of an attractive girl, Ruth Anne Preece. By Sister Ruth – his Spiritual Bride in Chief – he had two sons (named Glory and Power) and a daughter (named Life).

At Spaxton it was the Sunday ritual for thirty in the hundred-strong community to face the Master. As he sat in white robes embroidered with the Lion of Judah, he would call out the seven names of the spiritual wives who were to serve him in his private apartments on a daily roster during the coming week. They were generally young, beautiful girls endowed with sizeable fortunes.

This mode of behaviour did not appeal to the Bishop of Bath and Wells who served notice on the Messiah by registered post that he would be required to appear before a Consistory Court. During the hearing it emerged that Smyth Pigott, born in 1853, came of a good, fairly well-off family. He had sailed before the mast, been to Oxford, and, after attending a Highbury college of divinity, had been ordained in 1882. Before he succeeded Henry Prince as the Agapemonites' leader, he had served at a mission church in Dublin and in the Salvation Army, from which he had been expelled by General Booth.

In answer to the ecclesiastical court's queries about his relationship with Sister Ruth and their illegimate children, Smyth Pigott replied: 'I am God. There is no such thing as marriage at the Agapemone. We are all brothers and sisters of God.' On 9 March 1909 Smyth Pigott was defrocked for 'immorality, uncleanliness and wickedness of life'.

This did not greatly upset his way of life and he often retreated to Norway where he set up a branch of his sect and annually recruited fair-haired, blue-eyed fiord-maidens to join the Abode of Love. Periodically there were public outcries but they came to nothing: the police were powerless because all the women came voluntarily.

Over the years funds began to wane and in March 1927 Smyth Pigott died, tired, bent and no less mortal than Prince, the previous prophet. By then the number of Agapemonites had dwindled to about fifty. The Ark of the Covenant at Clapton had long since ceased to be used for services, but before she died in 1956 Sister Ruth told the self-styled Archbishop of the Ancient Catholic Church that she wanted him to have the building.

The Cathedral Church of the Good Shepherd is now attended by congregations concerned with the blessing of animals, faith healing and clairvoyance. With the winged beasts of the Book of Revelations staring belligerently from the tower, a bizarre aura still clings to this church in N.16.

We are back to murder – and a particularly wretched one – which took place in Islington and was discovered by a chauffeur when he arrived at 25 NOEL STREET on 9 August 1967. He had been sent to take the playwright Joe Orton to Twickenham Studios to discuss a film script with a producer.

The chauffeur went up the stairs of the little terrace house and knocked repeatedly on the door of the top floor flat. Getting no answer he looked through the letter box. It was nearly midday but inside the lights were on, and he saw a man lying on the floor.

When the police arrived they found that it was the body of KENNETH HALLIWELL, naked and covered in blood. Nearby was the tin of grapefruit juice he had drunk to wash down the twenty-two Nembutal pills that killed him.

There was a second body in the flat. On the bed beside a wall covered with a collage of magazine pictures lay Joe Orton. A tattoo of a blue swallow over an appendix scar identified the playwright who was otherwise almost unrecognisable. His face and head had been beaten in by repeated blows from a hammer.

Joe Orton's death at the hand of the man with whom he had lived for over fifteen years came at a time when his black comedies were winning international fame. Life appeared to be imitating art in a macabre fashion; the way he was beaten to death by his lover might well have been a scene from one of his own plays.

The reasons for the fearful end to their relationship were found in a diary kept by Orton which Halliwell had read and to which he called attention in his suicide note: 'If you read this diary all will be explained K H. PS. Especially the latter parts.'

The entries confirmed the reports of Halliwell's doctor that he had a hostility to life and a fear that Orton was edging him out. Orton wrote of 'exhausting wrangles over trivia' and of Halliwell shouting, 'This is Strindberg! You are quite a different person you know since your success.' Turning the pages Halliwell also learned that his lover no longer found sexual satisfaction with him.

When they met at the Royal Academy of Dramatic Art as students in 1951, Halliwell was 24, a strong and attractive personality; Orton was 18 and at that time still interested in girls. Halliwell, son of the chief cashier at Cammel Laird, the Liverpool shipbuilders, was a grammar school boy with a classical Higher School Certificate; Orton, whose father was a retired council gardener in Leicester, failed his 11-plus and was described by a teacher as semi-literate.

Mutually attracted within days of meeting at RADA, they were soon living together and moved into the Noel Street flat bought by Halliwell. These were the good times when they shared everything – practical jokes, periods of poverty, menial jobs, discussions about their writing. They made wills in each other's favour. They wore each other's clothes. They revelled in a curious form of vandalism. They would deface library books, writing bogus blurbs, and restyling the dust jackets by devices such as pasting pictures of female nudes on books of etiquette. For this pastime they were sentenced to six months in 1962.

The decisive change in their relationship came after the success of Orton's *Entertaining Mr Sloane* in 1964 and the fame of *Loot* in 1966. From then on Halliwell had a sense of failure and inadequacy. Six unpublished novels and a play lay hidden under his bed. He felt an appendage to the lover whose talents he had fostered. He became pathologically obsessed by his lack of height, his total baldness which forced him to wear a wig and a thickening of his former good looks.

As Orton acquired international fame, Halliwell went more and more on the defensive. While Orton shone in public, his friend seemed to lose all spontaneity; he just became aggressive and rude. But the greatest threat to their relationship was Orton's casual infidelities. These, we read in the diaries, occurred everywhere from building sites to public lavatories.

Despite Halliwell's entreaties Orton refused to end the encounters, and grew so tired of possessive jealousy that he threatened to move out. But their friends agree that, despite the mounting tensions, he would never have done so. And so the whole Strindbergian nightmare came to its climax in the murder summed up by the police as 'a deliberate form of frenzy'.

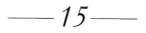

South-East London

Following a clockwise course round outer London we are again confronted by murder immediately we travel south-east across the river. Once more the victim is a playwright, but the death of Christopher Marlowe has an added dignity which comes with the centuries. It also faces us with a historical mystery.

Between Creek Road and the Thames the church of ST NICHOLAS, DEPTFORD GREEN, stands behind a gateway flanked by crumbling stone skulls. These reminders of death probably date from the eighteenth century; so it is on the church's tower which is contemporary with the Elizabethan playwright that our Black Plaque would be placed.

Somewhere in the weed-covered graveyard lies the body of the Muses' darling, that 'pure Elementall wit', Kit Marlowe, most violently done to death on the evening of 30 May 1593. The author of *Tamberlaine*, *Doctor Faustus* and *The Passionate Shepherd* was only 29. He died at about six o'clock from a dagger wound following a day's carousing with companions on Deptford Strand. The waterfront tavern where it happened is now lost under modern warehouses.

The name of the murderer is in the church records. In a tortuous Elizabethan hand it reads:

Christopher Marlow slaine by ffrancis ffrezer;
the.1. of June.

But this entry needs a little investigation and considerably more scrutiny. The man convicted of the killing was a servant of Thomas Walsingham named INGRAM FREZER (the name 'ffrancis' instead of Ingram was a clerk's error; 'ffrezer' is best modernised to Frezer: 1 June was the date of the inquest).

Her Majesty's coroner, William Danby, Gentleman, and a jury of

St Nicholas, Deptford. The murdered Christopher Marlowe was buried in the churchyard.

sixteen viewed the body and concluded that Christopher Marlowe had received the mortal wound of a dagger 'of the value of 12d.' and had 'there instantly died' at Frezer's hand. Their report, preserved in the Public Record Office, is remarkably detailed. It tells us that the wound was an inch long and two inches deep over the right eye but does not clear up the question of whether it was murder, accident, self-defence or premeditated conspiracy.

The coroner heard that Marlowe and the oddly assorted crew of Frezer, Robert Pooley, a government secret agent, and Nicholas Skeres, a servant of the Earl of Essex had been at the tavern since ten in the morning. They had been drinking 'in quiet sort together', had taken a walk in the garden, and after supper Marlowe was lying on a bed when trouble over 'the reckoning' flared up. He had seized a dagger from Frezer's waist and struck at him. In 'his own defence & for the saving of his life' Frezer struggled with the playwright and killed him.

Once the inquest was over the playwright was quickly put under ground. No stone marks the grave. It seems the authorities wanted the whole matter forgotten as soon as possible. But when we look deeper into the circumstances there appears something far too glib about a verdict which gives the impression that Marlowe was a quarrelsome roaring boy killed in a dispute about a bill. Something suspicious, too, about the sequel: Frezer was pardoned by the Queen only four weeks later, when the murder was described simply as 'the breach of our peace'.

Possibilities of conspiracy are raised because Marlowe had been brought before the Privy Council ten days earlier, suspected of atheism. He had satisfied his inquisitors and had been released on bail, but only the day before his death an informer had supplied the Privy Council with further reports of his blasphemies. Maybe Marlowe panicked and went to Deptford to take a ship abroad, and his assassination was planned and approved by the Privy Council to prevent his escape – and keep him quiet. Only as the day wore on would he have realised that the smiles of his companions were counterfeit and that the men with whom he had been carousing were really his gaolers and executioners.

This theory seems extreme but becomes more credible if, as is probable, Marlowe was not only a playwright but soon after Cambridge had served the government abroad as an anti-Catholic spy. Embarrassing secrets might come out if he were put on open trial; the Elizabethan Privy Council, steeped in devious actions, may well have preferred skulduggery.

In the last century reporting of crimes lacked the dramatic immediacy of television, but they were very widely covered by newspapers, and public involvement was frequently far greater than today. If people disagreed with a verdict they made it their business to protest.

On 17 July 1871 a truck was driven through the streets of Greenwich with a tableau mounted on the back showing a woman being hammered to death by a man. It drew up at 3 LONDON STREET (now the site of the future hotel facing the Mitre public house in Greenwich High Road), the home of EDMUND POOK, and a crowd estimated at 4,000 screamed and shouted outside. They believed that there had been a serious miscarriage of justice.

The young man against whom they were directing their anger was 20. Edmund worked in his father's printing firm and lived at home. His acquittal after trial for murdering a servant girl who had worked for the family provoked a series of demonstrations.

The girl, Jane Clousen, had been employed by the Pooks for two years when she was suddenly given her notice by Edmund's mother on the flimsy grounds that she was untidy. The real reason was that the parents were worried about her association with their son.

Jane found lodgings in Ashburnham Street, half a mile away. She was pregnant and confided to her landlady that she and Edmund were engaged and were shortly to be married. A fortnight after she moved she went to keep an appointment with him (or so her acquaintances testified), and the next that was seen of Jane was in the early hours of the following morning when a policeman patrolling near Morden College found the girl crawling on the ground in Brooke Lane. She had a ghastly head wound and died later at Guy's Hospital.

Public interest was intense. On the Sunday after the murder 20,000 people were reported to have visited the spot near Blackheath where she had been found. Edmund Pook was arrested for her murder and the prosecution showed that Jane had gone out to meet him and that a man similar to Edmund had been seen hurrying along Kidbrooke Lane. Edmund had enquired in Deptford about buying a hammer, and the murder had been committed with a hammer bought on the previous evening. There were bloodstains on his clothes.

It was not only because the evidence seemed so damning that Edmund's acquittal produced extreme reactions. There was social resentment. A 'son of the house' had got a servant into trouble and done away with her rather than face his responsibilities. 'She was poor but she was honest', the caption under one magazine picture of Jane, summed up the general feeling.

People saw Edmund going scot-free and were determined to protest. Yelling and hooting they converged in their thousands on the Pooks' house ('Disgraceful' the goaded father complained to *The Times*) and pamphlets were sold in the street. By insisting on Edmund's guilt newspapers risked libel. Then — the crowning horror for the family — came the grisly tableau of the murder paraded on a cart outside their windows.

The final word on the case appears scribbled on the Census Return for 1871, taken three weeks before the murder. Jane Clousen is listed as a servant at 3 London Street and in the column left open for comment the census officer showed he had no doubts about how she died. Cryptically he wrote: 'Murdered'.

In 1806 the Prince of Wales – the future George IV – was anxious to rid himself of the wife whom he heartily disliked and whose appearance had so appalled him on their first meeting that he had called for a stiff brandy. After eleven years of marriage, ten of which they lived apart, he instigated the Royal Commission set up to inquire into her behaviour in the vain hope of proving allegations of her immorality.

Among other charges facing PRINCESS CAROLINE at the 'Delicate Investigation' were accusations of 'guilty intercourse' with the painter Sir Thomas Lawrence, Sir Sidney Smith, hero of the Napoleonic Wars, and the future Rear-Admiral Thomas Manby. There were allegations that she was the mother of one if not two illegitimate children.

When the Commissioners' findings were published Caroline's reputation was cleared but she was rebuked for being indiscreet, and public gossip, rampant during the secret hearings at 10 Downing Street, still continued. Scandal hung over Montague House, overlooking Blackheath, where she lived for most of her unhappy marriage and where, it certainly seems true, she entertained admirers unwisely and too well.

Montague House, near to Chesterfield House, on the south-west corner of Greenwich Park, was vindictively demolished by the Prince Regent in 1815 shortly after Caroline went abroad, and for a visible reminder of her supposed indiscretions we have to go a quarter of a mile across the Heath to THE PAGODA, ELIOT VALE.

The Pagoda, an exercise in architectural chinoiserie built in 1760, served Caroline as a rustic pleasure house where she could escape

The Pagoda House, Blackheath, where malicious rumour accused Princess Caroline of bringing up illegitimate children.

from public gaze. There she tended a flourishing garden and, a lonely woman denied the company of her daughter, she ran a nursery for local children. Her enemies chose to regard the nursery as something rather more sinister.

Lady Douglas, a neighbour living in Montpelier Row, submitted a 20,000 word deposition to the Commission in which she contended that a small boy called William Austen was Caroline's son, born three and a half years before. Lady Douglas's husband stated that when Caroline had called on them during the summer of 1802 she 'appeared to be with child'.

Damaging statements were coaxed from servants at Montague House about Caroline's behaviour. They produced a picture of rowdy parties, visits by officers from the Royal Naval Hospital, Greenwich, and immoral comings and goings at all hours of the night. A page named Cole remembered Sir Sidney Smith sitting very close to Caroline on a settee and spoke of a mysterious, unidentified man 'in a great coat' who had gone away at an hour when no gentleman should be leaving a lady's house. The naval officer Thomas Manby had been observed kissing her; the painter Lawrence had once stayed overnight.

The tenuous stories of alleged bastards were demolished by the Commission. The boy's real mother was found in Deptford, and a little girl, Edwardina Kent, proved to have been abandoned on the Heath. The testimony of Lady Douglas and her husband was undoubtedly the result of the Prince of Wales encouraging them to vilify Caroline and 'not spare the horses'.

Caroline's vindication at the time was complete, but her reputation has remained tainted and a whiff of scandal still clings to the Pagoda because of her wayward behaviour subsequently. She further confused her supporters by wandering round Bayswater asking the bemused residents if she could rent their houses to accommodate her nine children.

There could be no denying her indiscretions abroad after 1815 when she travelled recklessly in Italy and the Middle East, visiting Lake Como and Jerusalem with Count Pergami, the so-called chamberlain of her household, as her companion. Once again she was faced with disgrace when George IV tried to divorce her, accusing her in a Bill before Parliament of 'a disgraceful, licentious and adulterous intercourse to the great scandal of the royal family'. The Bill was passed by a small majority at its third reading but was withdrawn by the Prime Minister.

Caroline, who had become Queen on George IV's accession in

1820, but was barred from attending the Coronation, died less than three weeks later on 7 August 1821.

Her end had long been keenly awaited by her husband: when Napoleon died earlier that summer a courtier informed him that his greatest enemy was dead. His absent-minded reaction was: 'Is she, by God!'

A light flickering in the back window of a large house in Blackheath – 2 ST JOHN'S PARK – led to the arrest of one of the most elusive and legendary Victorian criminals. A constable who knew that the owner of the house was away went to investigate the light, and with the help of two other policemen caught the man in the moonlit garden after a struggle in which one of them was wounded. The burglar was CHARLES PEACE who was so notorious that for years Victorian parents threatened their children with the frightening rubric: 'If you don't behave I'll set Charlie Peace on you.'

When arrested, the burglar was charged under the name of John Ward, and even when he was sent to prison for life it was still not known that Ward was really Charles Peace, the 'Gentleman Burglar' wanted for murder. At that time he had only been traced back to his previous alias of Thompson and an address in Evelina Road, Peckham, where, as Mr and Mrs Thompson, Peace and his mistress, Susan Grey, had been regarded as a model pair.

His neighbours knew Thompson as a family man, a regular churchgoer, animal lover and an excellent amateur violinist. They did not know that his real wife and son were living in the basement. He had given some guests a pleasant evening on the violin on the October night in 1878 before he went over to do the Blackheath job.

For shooting and wounding the policeman in St John's Park he was sentenced to life, and while he was in Pentonville it emerged that he was wanted for the murder of a man in Sheffield two years earlier.

Charlie Peace's colourful double, not to say multiple, life went back many years. Born in 1832, he served his first sentence at 18 and always carried on his career of crime with a plausible public front: at different times he was a picture-framer and gilder, an actor, and a music hall artiste. Burglary was for after midnight. A small wiry man, he was not particularly good-looking but this did not deter women; he often kept more than one mistress in his marital home.

Charlie Peace's exploits included sitting in the public gallery of a Manchester Court to hear a man convicted of a murder he himself

Charlie Peace, the gentleman burglar, struggling with a police constable after his attempted escape over the wall of the Blackheath house, (below).

had committed, and the same night going to the house of an Irish woman in Sheffield, to whom he had been making advances, and shooting her husband.

The discovery that he had committed murder in Sheffield meant that he was taken, not long after his arrival in Pentonville, to Leeds for a further trial. When this was delayed he was brought back to London. On the return train to Leeds he threw himself out of the window and survived the fall on to the line at 45 m.p.h. A month later, on 25 February 1879, Charlie Peace was hanged at Armley Prison, Leeds.

The Georgian crescent that is the pride of Blackheath was still unfinished in October 1800 when two women moved into 3 THE PARAGON. ELIZA ROBERTSON and her friend Charlotte Sharpe had to climb round scaffolding obstructing the front door and for a while lived in a small room in the basement.

This temporary inconvenience in no way inhibited the two women in a spending spree of vast extravagance. They took on servants including a footman. They bought a coach which had belonged to the Earl of Exeter and, without troubling to remove the coronets, went into Blackheath village and up to Soho to buy luxuries for their new house. One looking-glass alone cost £1,500. They spent £1,000 on beds and mattresses. Before they had finished they were in debt to the then astronomical sum of £20,000.

Born in Bermondsey in 1771, the daughter of a tradesman in oil, Eliza Robertson had enough education to become a governess and a teacher. She was 24 when she joined Charlotte Sharpe who was running a small school on Crooms Hill, Greenwich – now the Presbytery.

That two schoolteachers were able to take such a large new house in the Paragon and run up huge debts suggests that they must have been a remarkably plausible pair. Without depositing a penny they got the lease of the house and then using that as collateral raised an £850 mortgage to pay for extravagant decorations.

To this end Eliza put it about that her father was related to a government minister and to George Washington, and that she had great expectations from a wealthy family with whom she had formerly been a governess. She would be marrying one of them she said – Colonel Cunningham, a rich widower, who would be moving into the Paragon with her.

Talk of marriage, and some gossip about Eliza's relationship

The house beyond the first colonnade in the Paragon was leased by Eliza Robertson (right), who absconded after swindling local tradesmen.

with the father of one of her pupils, did not prevent the two women being looked at askance for quite a different reason. Lesbianism was not a subject much discussed at the time, but Eliza's tendency to go about in men's clothes caused gossip and eventually drew accusations in a sermon delivered by the minister of the Blackheath Congregational Church. Although she was to admit an 'attachment for many years' with Charlotte, Eliza ridiculed immoral implications, quoting the Bible and the innocent friendship of Naomi and Ruth as a defence.

Tradesmen were more concerned with debts than possible sexual aberrations. By the beginning of 1801 Blackheath was baying for money. An ironmonger was owed £485, a glazier £567; a bricklayer sued for £821; a carpenter who had built an aviary, a swing and furniture for their Paragon garden tried to have them arrested because they owed him £1,193. One close friend, fearing that he might be held finanicially responsible, put a paragraph in the local paper: 'Mr Creasy of Greenwich has contradicted the report that he had introduced the Swindlers of Blackheath to any tradespeople.'

Swindlers! The hard word was on them. Clearly the moment had come for flight. They covered up the expensive furniture in the big, gracious rooms and disappeared. But the law caught up with Eliza at Huntingdon where she was arrested, presumably because everything had been ordered in her name. Charlotte visited her during her imprisonment over the next seven months. So did other people. A figure of curiosity, Eliza was 'put on show' by her gaoler for the benefit of the Marquess of Salisbury, the Earl of Sandwich (whom she was let out to visit at nearby Hinchingbrooke House) and officers of the local militia.

The Fleet Prison for debtors became Eliza's next – and last – home. It wasn't exactly the Paragon, but she had well-furnished apartments, warm fires, and a servant to look after her. When her creditors met at the London Coffee House, Ludgate Hill, they roundly defamed her but seemingly they were unable to get any financial reparation.

During the next four years Charlotte came to the prison to comfort her and Eliza became a brisk pamphleteer and made a little money out of *The Life and Memoirs of Miss Robertson of Blackheath*, price 4s.

Elizabeth Robertson – 'of swindling notoriety' as the *Annual Register* put it – died in the Fleet on 7 June 1805 aged 32 and was buried at St Bride's, Fleet Street.

Sometimes it is difficult to decide the most culpable of several people involved in mutual misdeeds. This is certainly true when we come to put a Black Plaque on a small block of flats – WOODINGTON CLOSE, NORTH PARK, ELTHAM – the site of Wonersh Lodge (demolished 1964) and the scene of a great Victorian social and political scandal.

By the standards of the period KATHERINE O'SHEA was a wicked woman who for ten years lived in adultery with a man by whom she had three children. Responsibility for this liaison was shared with the man – the Irish statesman CHARLES STEWART PARNELL. Also deeply implicated was CAPTAIN WILLIAM O'SHEA, who connived at his wife's affair and condoned it. Only when Kitty's lover could no longer be useful to him politically, and when he found himself excluded from a legacy that went to Kitty, did O'Shea bring a divorce action.

The political events that precipitated Parnell's downfall are tangled, the sexual involvements fairly straightforward. Kitty had been married to Captain O'Shea for thirteen years and they had three children when she first met Parnell in the summer of 1880. Her husband, the ambitious MP for Co. Clare, had hoped to further his career by entertaining the newly elected leader of the Irish Party.

Kitty had invited him to dinner and he had not replied. So the pretty, volatile woman in her middle thirties went to the House of Commons to ask why. She sent up her card and waited in her carriage in Palace Yard until the tall, bearded figure of Parnell came down to apologise and promised to come the next time she asked him. As Kitty leaned forward to say goodbye a rose fell out of her bodice. Parnell picked it up, touched it to his lips, and put it in his buttonhole. He preserved the romantic memento until he died.

Shortly afterwards he came to dine and within two months when Kitty entertained him at Eltham it was usual for him to stay overnight with the excuse that he was in poor health. At that time Captain O'Shea was away from home a good deal, his marriage no more than a formality, and soon Parnell was spending more than single nights at Eltham. In 1882 Kitty gave birth to Parnell's child, who died in infancy. Two more daughters were born to them in the next nine years that they lived together at Eltham and Brighton.

During most of the time O'Shea appeared to accept the situation. Parnell's fellow politicians and many journalists knew about the liaison, but it was not until 1886 that the public had their first hint of the affair. When a paragraph appeared in the *Pall Mall Gazette* referring to Eltham as his 'suburban retreat', with all that implied,

Parnell's most serious political and private difficulties began.

The following year his reputation was tarnished when *The Times* published forged letters that suggested he had been implicated in the Phoenix Park murders of 1882. While Parnell was engaged in a libel action against the newspaper, O'Shea, angry that Kitty's rich aunt had died without leaving him a legacy, filed his divorce suit. O'Shea was also aggrieved that Parnell had not given him the political help for which he had hoped.

The case threw up a great deal of dirt. O'Shea's counsel called the couple's deception prolonged, squalid and degrading. He revealed that they had taken houses and stayed at hotels under false names. There was an uncorroborated story about Parnell making an escape from Kitty's bedroom by a fire escape and minutes later presenting himself like a visitor at O'Shea's front door. Parnell and Kitty put up no defence but O'Shea's connivance at the affair was an added scandal, as was the startling allegation that O'Shea had committed adultery with Kitty's sister.

O'Shea was granted a decree nisi and to Kitty's and Parnell's great distress he was granted custody of their two children. No political career could survive the public washing of so much dirty linen. Disgraced, especially among his Catholic countrymen, Parnell faced acrimony and abuse. Left with only a few loyal supporters, he was deprived of his leadership of the Irish Party; his chances of putting through the Home Rule Bill were ruined.

He was now able to marry Kitty but the strain of the previous year had weakened his heart and this was aggravated on a last courageous tour through the Irish countryside when insults were flung at him and he was pelted with stones. On 9 October 1891, three months after the wedding, Parnell died at the age of 45. O'Shea survived a further fourteen years – he was 65 when he died in 1905 – while Kitty lived on to write her memoirs in 1914, before her death on 5 February 1921.

Modern clergymen preaching to half-empty pews might envy the REVD ARTHUR TOOTH whose church in New Cross was always full. Sometimes he had as many people outside as in, and on the first Sunday in January 1877 attracted so vast a congregation that admission tickets had to be issued. There is, however, the less enviable thought that thousands came not to pray but to demonstrate, and that his church was stoned. He was arraigned at Lambeth Palace and sent to prison.

Mr Tooth's crime was that he permitted Romish practices.

'Spy' cartoon of Revd Arthur Tooth.

Wearing a biretta and a girdled red cassock, he led processions at services heavy with the smell of incense. He genuflected; he gave the sign of the Cross at the Absolution and Benediction; he chanted the *Agnus Dei*, tolled the bell at the Consecration and used an outsize crucifix. Wasn't there also an offending glint of gold to be observed on the wings of the carved angels in the church?

Coming shortly after the introduction of the Public Worship Regulation Act of 1874, all this was enough for the encumbent of ST JAMES'S, HATCHAM, a ragstone church in a cul-de-sac off the busy New Cross Road, to get into very hot water indeed.

In an age which took religion extremely seriously, a hint of 'High Church' ritual was enough to arouse angry passions and the law said that if any three aggrieved ratepayers objected they could have their complaint heard before the ecclesiastical Court of Arches. Three did, and the clergyman was ordered to appear before Lord Penzance, the President of the Court, when he was told his ritualistic services must stop. But Arthur Tooth carried on.

Again he was summoned. This time he was ordered not to hold a service for three months. The next Sunday Father Tooth was back, wearing vestments of a particularly defiant shade of purple.

On Christmas Eve, 1876, the bishop sent a minister to replace Mr Tooth. Mr Tooth declined to be replaced. On the Sunday after Christmas hecklers interrupted the Sung Eucharist, a fight broke out during *Adeste Fideles* and a thousand troublemakers assembled outside the church. The Sunday after that (admission by ticket only) organised dissenters broke through barriers and several thousand people defied the mounted police, threw stones and caused a riot.

The man who fermented this almighty row had come to St James's seven years before, when he was an ardent 28. Educated at

Tonbridge and Trinity College, Cambridge, Arthur Tooth belonged to a wealthy family and used his private income (from an
Australian meat preserving business) to improve a far from
flourishing church. He also opened a convent and orphanage
nearby to provide the choir and servers.

Pronounced 'contumacious and in contempt' by Lord Penzance,
Arthur Tooth was arrested and sent to Horsemonger Gaol near
London Bridge, an imprisonment which led to such an outcry by
his High Church supporters that the Home Secretary requested his
release.

Tooth then moved from New Cross to Croydon where,
diverting his zeal to education, he established Woodside, a boys'
and girls' school, and opened a home for inebriates. An enigmatic
personality who dearly loved his religion, he took a keen interest in
outdoor pursuits and encouraged his pupils to swim, shoot and
ride, and to learn about farming and camping. In later life he
became an enthusiastic motorist. He lived to a great age, and when
he was nearly 90 celebrated the fiftieth anniversary of his release
from gaol. The clergyman whose fervour had scandalised Low
Church worshippers was now respectable; the man who brought so
much notoriety to his church that his effigy was put in Madame
Tussaud's had become a hero.

The Revd Arthur Tooth, the first of five clergymen arrested for
High Church practices, died on 5 March 1931 and was buried at
Crystal Palace District Cemetery.

You will search in vain today for Forbes Road, Penge. When a
young woman named Harriet Staunton died there in a first floor
backroom the district assumed a bad reputation overnight.
Publicity about Harriet's grisly end caused fashionable houses to
lose value; Penge 'went down'. Residents demanded the name be
changed, and the house where she died – 34 MOSSLEA ROAD, PENGE –
is today part of an unoffending terrace of white stuccoed houses.
Neat steps lead up to a blue front door and it looks highly
respectable.

'The Penge Mystery' in 1877 provides a good example of how,
before the telephone and under the Victorian cloak of privacy,
inhuman crimes were committed behind firmly shut front doors by
people who could gamble on escaping detection.

Harriet, a truly pathetic figure, was the victim of nature and
conspiracy. At 33 she was feeble-minded and not very good-
looking, but had the human desire to get married. Her mother saw

the dangers, but Harriet was self-willed and with about £4,000 in her own right – a fortune in the 1870s – she quickly attracted an adventurer. He was LOUIS STAUNTON, an auctioneer's clerk.

They were married at Clapham in 1875 and as this was before the Married Woman's Property Act, Louis automatically took control of all her money. Fearing the worst, her mother called on Harriet at their first home in Loughborough Road, Camberwell, but after this visit she was forbidden the house. She was never to see her daughter again.

Within six months Staunton had hidden Harriet away in a remote house at Cudham, Kent. With his wife behind locked doors in an upstairs garret, he carried on an affair at a farm about a mile away with ALICE RHODES, a girl of nineteen, sister of the woman married to his younger brother, PATRICK STAUNTON.

A virtual prisoner in a room without a carpet, no wash-basin and three boards across trestles for a bed, Harriet was systematically starved to death. Her weight went down to 5 stone 4 lb. and she could hardly walk. As her life slipped away Staunton realised that if she died at Cudham there might be a nasty inquiry, and he brought her by train one dark April night to Penge East Station. From here she was carried round the corner to Forbes Road where he had rented a pair of rooms.

Harriet died within hours. With matted lice-ridden hair, horny feet and her emaciated body covered in dirt, she was reported to have looked like a woman of 60.

Staunton nearly got away with it. At first the Penge doctor accepted his account of 'cerebral disease', but by an astonishing coincidence Harriet's brother-in-law happened to be in the local post office when Louis came in to ask where he should register the death. This relative heard the word 'Cudham' and his curiosity was aroused. He got in touch with the doctor, the police were called and a post mortem was ordered (changing the cause of death to 'starvation and neglect').

Staunton, his mistress Alice Rhodes, his brother Patrick and Patrick's wife Elizabeth were all tried at the Old Bailey and sentenced to death for wilful murder. But the mystery – how much was Staunton to blame? – caused widespread public debate and the case was reopened (after agitation backed by 700 doctors, who signed a protest) to decide whether Harriet was killed by starvation or tubercular meningitis. The outcome was the pardoning of Alice Rhodes, death in prison of Patrick, the release after a few years of Elizabeth, and twenty years' penal servitude for Louis Staunton.

Just over a half a mile away a more famous woman, Eleanor Marx, died of poisoning at 7 JEW'S WALK, SYDENHAM, in 1898. Her macabre death in mysterious circumstances at the age of 43 suggests the guilt – moral if not actual – of DR EDWARD AVELING, the brilliant but unscrupulous man with whom she was living. Some of her friends were not satisfied with the coroner's verdict of suicide and put a more sinister interpretation on her death.

Eleanor, the youngest of Karl Marx's six children, was a zealous socialist worker, and the translator of books and plays. She bought the heavy Tudor-style Victorian house off Westwood Hill with money left her by Frederick Engels, a close friend of the Marx family and collaborator on *Das Kapital*. Three years before her death she went to live there with Edward Aveling, doctor of science, author and drama critic, whose name she took, calling herself Eleanor Marx Aveling.

On Thursday, the last day of March, 1898, a maid, Gertrude Gentry, coming into the bedroom at eleven o'clock in the morning found her mistress lying dead in the bed. She was dressed completely in white. A bottle of prussic acid stood empty on a table near her side. There was also a letter:

Dear. It will soon be over now. My last
word to you is the same that I have said
during all these long sad years – love

At the inquest it came out that on the morning Eleanor died a Sydenham chemist had been handed a note by the maid. It had said: 'Please give the bearer chloroform and a small quantity of prussic acid for the dog. – E.A.' Dr Aveling's card had been enclosed and the chemist had supplied the poison assuming that he was a medical doctor. It was stated in court that Aveling was out of the house at the time, on his way to London, and that the first he had heard of the tragedy was on his return.

'Had you any idea', asked the coroner, 'that she would destroy herself?' 'She had threatened to do it several times,' replied Aveling.

After censuring the chemist, the coroner gave his verdict that Eleanor had committed suicide in a state of temporary insanity. But a few years later H.M. Hyndman, founder of the Social Democratic Federation, put forward the theory that Aveling had told Eleanor that another woman was trying to force marriage on him and that he had suggested a suicide pact. According to Hyndman, he sent

Eleanor Marx

The house in Jew's Walk, Sydenham, where Karl Marx's daughter took poison in the main front bedroom.

Edward Aveling

for the poison and, when she had taken it, did not keep his side of the bargain. Because Aveling's handwriting and Eleanor's were indistinguishable, he could have forged the final note.

Colour is lent to his story by something which did not come out until many years later. In the previous June, Aveling under an assumed name had secretly married a young girl of twenty-two named Eva Frye. Somehow he had lived a double life between Eva and Eleanor for ten months. If Eleanor had just learnt of this, it might have precipitated her death. But however great Aveling's responsibility, suicide rather than murder is suggested by the remarkable parallel between her death and that of the heroine of Flaubert's *Madame Bovary*, a book which Eleanor was the first to translate into English.

Disillusioned after two love affairs, Madame Bovary tells a chemist she wants poison to kill rats, swallows the arsenic, goes to her bedroom, writes a farewell note to her husband and then lies down full length on her bed. After her death her husband insisted she be *dressed completely in white*. Eleanor's choice of the same colour makes similarity between fact and fiction seem too close for coincidence.

Aveling did not live long to enjoy his second marriage or the money inherited from Eleanor. Four months later he died at Stafford Mansions, Albert Bridge Road, Battersea, of a kidney disease. He was 47.

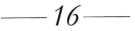

16

South-West London

I T is hardly cricket to kidnap someone half a mile away from the All England Lawn Tennis Club at Wimbledon. But this was what happened to Muriel McKay on the first Monday evening after Christmas 1969. The day started much like any other. First she got her husband Alex off to work; he went to Fleet Street in the company Rolls Royce. Then she picked up the daily help, did some shopping and visited the dentist. About five o'clock she took the daily home. As became widely publicised, she was wearing a green woollen jersey suit and cream leather driving shoes. Mrs McKay was never seen again.

Mr McKay got home shortly before eight o'clock after a day at the *News of the World* office where he was acting chairman in the absence of Rupert Murdoch who had just gone to Australia with his wife. He found the house in confusion; furniture had been thrown around, newspapers were all over the place. The phone was off the hook and the ex-directory number taken from the disc. No sign of his wife. Her overcoat was missing, and so was a small quantity of her jewellery.

The house which immediately became the focus of intense police activity was 20 ARTHUR ROAD, a pleasant, prosperous avenue near a church and a school with the All England Club not far down the hill. Whoever abducted Mrs McKay must have driven through the wide gates and pulled up on the gravel drive of her two-storey neo-Georgian home.

In the early hours of the following morning someone claiming to be 'M3 – the Mafia' came on the phone and demanded one million pounds by the following day. The kidnappers said they were holding Mrs McKay, but realised they had made a mistake: their intended victim was Mrs Murdoch, but they had been misled by the Rolls normally used by Mrs Murdoch, but that day taken by McKay.

Tension grew during the next five weeks during which the kidnappers made twenty-four phone calls, and pathetic letters were received from the terrified Mrs McKay. The kidnappers posted pieces of her woollen dress and Mr McKay was told that his wife would be killed unless the ransom was paid by 2 February.

A game of cat and mouse began between the family (advised by the police) and the kidnappers along fairly well-established lines. First a member of the family was told to go to a call box on the A10 Cambridge Road where he would be rung with a further message. Mrs McKay's son, Ian, was supposed to go, but was replaced by a policeman who, as instructed, carried a case full of banknotes – most of which were false with some genuine on top.

At the call box the police were directed to another phone on the Cambridge Road where they were told they would find a cigarette packet giving the place – High Cross in Hertfordshire – where the 'drop' was to be made. The police left the suitcase, and watching detectives noted a suspicious cruising blue Volvo saloon. But the occupiers of the Volvo spotted the detectives. The suitcase was not picked up.

So the whole routine started again. This time two detectives posing as members of the family were directed to a series of phone boxes leading to a drop at Bishops Stortford. The suitcase was left for two hours untouched. Again a blue Volvo was seen circling. It disappeared but on this occasion the police got the number.

The car was traced to Rook's Farm, a smallholding at Stocking Pelham, Hertfordshire, run by ARTHUR HOSEIN, a thirty-three-year-old tailor's cutter from Trinidad, and his younger brother NIZAMODEEN HOSEIN. They were arrested and charged on seven counts but the prosecution's main problem was the absence of a body. However, it was proved that Nizam Hosein had visited County Hall and spun a story to get the registration number of the Rolls.

Although well-dressed and speaking good English Arthur Hosein revealed himself at the trial to be a megalomaniac hysteric. His wildest story was that the crime had been committed by an international gang led by rival press proprietor Robert Maxwell. They had forced the Hoseins to let them operate from their farm.

Though there was no body, and the jury was out four hours, a unanimous verdict of guilty was reached. Arthur Hosein received the maximum sentence of twenty-five years; his brother (with a recommendation for leniency) fifteen.

Various solutions have been suggested for Mrs McKay's total disappearance, not the most attractive of which is that her murderers fed her body to pigs on the farm.

It looked rather like a party for somewhat mature guests when, around lunchtime, on 6 December 1978, fifty middle-aged and elderly men began to arrive at 32 AMBLESIDE AVENUE, STREATHAM. Thirteen women callers at the large detached Victorian house named Cranmore were rather younger.

During the previous ten weeks the police had observed 247 men and 50 women calling at this same address in the suburban road near Tooting Bec Common. They decided the moment had come to find out what was going on. When they entered shortly after four o'clock on that Wednesday afternoon the first person they saw was a naked woman, the second was clad only in bra and pants. Queuing on the staircase were a number of men in their underclothes.

A search round the house produced a box filled with vouchers valued at 10p and 15p. A puzzled constable asked the owner of the house, CYNTHIA PAYNE, what these were for. 'Oh,' she told him, 'they are my luncheon vouchers. They are for my gentlemen friends to satisfy their appetites.'

Everyone got dressed, and at Streatham police station Mrs Payne and her luncheon guests were questioned. It emerged that on entering Cranmore each man had paid £25 – there was a £3 discount for OAPs – and at the ensuing party they were given drinks, a film show and a lesbian display. The men surrendered their luncheon vouchers to the girls of their choice. At the end of the party the girls handed over their vouchers to Mrs Payne, who paid them.

The hostess at the Streatham house for these afternoon parties was a handsome and shapely woman of forty-six. Her progress to Streatham had taken her through various jobs: at an Aldershot hairdresser's, as a waitress in Brighton, and in London at Swan and Edgar's. At a café where she worked the proprietor taught her to poach eggs, which was to come in handy later on.

There were pregnancies and abortions and a meeting with a prostitute who asked if she could rent her room during the day. This gave Cynthia the idea of becoming a landlady and within a few months she had four flats in Victoria. Business provided enough money to buy a house in Edencourt Road, Streatham, and then the larger house in Ambleside Avenue.

Mrs Payne maintained that her sex parties were a social service and that she was giving self-confidence back to elderly men. Her lowest age limit was 40, and she was particularly solicitous about the needs of the disabled. She wanted the parties to be friendly not commercial. Believing, so she said, that her guests were romanti-

Cynthia Payne and the innocent-looking house in Ambleside Avenue where she says she would like her Black Plaque to read that she 'lived and worked here'.

cally inclined, she issued the luncheon vouchers to save them from paying her girls direct.

Her benevolent therapy extended to cheaper rates for less wealthy guests, and giving little snacks to exhausted gentlemen. There would be a chat over a cup of tea in the kitchen and sometimes she recalled her old skills and made them a poached egg on toast. 'There aren't', she observed righteously, 'many brothels that offer that kind of service.'

Requests received by Cynthia Payne show that not all her guests had uncomplicated requirements. There was a solicitor who enjoyed pretending he was a sergeant-major and would yell 'Get them OFF!' in a parade-ground voice to a girl wearing nothing but seven pairs of frilly knickers. A clergyman, we are told, informed her, 'I crave an ample angel', and she complied by providing a voluptuous blonde in a flowing white gown with wings she hired from a theatrical costumier.

It was hardly to be expected that the law would see Mrs Payne's activities in the same humanitarian light as she did or the vouchers as anything but an attempt to evade prosecution. At her trial, when she faced ten charges, there were more mundane phrases like 'keeping a disorderly house' and 'exercising control over three prostitutes'. Her defence that some of her girls were amateurs raising money for Christmas did not carry much weight. She was sentenced to eighteen months, fined £1,950 and ordered to pay £2,000 legal costs – but on appeal her imprisonment was reduced to six months. It did not pass unnoticed that it was she who was punished rather than the clergymen, lawyers and others who enjoyed her hospitality.

When she was released from Holloway, Cynthia Payne was driven home in a Rolls Royce, possibly provided by one of her former guests. For a while No. 32 Ambleside Avenue appeared to have become a respectable address with Mrs Payne sitting in her lounge weaving a fantasy in which she was mistress of an old people's home dispensing sexual medicine to her patients on the National Health.

However, these mild imaginary ministrations gave way to stronger actual dosage within three years. Once again elderly gentlemen began to pass under the wooden porch to be comfortably greeted. They were closely followed by the Metropolitan Police, two of whose constables posed as businessmen and one of whom pursued his investigation as far as a bathroom where a tattooed lady obligingly removed her leather top.

The renewed activities of 'Madam Cyn' (as the papers named her) in 'The House of a Thousand Delights' (Mrs Payne's description) led early in 1987 to her further trial on ten charges of controlling prostitutes. The case lasted two and a half weeks and cost the taxpayer £84,000. Police costs, estimated at a further £16,000, involved up to forty undercover investigators and perhaps included danger money to a constable who was faced with a transvestite dressed as a French maid.

As before, the activities in Ambleside Avenue were revealed as bizarre in the extreme, but a certain light-hearted circus element prevailed in court. People found some difficulty in keeping straight faces. Blithe and cheerful in the box, Mrs Payne acquired the status of a national heroine. No one was the least surprised when (despite evidence to the contrary) she was acquitted. It was generally felt that she deserved no less for bringing warmth and laughter to a particulary cold snap of winter weather.

You can't miss the Priory. As you cross Tooting Bec Common from the south, the big house – Victorian Gothic, crenellated and gleaming white – appears dramatically between the trees. What took place there in 1876 was also dramatic. There was a death which stirred up enormous controversy and has remained a classic Victorian mystery ever since.

THE PRIORY, which has the modern address of 225 BEDFORD HILL, BALHAM, is now divided into flats, but when leased in 1874 by Florence Ricardo, a rich widow of twenty-nine, it was a single house of fifteen rooms. MRS CHARLES BRAVO (as Mrs Ricardo was soon to become) had a staff of twelve, a companion called Mrs Cox and an elderly close neighbour, Dr James Gully.

Florence's first husband, from whom she inherited considerable wealth, had been a brutal alcoholic. In an effort to cure his condition, he and Florence had visited a private hydro run by Dr Gully in Malvern. Manifestly the cure was not a success; within a short time Ricardo died after another bout of heavy drinking. That his body was found to have a small amount of an emetic (now known as antimony) was not thought significant at the time. What does seem of more consequence is that Florence, a handsome, full-bosomed woman, became the mistress of the owner of the hydro. Their tolerably discreet liaison, which lasted for more than a year, and took them on holidays abroad, was brought to an end by Florence after a miscarriage – possibly induced by Dr Gully. After that Gully, married to an invalid wife reluctant to die, seemed

The Priory, Balham. The husband of Florence Bravo (right), died of poisoning in the bedroom with the main casement window on the first floor.

happy to become just a friend to the neighbour who was 37 years younger than himself.

This was the situation when in December 1875 – four years after her first husband's death – Florence remarried. On this occasion her husband was Charles Bravo, a young South Kensington lawyer, the same age as herself, who was attracted by her and her money.

Four months later Bravo was taken violently ill in the night, and made a dramatic appearance in his nightshirt on the landing of the Priory shouting: 'Florence! Hot water! Hot water!' Two days later he died. A post-mortem revealed a massive amount of antimony in his stomach.

At this point the mystery begins. *Did Bravo himself take the tartar emetic poison, either deliberately or by mistake?* The companion, Mrs Cox, attested that she thought he had committed suicide. The coroner's jury did not think so, and a second inquest was called. *Was the poison in the burgundy Bravo drank at dinner that night or in the glass of water which he customarily took before bed?* Mrs Cox now enlarged on the situation to the coroner, revealing Florence's previous relationship with Dr Gully. This excited suspicions of his complicity in the death. *Had Dr Gully provided the poison?* He had some in his pharmacy but had had no opportunity to administer it. *Had Florence put poison in the drink?* She had the opportunity but was not, as far as was then known, in possession of the drug. Later it became known that Florence's groom (previously employed by Dr Gully) had obtained supplies of tartar emetic in the doctor's name, to worm Florence's horses. This had been kept in the Priory stables.

The second jury delivered their verdict that Bravo had been wilfully murdered but, whatever their suspicions, there was no proof of Florence's or Dr Gully's guilt.

Florence died of drink four years later, in 1880, and Dr Gully (ruined by gossip) three years after that. Their deaths reopened the *cause célèbre*. Innumerable books fuelled further speculation. Hardly a permutation has not been presented or probed. But, while nothing has ever been proved against Florence Bravo, for a wife to lose one husband may be regarded as a misfortune; to lose both looks like carelessness; and for two to have consumed some of the same poison invites suspicion.

Except for Cock Lane we have given ghosts a wide berth. Poltergeists haven't had a look in. But it would be difficult to pass 8 ELAND ROAD, BATTERSEA, without stopping to listen for the sound of breaking crockery. Things may be quiet now in the two-storey terrace house going down from Lavender Hill but in November 1927 this little Victorian house was very noisy indeed.

Trouble started on the last Saturday of that month. Lumps of coal, copper coins and pieces of sods started landing on the roof of the conservatory and broke the glass. A constable who was summoned had his helmet knocked over his eyes by a bit of coal. He reported that he could not see where the bombardment had come from and the police ordered a day and night watch on the house.

Round about Christmas there was loud banging in every room, ornaments crashed to the floor and window-panes were broken. Chairs were said to have 'marched down the hall in single file'. In an upstairs bedroom the windows caved in and as a frightened old man of eighty-five, who was an invalid and lessee of the house, was carried down the stairs a chest of drawers toppled over. He was taken to hospital suffering from shock and died shortly afterwards.

Testimony for all this came primarily from the old man's son, FREDERICK ROBINSON, who told the police and journalists of how on that same day he had seen the hallstand swaying but as he went to steady it 'some strange power seemed to tear it from my hands, and it fell against the stairs. It broke into two parts.'

The occupants of the house, in which the family had lived for twenty-five years, were Frederick Robinson's father and his sisters – schoolteachers, one of them a widow with a son of fourteen. As Frederick Robinson was a twenty-seven-year-old teacher, his testimony might be regarded as likely to be rational and accurate.

Once the story broke Eland Road was besieged by reporters and

The Battersea 'Mystery House' investigated in 1927 by the Society of Psychical Research.

photographers and on 19 January 1928 Harry Price, the ghost hunter, arrived. After hearing the story and going out into the garden the investigator for the Society of Psychical Research asked about a house some eighty yards away. He was told it was a private asylum mostly for shell-shocked patients from the First World War. This was obviously suspect but from that distance he reckoned the inmates would have had to catapult the missiles, and this, anyway, did not account for the damage inside the house.

Strange disturbances continued, once with Price as well as a well-known woman medium and a reporter present. The idea that they were caused by a practical joker was considered. Robinson's nephew was sent away for a few days although the idea that he might be responsible seemed nullified by his obvious fear. Really Price wanted to test a theory that as a sensitive adolescent he might be the object of a poltergeist's attention. Manifestations went on in his absence.

A strange feature of the case was that Frederick Robinson, whom Price regarded as 'extremely intelligent and absolutely normal', suffered a breakdown and was detained under the Lunacy Act for ten days.

While Robinson was away being examined, Price and a reporter visited the house and when they were in the kitchen heard a thud behind them. A search revealed a small bronze cherub lodged in a shoe. The cherub had been projected from the front room – a flight involving the turning of two or three corners. Price testified that no one, other than those in the kitchen, was in the house.

As there were aspersions against his honesty in the affair, when Frederick Robinson was allowed home (declared perfectly sane) he declined any further questioning and arranged for the whole family to move house at once. Thirteen years later, however, he was reported in a psychical journal as saying that slips of paper at one time had rained down 'out of nowhere' at Eland Road. On one he said was a message, 'I am having a bad time here. I cannot rest. I was born during the reign of William the Conqueror'. It was signed 'Tom Blood'.

This was not calculated to remove the suspicions of sceptics and hardly makes a true psychical experience seem more probable. It may be unjust to brand Robinson as the perpetrator of the strange manifestations. Perhaps not he but the mysterious poltergeist (from the German meaning 'noisy ghost') should be on the Black Plaque. Whatever the answer, 'the Mystery House', as the press called 8 Eland Road, has not provided a solution.

We saw what can happen if a difficult employer continually picks on a servant when the owner of a home in Park Lane was choked to death by her cook in 1871 (p. 95). Eight years later the situation was repeated when a widow dismissed an Irish domestic.

Mrs Julia Thomas was fanatical when it came to tidiness in her little home, 9 PARK ROAD (then 2 Vine Cottages), RICHMOND. The clumsy, untrained KATE WEBSTER whom she employed without asking for references failed to reach her exacting standards. Mrs Thomas gave her notice and as a result came to a very nasty end.

The February of 1879 was a month of growing tension between the pernickety Mrs Thomas and the truculent Irish woman of forty with a background of petty crime and an illegitimate baby. Mrs Thomas may have behaved like a tartar but Kate Webster gave as good as she got. Mrs Thomas's friends observed that she became increasingly afraid of her servant.

On Sunday, 2 March – the last day of her notice – Kate spent part of the day next door in the Hole in the Wall public house and may well have taken too much to drink. Mrs Thomas attended Morning Service and Evensong and when she returned home in the evening was confronted by the servant due to leave the next day.

There was an argument which turned into a violent quarrel. 'In the height of my anger,' Kate stated, 'I threw her from the top of the stairs to the ground floor. I lost all control of myself.'

What followed carries an unpleasant but mundane murder into the realms of the macabre. When she found her employer was dead, Kate Webster dragged her body into the kitchen and began, rather crudely, to cut her up. The next day she boiled down the flesh but found herself in difficulty about disposing of the head.

Her solution was to take it to Hammersmith in a black bag. She went to visit some old friends and, to explain her improved wardrobe, told them that since they had last met she had married, been widowed and come into money. While they were talking in a public house by Hammersmith Bridge she slipped away for twenty minutes. She had no bag when she returned.

Later that night with the help of the friends' sixteen-year-old son, Kate took a heavy corded box to Richmond Bridge. When they reached the centre of the bridge about 11 p.m. she told the boy to walk on ahead. He heard a splash.

The box, but not the bag – the dismembered body of the murdered woman but not her head – was found in the Thames, and a missing foot at Twickenham. Half-way through the month a suspicious next-door neighbour, seeing furniture from Vine

The cottage in Richmond where Kate Webster (below) decapitated her mistress and boiled down her remains.

Cottage being loaded on to a van for the saleroom, raised the alarm and before long the police started a hunt for Kate, who had fled to Ireland. She was arrested in her home county of Wexford.

Her testimony at the trial was such a mixture of lies and contradictions that, before sentencing her to death, the judge wearily admitted that only God knew what was true or false. The landlady of the Hole in the Wall supplied an horrific footnote to the story. She said a day or two after the murder Kate Webster had come into the pub and offered to sell her two jars of fat – the best dripping, she said.

In the autumn of 1962, BUSTER EDWARDS, a round-faced, cheerful-looking man in his early thirties, moved with his wife and daughter into a flat at 214 ST MARGARET'S ROAD, TWICKENHAM. In this tall, narrow Victorian house he helped to plan the biggest mail hold-up in history – the Great Train Robbery.

The daring and intricate crime, involving two gangs and at least fifteen men, took place in August the following year. The mail train from Glasgow was ambushed at Cheddington, Buckinghamshire, and the robbers escaped with 120 mailbags containing over £2,500,000 in banknotes.

Edwards, who grew up in South London near the Elephant and Castle, was a wartime evacuee who left school at 14. After a number of menial jobs and two years in the Royal Air Force, he drifted into petty theft which grew into large-scale crime. A £62,000 bank robbery at Heathrow involved him with criminals who later provided the information that big sums of money in old notes ready for pulping were regularly brought from Scotland to London by train. An exceptionally large amount was expected to travel south after the August Bank Holiday.

To hold up and rob the train, and make good their escape, was a complicated operation calling for varied criminal skills. Edwards helped to recruit a team of experts who regarded this as the big one – the job on which all of them could retire.

It also called for capital and there is an uncorroborated story that the Great Train Robbers were backed to the tune of £80,000 by ODESSA, an organisation of former Nazis thought to have been run by the late Otto Skorzeny, a famous wartime SS commando.

Plans were carefully laid during the spring and early summer of 1963 at the Edwardses' flat in the busy Twickenham road. The gang's other varied rendezvous were the Regent Palace Hotel, an Elephant and Castle club, and parks all over London. Preparations involved leasing a farm south of Bicester, about twenty miles from the place where the train was hi-jacked and where afterwards the gang remained hidden with their vast haul.

They purchased army uniforms and vehicles to give the impression of military operations. Buster Edwards and three others, disguised as railway workers, sought out the actual mail train they were to rob in a marshalling yard so that they could examine padlocks and the wire cages in which the mailbags were carried on the journey.

Having prepared alibis, the gang moved into Leatherslade Farm two days before the operation, planned for 3 a.m. on Thursday, 8 August 1963. Edwards checked uniforms, gloves, coshes and stocking masks, and handed out pep pills to the men as they dozed on air beds. They set off in convoy after midnight and reached the Tring-Leighton Buzzard road at 1.30 a.m. It was a warm night, not too dark: perfect conditions.

They cut telephone wires to prevent alarms being raised. Deftly they changed to red the signal half a mile short of the bridge. When the diesel train came to a halt, five of the masked men leapt up from the embankment, uncoupled the back coaches and forced the driver – whom they coshed – to move the engine with the mail vans still attached to the bridge where they could be unloaded.

They ordered post office sorters to lie face down as they smashed padlocks into the cage where the bags were stacked. Forming a human chain they passed 120 of these heavy sacks tightly packed with banknotes down the embankment to the road and the waiting vehicles. The whole operation was completed within thirty-five minutes of stopping the train.

Exhausted but exhilarated, the men opened the sacks in the farmhouse kitchen and piled up a great wall of notes – just over £1,200,000 in £5 notes and £1,300,000 in £1 and 10/- notes. It was half what they had hoped for, but they went wild with excitement and with extravagant bravado lit cigarettes with pound notes.

The haul was divided into eighteen 'whacks', roughly £150,000 for each of the gang. They had planned to stay in hiding until Sunday, but fearing their hideout would be discovered they moved out on the Friday taking the money and themselves to various safe houses. While the police were carrying out their nationwide search, the final distribution took place.

The great coup brought little lasting enjoyment to the men who took part. Much of the money faded away – 'laundered' by the fences whom they had to employ to dispose of it. Before the end of the year nine had been arrested, and at their Aylesbury trial were given sentences of up to thirty years. Two made sensational escapes from prison, but only Ronnie Biggs (whom the others had reluctantly included in the gang) has never been recaptured. He now lives in Brazil.

Buster brought £90,000 back to a friend's house in Kingston-upon-Thames in the boot of a car and after months of lying low in Wraysbury he went to Germany to undergo plastic surgery. He eluded police for three years, one of which he spent with his wife and daughter in Mexico City. But the high life held few attractions: homesick for the pubs round the Elephant and Castle, he decided to give himself up.

At his trial he pleaded that he had not been at the robbery and had been paid only £10,000 to help clear up at the farm. Optimistically he had hoped for a short sentence, but, though he went down for roughly half the time of the other ringleaders, he was given fifteen years. Buster Edwards was released in 1977 and, not shy of the press, this grey-haired, youthful and seemingly happy man has subsequently sold flowers at Waterloo Station.

—— 17 ——

North-West London

For the last two years of her life a celebrated courtesan lived quietly in a house overlooking the Thames at Chiswick. In her heyday she had known luxury at the Palace of Whitehall, had kept a retinue of servants at a fine house in St James's, and had owned Nonesuch Palace at Ewell. But now the years of extravagance and scandal were over; in her middle sixties she was content to be out of the public gaze, safe at last from the censure and jealously of the world.

Called by a contemporary pamphleteer 'the fairest and lewdest of the royal concubines', she had been a king's mistress, and by the King she had given birth to five children. Different men fathered other illegitimate offspring. By the time she came to the pleasant modest mansion at Chiswick her royal lover had been dead for more than twenty years, but she had memories of at least ten other love affairs and two marriages.

In her lifetime she had gone through several fortunes; she had appeared at banquets and the theatre wearing jewels worth £40,000; one of her expensive habits was to travel in a coach with eight horses. Now in the twilight of her life she was thankful for a small revenue from Nonesuch Park.

For a time, long ago, she had exerted inordinate influence over the King, and at Court had been hated for her say in the affairs of the nation. She had replaced statesmen with her favourites. She had sold appointments. In love as in money matters she had schemed unscrupulously. When her royal lover married, she pretended acquiescence but became lady-in-waiting to the Queen so that she had an apartment next to him and their relationship was hardly interrupted.

With dark auburn hair and blue eyes, she had been a great beauty, frequently painted by Lely. But in the summer of 1709 her appearance changed alarmingly. She swelled 'gradually to a monstrous bulk'. Her physicians diagnosed dropsy that could not long be stayed.

On Sunday, 9 October 1709, BARBARA VILLIERS died aged 67 at what is traditionally identified as her home – WALPOLE HOUSE on CHISWICK MALL. As she leased the house and refused to contribute to the local Church of England she does not appear in the parish rate books, but in 1723–8 her son Charles Fitzroy, Duke of Cleveland and Southampton, was paying thirty shillings from what has been deduced to be this house.

Four days later she was buried at Chiswick parish church with two dukes and two earls among her pallbearers. Perhaps because she had become a Roman Catholic no memorial was raised; there was nothing to remind the world that the girl who had become Charles II's mistress when she was 19 was Countess of Castlemaine, Duchess of Cleveland, Baroness of Nonesuch and Countess of Southampton. The last three titles had been given by Charles in 1670 (along with a gift of £30,000 and Nonesuch Palace) to smooth stormy waters when he turned his favours to Nell Gwyn.

Barbara Villiers, born at Westminster in 1641, the daughter of a Royalist general, was 16 when she had her first affair. This was with the second Earl of Chesterfield, a liaison which continued after her marriage a year later to Roger Palmer. Her relationship with Charles began two years after that. At the Restoration she was so readily available that when the King rode into London in May 1660 she contrived to share his very first night in Whitehall.

For the next ten years the woman whom Pepys called 'the curse of the nation' held complete sway over the King. He lavished money and jewellery on her, gave her houses and bestowed a title on her husband so that she became Lady Castlemaine. Children born to them were duly ennobled, so that Barbara's direct descendants are the present Duke of Grafton and the Earl of Southampton. The Princess of Wales, the Duchess of York and the Marquess of Hertford are also descended from her.

All this sounds connubial, dynastic, almost respectable. But Barbara's relationship with Charles was not exclusive. Quite early in their affair there was gossip of her liaisons with three other men. A rumour about her association with Henry Jermyn was so strong that the King declined to acknowledge one of her babies, protesting that he couldn't remember having lain with her for months. 'God damn me, you shall own it!' responded the fiery-tempered Barbara, who threatened if he didn't she would dash the

Walpole House, Chiswick Mall, last home of Barbara Villiers (right) Charles II's mistress.

baby's brains out in full view of the Privy Gardens gallery at Whitehall.

Barbara's infidelities during the decade when she was closest to Charles were apparently few but these increased noticeably with the advent of Nell Gwyn. A procession to her bed was formed by an acrobat in the royal troupe; an actor; John Churchill (later Duke of Marlborough) by whom she had a daughter; an Under-Secretary of State and the English Ambassador in Paris. There were intrigues with the playwright William Wycherley and several other men. At the court of Charles II such misbehaviour was not exceptional, but hostility to Lady Castlemaine was intensified because of her arrogance, her greed and the large sums of public money diverted to her by the King.

After Charles II died in 1685 there was another affair with an actor and a liaison with an adventurer, Robert Fielding, whom Barbara, by then a widow, married only to discover he had a wife. The scandal and humiliation of this late bigamous marriage in her sixties made her leave St James's for Chiswick. Here there was peace, though a grandson living with her was a reminder of the fitful fever of her earlier life. He was the illegitimate son of her own illegitimate daughter by the Duke of Marlborough.

Half a mile west of Chiswick Mall is Lord Burlington's Palladian villa, Chiswick House. In the grounds stood OLD CHISWICK HOUSE, a Jacobean mansion which was the home of FRANCES HOWARD for the last eight years of her infamous life. She plotted the notorious murder of Sir Thomas Overbury in the Tower.

Both an adulteress and a poisoner, Frances, Countess of Essex and later Countess of Somerset, richly deserves a Black Plaque, which will have to go up on the broken wall attached to the Inigo Jones gateway close to the villa; this is all that remains of the former house demolished in 1756.

In 1606 Frances, a member of the powerful and ancient Howard family, was contracted in a child marriage to Robert Devereux, Earl of Essex. Both were in their early teens and they parted immediately. After Oxford he went abroad and became a soldier; she was sent to Court where, says a contemporary, her 'sweet and bewitching countenance' was allied 'to a lustful appetite'. She had a brief affair with James I's son, Prince Henry, and then fell in love with Sir Robert Carr, a favourite of the King and his private secretary.

At the age of 18 and passionately involved with Carr (soon to be

Frances Howard, poisoner. She died at Old Chiswick House.

created Viscount Rochester), Frances found herself faced with the return of her young husband from the Continent eager to enjoy the delayed pleasures of marriage. She did everything to fend him off and visited the widow of a doctor of physics in Hammersmith, Mistress Anne Turner, with a request for a bromide to reduce her husband's desires.

Mistress Turner, who dabbled in the black arts, provided the potion and introduced Frances to an occult circle in Lambeth run by a quack doctor and from these people she learnt about the poisons she would soon employ.

Into this fraught situation now appears Sir Thomas Overbury, recently knighted, and the close friend of Rochester, the Countess's lover. A scholar and poet, he also acted as Rochester's secretary.

While his friend's liaison remained simply an affair, Overbury willingly acted as a go-between. But when Frances arranged to divorce Essex in order to marry Rochester, his attitude changed. He did not consider her a suitable person to be his friend's wife.

Intensely resentful of Overbury's interference, Frances decided he must be got rid of. Using her family influence, she deviously arranged for the King to offer him a post of ambassador abroad. When he declined she went further. In 1613 Overbury suddenly found himself arrested and taken to the Tower on a trumped-up charge of 'high contempt' for opposing the King's wishes.

Originally it may not have been intended that his imprisonment should last more than a couple of months – time for Frances's marriage to Rochester to go through smoothly – but this did not satisfy the Countess. Still under 21, she now revealed herself as not only unscrupulous but diabolically wicked.

She conspired to have the Lieutenant of the Tower replaced by a friend of the family, and for a creature in her pay, Richard Weston, to become Overbury's personal gaoler. She then resorted once again to Mistress Turner of Hammersmith, who arranged with James Franklin, a City apothecary, to supply phials of white arsenic. These were passed on to Weston to mix in Overbury's meals. On one occasion tarts arrived at the Tower so black with poison that they were thrown out.

Except for the tarts, the City apothecary did his work well; his poisons acted slowly and deceptively. For a long time Overbury somehow withstood a combination of the arsenic and aqua fortis (nitric acid), mercury, powdered diamonds, lapis costitus, great spiders and cantharides (Spanish Fly). It was three months before this lethal brew took effect and then was not diagnosed by physicans called by Overbury to his bedside. The coroner gave a verdict of natural causes when Overbury, reduced to skin and bone, died after three and a half months of consistent poisoning in his dark cell.

Overbury's death occurred on or around 14 September 1613. In November Rochester was created Earl of Somerset. On Boxing Day he and Frances were married. The bride wore white.

Frances seemed to have got away with it, but when, two years later, the truth leaked out in a roundabout way the King called for an investigation with Lord Chief Justice Coke in charge.

The gaoler Weston, the apothecary Franklin, the collusive Lieutenant of the Tower and Mistress Turner were all arrested and convicted in November 1615. Frances, in poor health after two years' dread of discovery, was tried with her husband in the following May. She pleaded guilty; he innocent. They were sentenced to death, reprieved, and pardoned (at the King's instigation) after six years' imprisonment.

The Earl and Countess were released in 1622 and two years later went to live permanently at Old Chiswick House. Their relationship is said to have deteriorated into deep hatred. Frances died of an extremely painful disease at Chiswick in 1632, aged about 39. Her husband lived on in obscurity and died in London in 1645. Their daughter, Anne, born while they were in the Tower, married William Russell, first Duke of Bedford, in 1637, when Old Chiswick House was sold by her father for her dowry.

The bungalow, brightly painted in orange, maintains a look of innocence. In a cul-de-sac off roads lined with identical suburban houses to the north of Western Avenue, 45 CRANLEY DRIVE, RUISLIP, has an anonymity that exactly suited PETER and HELEN KROGER who were living there from 1958 until they were arrested in 1961.

Neighbours and close friends across the road knew Kroger as an antiquarian bookseller. They found him and his wife who had come

Detectives leave the Cranley Drive bungalow with evidence to convict the Krogers (left). They transmitted secrets to Moscow by radio from the room under the dormer.

to England from Canada quiet and charming people, and were sorry to hear that they were having a struggle about the mortgage.

When they first came to this country the Krogers lived at Catford in south London, and when they moved to Cranley Drive, close to the Ruislip US airbase, they did so with a reason. They wanted to send messages to Moscow and these short coded transmissions, never longer than thirty seconds, were insinuated and engulfed in the volume of radio signals from the base, which made their detection impossible.

For three years information about secrets from the Portland Underwater Weapons Research Establishment, the Holy Loch nuclear submarine base in Scotland, and from agents all over Britain, was sent to Russia from a small transmitter which, taken from under the kitchen floorboards, was operated in the attic. The large oblong dormer from which the calls went out still exists.

At their trial it was claimed that the Krogers were innocent – their premises, they said, had just been used to store equipment – but this hardly plausible story was exploded when the CIA identified them as Morris and Lena Cohen, two escaped KGB agents. The affable good-looking Morris Cohen, alias Peter Kroger, born in the Bronx in 1910, had been a Communist since the 1920s when he was at a university in Illinois. His wife, three years younger, had been a domestic servant, and during the war worked in an aircraft factory. They were sentenced to twenty years' imprisonment, but in 1969 were released in exchange for Gerald Brooke, who had been held by the Russians.

A man of just under forty who stood trial with the Krogers had been a frequent weekend visitor to 45 Cranley Drive. Neighbours were told that GORDON LONSDALE had been lent the keys so he could keep an eye on the valuable antiquarian books when the Krogers were away. Ostensibly a Canadian business man hiring juke boxes to pubs and clubs, Lonsdale had an office in Wardour Street and a flat at the White House, Regent's Park.

Lonsdale had met the Krogers in Paris in 1955 and had brought them in on what became known as the Portland Spy Ring. They had decided on the suitability of Ruislip for transmitting information to Russia and, as the technician, Lonsdale installed radio equipment under the kitchen floorboards and set up a darkroom in the bathroom for processing secret film.

Surprisingly little came out about Lonsdale at the trial, as may be gauged by the Lord Chief Justice's barely adequate remark ('Gordon Arnold Lonsdale, you are clearly a professional spy') before sentencing him to twenty-five years 'as the directing mind' of the ring. Not until eight months later did the FBI reveal his true identity as Konan Trofimovich Molody, a Russian born in 1922 who was taken to the United States in 1929 and educated at Berkeley. He had returned to Russia, in the war had served in the Red Army and had been trained in a spy school before making his way to London where he studied at the London School of Oriental Languages.

The twenty-five year sentence suggests that the judge may have known more about his background than he announced. Lonsdale served only three years and one month in prison before the Russians bartered Greville Wynne to secure his release.

Yet two more names must be squeezed onto the Ruislip Black Plaque: HARRY HOUGHTON and ETHEL GEE who, though they lived in Dorset not London, were tried with Lonsdale and the Krogers. Their information from Portland went out from the loft in Cranley Drive.

Houghton, a former petty officer in the Navy, was initially drawn into the spy net by a girl while serving as a clerk to the naval attaché in the British Embassy in Warsaw. Sex was always his undoing. He was posted by the Admiralty to the experimental station at Portland where he began his relationship with 'Bunty' Gee, an attractive thirty-eight-year-old clerk in an adjoining office. Houghton's recruitment has a cloak and dagger flavour; he met his Russian contact at Dulwich Picture Gallery, identifying himself with a copy of *The Times*. When he was transferred from work dealing with classified material his mistress helped provide him with secrets of our anti-submarine defences. These reached Lonsdale at meetings opposite the Old Vic Theatre and were taken to Ruislip.

Houghton, aged 56, and the woman who was infatuated by him, were both sentenced to fifteen years. They served ten, were released in 1971 when they married, and settled down to a quiet life with changed names.

In 1961 spies toppled each other over with knock-on confessions and clues leading to their unmasking. Twelve days after the trial which sent the five Portland spies to gaol, the double-agent GEORGE BLAKE arrived in England and was arrested the next day. A traitor probably second only to Philby, Blake went to prison for forty-two years, a sentence unprecedented in English legal history.

Except for a short period in Bromley, Kent, in the 1950s, Blake spent most of his life abroad, but he deserves to be remembered by a Black Plaque either on the tall walls of Wormwood Scrubs Prison in Artillery Road, from which he escaped, or better still on the little terrace house, 28 HIGHLEVER ROAD, where he hid just round the corner.

A message from Blake to Moscow, intercepted by MI6, saying that Lonsdale was going to be arrested, was probably the link in the chain of clues that led to Blake's unmasking. Referring to his nine and a half years in MI6 as a double agent, Blake confessed: 'I must freely admit that there is not an official document to which I had access which was not passed over to my Soviet contact.'

Like a number of other post-war British traitors, Blake claimed his motives were ideological. He never took any money for spying. He joined the Communist side believing their system most likely to produce 'a balanced and more just society'.

Born in Holland in 1922 and brought up there, Blake was the son of a Jew with British nationality and a Dutch mother. He was interned in 1940, escaped, joined the Resistance and fled to England where he enlisted in the Royal Navy. From Naval Intelligence he went to the Foreign Office in 1947, learnt Russian at Cambridge, and after being interned in Korea (where he was British Vice-Consul) his political convictions changed. When he returned to London – and MI6 – in 1953, he began his life as a double agent.

Great secrecy persisted at Blake's trial so that the full extent of his treachery is not known. But as well as photographing everything that came into his office for the KGB, he supplied the Russians with the names of every important East German who defected to the West. He betrayed the names and supplied descriptions of MI6 agents going abroad, so rendering them useless. He gave away a giant monitoring system set up by the Allies in West Berlin to listen to conversations from the East.

Worried that his cover might be blown by a German double agent, Blake requested a transfer from Berlin in 1961 and it was while in Beirut that his activities were discovered and he was called to London (for what he assumed was a routine Whitehall interview) to be arrested on five charges.

The most dramatic event in Blake's career was still to come. In Wormwood Scrubs during 1965 Blake made friends with an Irish prisoner, Sean Bourke, who on his release set up an escape plan with a code signal by two-way radio. The opening line of Richard Lovelace's poem: 'Stone walls do not a prison make...' was Blake's cue to force the loosely cemented bars of his cell window, race across the prison yard and climb a rope ladder thrown over the wall by Bourke on the outside. He dropped into Artillery Road, broke his ankle, gashed his forehead and climbed bleeding into a cheap second-hand car. With Bourke at the wheel they drove to the flat rented in Highlever Road. While police manned road blocks, and searched airfields and harbours all over the country, Blake stayed there for a week, watching it all on television less than half a mile from the prison.

After that he moved to a flat in the Cromwell Road, and Dover, Berlin and Moscow were the final stages of George Blake's journey to the country of his ultimate choice.

If one street in London may be said to have been completely erased and without regret, it is the cul-de-sac in Notting Hill that made headlines in 1953. Along with the other drab terrace houses in the road, 10 RILLINGTON PLACE has disappeared, leaving only gruesome memories of the perverted murders committed by JOHN REGINALD HALLIDAY CHRISTIE.

After a trial which followed the discovery of six bodies, the name of Rillington Place was changed to Rushton Close. Pulled down in the early 1970s, this is now Bartle Road, so extensively rebuilt that the nearest we can come to an accurate location for the murders is in a modern block of maisonettes – also No. 10.

The subject of innumerable books, the Christie killings (there were seven, possibly eight, in all) need not long detain us. The pathological details, here much curtailed, make grim reading.

We are dealing with a murderer and a necrophile, the bespectacled Yorkshireman with the high-domed bald head who came to Rillington Place in 1938 when he was 40 and who, during the war, was a special constable. Separated from his wife, who was evacuated, his first victim was an Austrian girl of twenty-four. He took her back to the house, strangled her during sexual intercourse, and buried her in the back garden. Another girl was killed and buried in much the same way the following year.

In 1952 Christie strangled his wife and put her under the floorboards in the front room. Three prostitutes met similar fates in the next few months with slight variations of a routine which consisted of getting them to inhale coal gas and strangling them as he copulated with them while sitting in a deck chair threaded with string mesh.

The discovery of one of the bodies by a Jamaican tenant of the house led to Christie's arrest on the Embankment near Putney Bridge in March 1953 and to his execution at Pentonville four months later. He had been responsible for the killing of six women in the most squalid and perverted ways. In addition he also confessed to killing Beryl Evans, who had a flat in the house, but not to the murder of a baby daughter, Geraldine, for which her husband, Timothy Evans, was hanged in 1950.

Whether Christie also killed the baby (as Evans had accused him at the time) remains uncertain. 'The more the merrier!' was his imprecise jocular reply when asked the total number of his murders. As he was seeking a verdict of insanity, Christie may have reckoned that the inclusion of a baby in the list of adult, predominately sexual, crimes would not help his plea. But whether there were seven murders or eight, a grim joke at the time dubbed them the Feast of Corpus Christie.

During the January sales in 1907 a good-looking man of twenty-seven arrived at what was then the main entrance to Whiteley's at 43 WESTBOURNE GROVE, BAYSWATER. Impoverished, but carefully dressed for the occasion in frock coat and top hat, HORACE RAYNER asked to see the owner of the store. It was a busy day but William Whiteley found time to receive the visitor.

The staff in the outer office were surprised at the length of the interview; their employer usually gave anyone without an appointment only five minutes. Normally he went out to lunch sharply at one o'clock but it was four minutes past when he appeared. Greatly agitated, he asked for a policeman to be called. Hardly had he returned before there was the sound of three revolver shots.

When the police arrived they found Whiteley lying dead. Beside him was the visitor who was alive though he had put a bullet through his right eye. Searching through the man's pockets a detective found two leaves torn from a notebook on which was the message: 'To all whom it may concern; William Whiteley is my father, and has brought upon himself and me a double fatality by reason of his own refusal of a request perfectly reasonable. R.I.P.'

An extraordinary story slowly was unfolded at the trial of Whiteley's murderer. According to Horace Rayner's story, when they were seated at that fateful meeting on 24 January 1907, Whiteley asked what he could do for him, and he answered: 'I believe I am right in stating that a son is speaking to his father?' It was a disconcerting question which Whiteley countered by saying: 'Is that so? And when did you see me last?' Rayner said it was when he was a small boy – at Greville Road, Kilburn, where his aunt was living under Whiteley's discreet protection.

It was a reference to set the years rolling back for Whiteley, the 'Universal Provider', a self-made Yorkshireman who bought his first London shop in Westbourne Grove in 1863 and who, a decade later, had 622 employees and ten shops ready to become one great store boasting it could supply 'anything from a pin to an elephant'.

More acutely it was a reminder of how in his late forties – married with two children – he had slipped from the path of respectability. He and a friend in the City, George Rayner, took apartments on the Steyne at Brighton. There they spent pleasant weekends with two sisters, Louisa (who worked at Whiteley's) and Emily Turner (a nurserymaid). Louisa was Whiteley's girlfriend; Emily was Rayner's.

There seems to have been a certain informality about this arrangement with the result that the paternity of a boy, Horace, born to Emily in 1879 was a matter of doubt. That, anyway, was what George Rayner later explained to the boy. 'Your real father' Rayner told Horace, 'is William Whiteley.' His mother had also told him that if he were in trouble he should go to see Whiteley and mention her name. And this was what Horace finally decided to do.

There could hardly have been a greater contrast between the desperate young man of twenty-seven and the seventy-five-year-old, immensely prosperous owner of the country's first department store. Horace had suffered a disturbed upbringing and had been constantly in and out of jobs. He had left a wife and two children whom he could not support. The previous Christmas he had spent at Rowton House for down-and-outs at Hammersmith.

He was contemplating suicide when he decided to take one last chance and confront the man whom he believed had seduced his mother and was his father. But the Universal Provider did not live up to his name; instead of offering help, he suggested Horace go abroad.

'Do you refuse to help me either in kind or employment?' Horace said he asked. When Whiteley answered 'Yes', he had taken a revolver from his pocket. His threat to kill himself caused Whiteley to call for the police.

Horace claimed that he had no recollection of anything after that and at his trial he pleaded 'impulsive insanity'. But for the jury the phrase 'double fatality' which Horace had scrawled on his note while Whiteley was out of the room established his guilt.

The murderer did not hang, however. The public, taking the romantic view that Horace Rayner was a destitute son repudiated by a rich father, petitioned the Home Secretary. Signatures poured in – 180,000 within a week – and he was reprieved even though he said he would prefer death. Rayner twice attempted suicide in prison before he was released in 1919.

Nearly forty years ago a flat over a greengrocer's shop near Golders Green underground station came under intense police investigation. The flat at 620 B FINCHLEY ROAD is a long way from the Essex Marshes but in October 1949 Scotland Yard established a close connection between Golders Green and a grisly package found in the mudflats.

A sportsman in a punt near Tillingham hauled aboard a soggy rope-bound parcel which he opened to reveal a disagreeable sight: a headless, legless human torso with five stab wounds in the chest. The identity of the body was the first problem for the police. Arms and hands were intact and a pathologist succeeded in peeling the skin off the fingertips and making prints. They proved the body to be that of Stanley Setty, a dubious second-hand car dealer whose fingerprints were on police files and had also been recently found on his car lying in a mews garage.

Setty had been missing for seventeen days and the next question was how the body had got to the mudflats. Nearly every bone in the torso was broken, which suggested it had been dropped from a height. Could it have been from an aeroplane, wondered Chief Inspector Jamieson? If so it would be the first time in criminal history that an aircraft had been used to dispose of a body.

A check made at local airfields revealed that three weeks earlier a plane had been taken up by a club member, and a mechanic remembered the pilot with a package. The flyer, BRIAN DONALD HUME, was traced to the Golders Green flat where he was living with his wife and two-months-old baby.

Hume admitted being the pilot of the plane and dumping the body but he said he was paid to do so by three men who had brought the body to his home. They had paid him with notes that they had stolen from Setty. Detectives found bloodstains of Setty's blood group on the carpet but could produce no one who saw Hume in Setty's company on the day of the killing. Hume was charged with the murder (which he violently denied) and alternatively with being an accessory after the fact.

Because the evidence was circumstantial the jury disagreed. A second jury was formally ordered to find him not guilty: Hume pleaded guilty to disposing of the body and was sentenced to twelve years. After serving eight he was released and promptly sold his story ('I did kill Setty') to the *Sunday Pictorial* for £10,000.

Born in 1919, Hume grew up resenting his mother, who had sent him to an institution and gave him no idea who his father was. He was clever enough to win a secondary school scholarship but ran away to become a kitchen boy. He trained as an electrician, became a wartime aircraftman in the RAF, was invalided out, but posed as a Battle of Britain officer. His marriage in 1948 ended when his wife divorced him two years after the Setty killing.

Within months of his release a bank was raided and a manager shot in Brentford, a crime to which he subsequently confessed. In January 1959, Hume snatched money in a Zurich bank and shot dead a taxi driver who blocked his escape. He was released from a Swiss prison after sixteen years – the authorities said they couldn't deal with his attacks on staff and unco-operative behaviour – and was brought back to Britain, where he was sent to Broadmoor.

Now, twelve years later, Hume is still alive, a grey-haired portly man nearing 70 who as recently as April 1985 was reported to have been seen in Windsor on an outing of the kind granted to prisoners before they are paroled. In Switzerland he was known as 'The Beast' but a Broadmoor nurse has said that Patient 21332 B.D. Hume is 'as good as gold'.

Among the large houses standing on a tree-lined hill between Hampstead Heath and Finchley Road, 25 HEATH DRIVE has a look of solid prosperity. It is not in the least surprising to learn that when he died in 1937 the owner left £138,000 and had a library worth another £60,000.

A portrait of the owner shows a scholarly figure in cap and gown. An Honorary Fellow of Worcester College, Oxford, with a firm chin above a winged collar and a book held to his right breast, THOMAS J. WISE lives up to the popular conception of a bibliographer and book collector.

It therefore comes as a shock to learn that we are actually in the presence of a forger. For nearly half a century Wise deceived the entire literary world.

When a book with the apparently innocent title of *An Enquiry into the Nature of Certain Nineteenth Century Pamphlets* was published in 1934 it was a bombshell. Book collectors realised they had been duped by a man long respected as an international authority. Auctioneers like Sotheby's and booksellers as fastidious as Maggs Brothers found they had been trafficking in fakes perpetrated by Wise. Catalogues had to be radically overhauled at the British Museum and other learned libraries.

Over fifty first-edition pamphlets of authors including Thackeray, Dickens, Tennyson, Rossetti and Wordsworth were shown to be forgeries. Wise had passed off facsimiles as authentic. One of the

Forgery and vandalism long past, Thomas J. Wise seemed the epitome of scholarly respectability both in his appearance in later life and from the prosperous look of his Hampstead home. The scandal broke during his last years in Heath Drive.

most prized items in bibliographical history – Elizabeth Barrett Browning's love poems to her husband – had appeared with an entirely bogus early imprint to increase its value.

Among the devices employed by Wise was to get a printer to produce a facsimile of a work by a famous author. The printer assumed it would be sold as such, but Wise gave it a date earlier than any previously known first edition and declared it a rare or unique discovery. He couldn't be caught out because, of course, no genuine original existed with which it could be compared.

When Wise started his forgeries in the last century no scientific tests existed to analyse paper. John Carter and Graham Pollard who exposed the forgeries in their *Enquiry* discovered that there was esparto grass in the paper used for a number of items which Wise had given false early dates. Esparto hadn't then become an ingredient of English paper.

Thomas Wise was born in Gravesend in 1856, the son of unlettered parents. Long regarded as a scholar, he had little formal education, grew up in Holloway, and from being an office boy in a commodities firm in Mincing Lane rose to be managing director. But combined with his business career was a fascination with books, derived from bargain hunting in Farringdon Road bookstalls. When he was about 26 he started his criminal deception and found that with ingenuity he could augment his small salary as a cashier.

Wise's manufacture of forgeries lasted only about twelve years. When the game became too risky he changed to an unusual form of theft. Over some ten years he stole leaves from as many as two hundred original editions of plays, mostly Restoration, in the British Museum and used them to improve his own blemished copies. This vandalism seems to have ended in 1912 and his distribution of forgeries on any scale finished about the same time. From then on Wise disposed of occasional fabrications but was more concerned with becoming a bibliographical authority in the specialised field of poetry from Jacobean to late Victorian times. When it came to literary attributions his word was law. Ironically he was regarded as the final arbiter on authenticity.

Having succeeded in business – he was rich enough to buy the Heath Drive house in 1910 – he found the production of the spurious to make money less interesting than genuine acquisitions. Prosperously retired in 1930, he concentrated on his Ashley Library (named after the road he lived in when he started collecting) which he proposed to bequeath – but which was eventually sold – to the British Museum.

His horror when he learnt that Carter and Pollard were burrowing away at his secret past can be imagined. He tried to plug all the holes, and in the autumn of 1933 – the year before the publication of the *Enquiry* – he visited his old printers, Clay and Sons, in the City. Fortunately for him, they had destroyed all their records before 1911 but he received a short answer when he asked if they would be prepared to say they had nothing to do with the printing of any of his pamphlets.

When the *Enquiry* shattered the peace of Heath Drive Wise was ill. The authors, both booksellers, had exposed the forgeries, but spared the man. They simply pointed the finger: 'We find it difficult to believe that Mr Wise cannot now guess the identity of the forger ...'

With a great show of injured innocence Wise took refuge in silence and after a few weak protests declined all interviews. His wife claimed he was too ill to issue statements. He died on 7 May 1937 and went to his grave in Golders Green Cemetery without confessing the truth.

Wise made thousands of pounds from his deceptions but, except at the beginning, money does not seem to have been his main motive. He probably enjoyed the fame that he gained from his 'discoveries'. Perhaps he derived excitement from the Jekyll and Hyde existence in which dishonesty alternated with probity. Bernard Shaw excused his deceptions as 'jokes'. 'An uncanny genius' was the verdict of his biographer.

The house in Hilldrop Crescent where Crippen buried his wife in the cellar (p. 251) has gone but a visible link with the killing still exists at 30 CONSTANTINE ROAD, HAMPSTEAD. Now a one-way street of red-brick terrace houses, this is the address to which ETHEL LE NEVE came in September 1908 and where she was living at the time of the murder in 1910. The unresolved question is how much she knew or suspected about the crime.

Ethel, born at Diss in Norfolk, the daughter of a railway clerk, went to work for Dr Hawley Crippen at a patent medicine firm in 1900. She was 17, a shorthand-typist from Pitman's, who developed a father-figure crush on the doctor, then 41. With her large grey-blue eyes and a small slim figure Ethel was very unlike his wife Belle Elmore. Crippen found her attractive and three years after she came to the firm she began to play an increasingly important part in his life.

The Hampstead house where Ethel le Neve (right), was lodging at the time of the Hilldrop Crescent murder. Here she miscarried Crippen's child.

Accounts are inclined to telescope a relationship which ripened only slowly over a ten-year period. At first it was a matter of evening meals at Frascati's in Holborn and day outings, a courtship which became more intense as Crippen grew further estranged from his wife. It did not become a physical affair until 1906. Then their assignations in seedy King's Cross hotels were romanticised; they both talked of the affair as a marriage, with Hawley calling Ethel 'wifie'.

Whether Ethel's move to Constantine Road in 1908 meant that they had a more congenial place for their meetings is not certain. Crippen may have visited her there, for her motherly landlady, Mrs Emily Jackson, spoke of him as 'one of the nicest men I ever met'. To 'Ma' Jackson, who saw her through a miscarriage, Ethel confided worries about her status and her chances of ever marrying her lover.

Crippen killed his wife on 1 February 1910, and the following day Ethel found a note from him tucked into her typewriter at their Oxford Street office. It read in part: 'B.E. has gone to America ... Shall be in later when we can arrange for a pleasant little evening.' This was Ethel's first intimation that his wife had gone abroad or was even contemplating it. The pleasant little evening ended at 39 Hilldrop Crescent – their first night together at the house. Barely twenty-four hours earlier Crippen had buried his wife's headless and legless body wrapped in his pyjama top under the floor of the coal cellar.

Until just before Easter, six weeks later, Ethel stayed sometimes at Hilldrop Crescent, sometimes back with Mrs Jackson. Her domestic future was still uncertain; she must have thought that Belle Elmore might come back at any time. But at least things now looked more promising and she admitted 'a spark of pride' at wearing her rival's jewellery – the fatal mistake which started neighbours gossiping.

Crippen told her (as he later informed the police) first that his wife had gone to visit a sick relative in the States; then that she had died there of pneumonia; and – a final change of story – that she was not dead at all, but living with a lover near Chicago, address unknown. Later Ethel insisted: 'Trusting him as I did, of course I believed him'.

It is hard to credit that she wasn't suspicious. Even if she had not the faintest knowledge of the body in the cellar, Ethel must have thought Belle's absence strange and Hawley's varying explanations unconvincing. Only fears that something dreadful had happened, and that Hawley faced arrest, would have induced her to cut off her hair, dress as a boy and, posing as his son, flee the country with him in July.

Despite many unresolved questions, a jury took no more than twenty minutes to acquit her of being an accessory after the fact. Absolved of the crime, but internationally notorious, Ethel took refuge in Canada, calling herself Allen. After six years she returned to England and, under the name of Ethel Nelson, married an accountant, Stanley Smith, in the furniture firm of Hampton's, Trafalgar Square, where she was a typist. They had two children (still living in 1986) from whom her past remained a secret for the many years they lived at Parkview Road, Addiscombe. Widowed, Ethel le Neve died in Dulwich Hospital on 9 August 1967.

Heading towards Highgate across Hampstead Heath we pass a number of roads on the north side of Hampstead Lane with houses of Hollywood-style opulence. Each is a symbol of wealth and status. Sleek cars slide into triple garages through radio-controlled doors. Self-made millionaires live behind white walls and under roofs of green Dutch tiles. Reproduction Louis XIV furniture and dubious Renoirs are protected by complicated burglar alarms and very large dogs.

One house, slightly more subdued than most, is the neo-Georgian BISHOPSTONE in WINNINGTON ROAD, HAMPSTEAD. With Venetian windows, a huge quasi-royal coat of arms over the crescent-shaped portico and an outside light provided by a naked cherub holding a torch, this was the home of the property dealer who gave a new word to the language. In the *Concise Oxford Dictionary* an entry reads: 'Rachmanism = n. Exploitation of slum tenants by unscrupulous landlord' and provides its derivation: PETER RACHMAN, who lived there from 1959 until his death in 1962.

In his last ten years Rachman controlled property through forty companies operating in Paddington and Notting Hill. His empire extended to Shepherd's Bush, Battersea, Maida Vale and Earls Court. His lifestyle was one of large cars and large cigars, rooms at the Savoy, tables at Les Ambassadeurs, jewellery from Kutchinsky's, nightclubs which he owned and glamorous mistresses like Mandy Rice-Davies and Christine Keeler.

All this had been acquired since his unpromising arrival in Britain after the war in 1946. Son of a Jewish dentist, born in East Poland, Rachman was a penniless refugee, a stateless person (which he always remained). At the age of 28, when he left a resettlement

Elaborate portico of the Winnington Road home of property racketeer Peter Rachman (below), at the time of his death in 1962.

camp near Reading in 1947, his first job was at Cohen's Veneer Factory in the East End where he earned £4. 10s a week while living in a bedsitter in Stepney Green. Next he worked for a Jewish tailor in Wardour Street.

Rachman had been toughened in a hard school – seeing his parents taken to German concentration camps, working on a road gang, escaping into Russia, being captured and taken to Siberia and, when freed, serving in the Polish 2nd Corps in Italy.

This was preparation for the hard graft of selling cheap suitcases and making Black Market deals from public call boxes before he got his first break in 1950 thanks to a Bayswater prostitute. She lent Rachman her savings to set up a flat-letting agency. From a basement in Westbourne Grove he rented flats, mostly in the Sussex Gardens area, to prostitutes at a rent-book rate of £5 a week plus £10 cash in his hands. One girl to a flat, he stipulated, so he couldn't be accused of brothel-keeping.

In conjunction with a former lieutenant-colonel he began to buy up end-of-lease properties, and within six years he had thirty houses in Shepherd's Bush, thirty more in Notting Hill and twenty flats in Maida Vale.

A typical Rachman deal was to buy a block like 1–16 Powis Terrace, Notting Hill, for £20,000, install a landlord – there a Nigerian – who had to guarantee him an income of £300 a week. Soon there were 1,200 people living in a property which should have housed 200 with an Asian family packed into each room paying £10 a week. Rent collectors with Alsatian dogs made the rounds. If he wanted to get rid of an awkward sitting tenant his henchmen cut off electricity and essential supplies.

Now was the time for the big cigars, a Rolls Royce and flamboyant friends like Dennis Hamilton (Diana Dors's husband) with whom he shared a passion for gambling. He enjoyed the company of swinging socialites in shady nightclubs. He part owned El Condor in Wardour Street where he greeted younger members of the Royal Family and instead of cashing a cheque from the Duke of Kent kept it as a souvenir.

With money rolling in there was every chance for a promiscuous life. In 1960 he married a nurse and secretary with whom he had been living for several years, but this didn't inhibit his visits to Bryanston Mews West where he installed the seventeen-year-old Christine Keeler (p. 159) before moving on to Mandy Rice-Davies (p. 160), whom he set up in the same flat.

On a November weekend in 1962 Rachman made his usual

round of nightclubs, and in the early hours of Monday, was being driven home to his wife (as was his rule) when he was taken ill and had to stop. He died of a heart attack in the afternoon of the same day, 29 November, in Edgware General Hospital with his faithful wife Audrey at his bedside.

The house in Winnington Road was besieged by property men to whom Rachman owed money, but most came away frustrated. Rachman had not been one to put much on paper. There was little ready money out of the vast sums he had made from his huge property rackets. Everything was mortgaged. Audrey knew about Mandy (who had been in Paris that weekend) and when she came to Bishopstone chatted with her in the hope that the girl might be able to throw light on some of his tangled business dealings.

When he died aged 42 the general public knew virtually nothing about Rachman. His name was unknown. Only with the Profumo case and other spy scares in the summer of 1963 did his activities begin to make headlines. Fleet Street, inhibited by libel problems and *sub judice* proceedings, at last had someone they could write about who couldn't sue. With difficulty the papers began to disentangle and expose the countless rackets in which he had been involved. The word 'Rachmanism' was born.

The next road to the one where Rachman lived is even more affluent. Into this 'Millionaires' Row' moved an even more spurious financier, EMIL SAVUNDRA, in the early 1960s. WHITE WALLS (now Eliot House), BISHOP'S AVENUE, HAMPSTEAD, was set in a floodlit two-acre garden. Furnished with white leather suites and a gold and ivory piano, the large house with servants' wing had a gaudy extravagance that made Rachman's Bishopstone look almost dowdy.

Comparisons between the Ceylon-born insurance swindler and the Polish-born property rogue are inevitable. Both cashed in on the 'never-had-it-so-good' boom in the early sixties; they shared the same life-style; the same taste in expensive cars; and even the same women – Christine Keeler and Mandy Rice-Davies. It is hard to decide who was the greater villain.

Savundra's arrival in Bishop's Avenue with his fleet of cars – two Aston Martins, a Jaguar and a Rolls Royce with CD plates to which he wasn't entitled – came soon after his formation of Fire Auto and Marine, a low-cost motor insurance company with offices in Jacqueline House, Hendon. Apart from this enterprise, which was to be disastrous for thousands of motorists, Savundra had thirty-two firms registered at this address. 'Some people collect stamps, and others dogs', he once said. 'I collect companies.'

The larger-than-life man with silver hair who called himself 'God's own lounge lizard' enjoyed phrase-making. 'When the English find a loop-hole in the law they drive a Mini-Minor through it. I drive a Rolls Royce' was another of his boastful aphorisms, and his career showed that here, at least, he spoke the truth.

Born in 1923 into a respected legal family in Ceylon, Emil Savundra grew up to a life of fast motor bikes, fast cars, private planes and speed boats. At his 1949 marriage into an aristocratic Ceylonese family there were 3,000 guests. With his bride came a large dowry, part of which he invested in deals which involved him in forgery and Belgian currency infringements before he fled to England in 1954.

When the Belgian police tried to extradite him, Savundra simulated a heart attack and moved into the London Clinic, where a court was convened and from which he was taken to the Continent on a stretcher. In Brussels he was sentenced to five years and a large fine. Somehow he contrived to halve the fine and secure his release within a few months.

After an abortive attempt to secure all mineral rights in Ghana, Savundra returned to London in 1959 and received the naturalisation papers which Rachman always wanted but never obtained. In the same way as he used CD plates on his car, he put Ph.D. after his name, and styled himself doctor, a degree, he explained when pressed, conferred on him by a university in Kensington. His world soon became that of Lord Lucan, Stephen Ward and Mandy Rice-Davies, with whom he had an affair. He was the 'Indian doctor' who gave evidence at Ward's trial.

The loop-hole in the law (through which he drove his Rolls Royce in 1962) permitted anyone to set up an insurance company, regardless of experience or qualifications, provided he could show a capital of £50,000. This enabled Savundra to launch Fire Auto and Marine whose premiums were so low that they attracted 400,000 motorists. He was raking £40,000 a week into Jacqueline House but claims grew alarmingly and soon far exceeded money available. When the crash came in July 1966 Savundra promptly took to a Swiss clinic with a heart attack.

Liquidators were appointed and all the share certificates in Savundra's insurance company were found to be bogus. Fire Auto and Marine, with a deficit of almost £3 millions, owed £300,000 to

White Walls, now renamed, in 'Millionaires' Row', Hampstead, the extravagant home of Emil Savundra, fraudulent financier.

43,000 claimants. Some 400,000 motorists found themselves without insurance coverage.

For no clear reason except that he was vain and basked in publicity, Savundra decided to return from Switzerland and brazen things out. He had not then been charged with anything and in February 1967 he made television history by ringing up David Frost and volunteering to go on his programme. In an extraordinary confrontation – a trial by TV – millions saw Frost quiver with anger during their furious exchanges, Savundra losing his temper and the studio audience booing him for calling them 'peasants'. The Director of Public Prosecutions, who was watching, rang the Fraud Squad.

Within days Savundra was charged on technical financial

grounds sufficiently serious for him to be sentenced to eight years' imprisonment which was to be extended to ten if he failed to pay a fine of £50,000. The trial lasted forty-two days. Most of his sentence in Wormwood Scrubs was spent in the hospital wing with diabetes and heart disease and he was freed after six and a half years.

By now White Walls in Millionaires' Row (shrewdly bought in his wife's name) was exchanged for a house he had in Old Windsor and Savundra devoted the next two years to a grandiose scheme for selling the estates owned by his wife's family in Ceylon to the US Government as a nuclear base. He planned to receive 200 million dollars from the deal and hoped his wife would be made Queen of Jaffna in the north of Ceylon.

Emil Savundra died on 21 December 1976 of the heart disease he had so conveniently cultivated.

Briefly we return to south-east London to put up one final Black Plaque on LINDSEY HOUSE, LLOYD'S PLACE, BLACKHEATH. We are – to readjust a Biblical precept – doing unto ourselves as we have done unto others. It was mostly in the top floor study at this address during 1985–6 that two pitiless chroniclers, FELIX BARKER and DENISE SILVESTER-CARR, the Devil's Topographers, uncharitably recorded the misdeeds of others.

Lindsey House · *Blackheath*

THE END

Personalised Bibliography

Unlike many bibliographies this book list is not designed to display prodigious research; it is simply to tell people where they will find more about the characters awarded Black Plaques. Although hundreds of varied sources have been consulted, we have cited only one book for each person and this is not necessarily the definitive biography or our main reference. Where possible we have chosen modern rather than older titles as they are likely to be easier to come by. Even so many are out of print; the best hope then is a public library where the *Dictionary of National Biography* (still the best source for some historical villains) should also be on the shelves. Where no book is given we have relied entirely on contemporary newspaper reports.

Chapter 1: The Strand and Covent Garden

JOHN ROBINSON. *Commander Burt of Scotland Yard* by Leonard Burt. (Heinemann. 1959)

KLAUS FUCHS and ALAN NUNN MAY. *The Traitors* by Alan Moorehead. (Hamish Hamilton. 1952)

ALI KAMEL FAHMY. *The Life of Sir Edward Marshall Hall* by Edward Marjoribanks. (Gollancz. 1930)

WILLIAM IRELAND. *Grand Deceptions* edited by Alan Klein. (Faber and Faber. 1956)

TITUS OATES. *Titus Oates* by Margaret Lane. (Dakers. 1949)

EDMUND CURLL. *A History of Erotic Literature* by Patrick J. Kearney. (Macmillan. 1982)

JAMES HACKMAN. *The High Tide of Pleasure* by Henry Blyth. (Weidenfeld & Nicolson. 1970)

JOHN WILMOT, EARL OF ROCHESTER. *Lord Rochester's Monkey* by Graham Greene. (Bodley Head. 1974)

CLAUDE DUVAL. *The Romance of London* by John Timbs. (Frederick Warne. 1985)

W.T. STEAD. *The Age of Consent* by Michael Pearson. (David & Charles. 1972)

TERESIA CONSTANTIA PHILLIPS. *Twelve Bad Women* edited by Arthur Vincent. (T. Fisher Unwin. 1938)

Chapter 2: Trafalgar Square to St James's

COUNT CHARLES JOHN KONIGSMARCK and OTHERS. *Dictionary of National Biography:* ref. Thomas Thynne

ARABELLA CHURCHILL and CATHERINE SEDLEY. *The King's Mistresses* by Alan Hardy. (Evans Brothers. 1980)

NELL GWYN. *The Dictionary of National Biography*

DR JAMES GRAHAM. *The Survey of London, Vol.XXX* (University of London for London County Council. 1960)

HORATIO BOTTOMLEY. *The Rise and Fall of Horatio Bottomley* by Alan Hyams. (Cassell. 1972)

JOHN CLELAND. *John Cleland: Images of a Life* by William H. Epstein. (Columbia University Press: New York & London. 1974)

THE DUKE OF CUMBERLAND. *Ernest Augustus, Duke of Cumberland and King of Hanover* by G.M. Willis. (Arthur Barker. 1936)

Chapter 3: Buckingham Palace through Victoria to Westminster

QUEEN VICTORIA. *Enter Rumour* by R.B. Martin. (Faber & Faber. 1962)

DR WILLIAM DODD. *The Macaroni Parson* by Gerald Howson. (Hutchinson. 1973)

CORA PEARL. *The Pearl from Plymouth* by W.H. Holden. (British Technical & General Press. 1950)

SIR OSWALD MOSLEY. *Rules of the Game* by Nicholas Mosley. (Secker and Warburg. 1982)

COL. THOMAS BLOOD. *Dictionary of National Biography*

RICHARD DE PODLICOTE. *Historical Memorials of Westminster Abbey* by Arthur Penrhyn Stanley. (John Murray. 1876)

GUY FAWKES. *Portrait of Guy Fawkes* by Henry Garnett. (Robert Hale, 1962)

JOHN BELLINGHAM. *Chronicles of Crime, Vol I.* edited by Camden Pelham. (Reeves & Turner. 1886)

JOHN WILKES. *Wilkes 'A Friend of Liberty'* by Audrey Williamson. (Allen and Unwin. 1974)

J. MAUNDY GREGORY. *Maundy Gregory: Purveyor of Honours* by Tom Cullen. (Bodley Head. 1974)

CHARLES I. *The Trial of Charles I* by C.V. Wedgwood. (Collins. 1964)

LADY CAROLINE LAMB. *Byron's Letters and Journals* edited by Leslie A. Marchand. (John Murray. 1973–82)

Chapter 4: Piccadilly, Park Lane and Mayfair

EMMA HAMILTON. *Beloved Emma* by Fiona Fraser. (Weidenfeld & Nicolson. 1986)

LORD BYRON. *Byron: A Biography* by Leslie A. Marchand. (John Murray. 1957)

MRS OLIVIA SERRES. *The Annual Register*. 1823 and 1866

SARAH RACHEL LEVENSON. *Stories of Famous Master Criminals* by Leonard Gribble. (Arthur Barker. 1973)

LORD CAMELFORD. *The Half-Mad Lord* by Nikolai Tolstoy. (Jonathan Cape. 1978)

WILLIAM POLE-TYLNEY-LONG-WELLESLEY. *Black Sheep* by Christopher Simon Sykes. (Chatto & Windus. 1982)

JOHN MURRAY AND OTHERS. *The Late Lord Byron* by Doris Langley Moore. (John Murray. 1961)

SIR FRANCIS BURDETT. *The Dictionary of National Biography*

EDMUND KEAN. *Six Studies in Hypocrisy* by Giles Playfair. (Secker and Warburg. 1969)

DENNIS O'KELLY AND CHARLOTTE HAYES. *The High Tide of Pleasure* by Henry Blyth. (Weidenfeld & Nicolson. 1970)

LORD PALMERSTON. *Lord Palmerston* by Jasper Ridley. (Constable. 1970)

LORD WILLIAM PAGET. *Black Sheep* by Christopher Simon Sykes. (Chatto and Windus. 1982)

ALEXANDER KEITH. *Mayfair: The Years of Grandeur* by Mary Cathcart Borer (W.H. Allen. 1975)

MARGUERITE DIBLANC. *Unfair Comment* by Jack Smith-Hughes. (Cassell. 1951)

WHITAKER WRIGHT. *'Fraudsters'* by Michael Gilbert. (Constable. 1987)

LADY TWISS. *Painful Details* by Michael Harrison. (Max Parrish. 1952)

FRANCOIS BENJAMIN COURVOISIER. *Chronicles of Crime of the New Newgate Calendar. Vol II* by Camden Pelham. (Reeves & Turner. 1886)

THOMAS, LORD COCHRANE, EARL OF DUNDONALD. *A Matter of Speculation: The Case of Lord Cochrane* by Henry Cecil. (Hutchinson. 1965)

CAPT. ANDREW STONEY. *The Unhappy Countess* by Ralph Arnold. (Constable. 1957)

Chapter 5: Inner Mayfair

BARONESS MELUSINE VON DER SCHULENBURG, DUCHESS OF KENDAL. *The King's Mistresses* by Alan Hardy. (Evans Brothers. 1980)

HENRIETTA, LADY GROSVENOR. *The Letters and Journals of Lady Mary Coke.* (Kingsmead Reprints. Bath. 1970)

LAURA BELL. *They Startled Grandfather* by W.H. Holden. (British Technical and General Press. 1950)

MRS FITZHERBERT. *The Life and Times of George IV* by Alan Palmer. (Weidenfeld and Nicolson. 1972)

LILLIE LANGTRY. *The Prince and the Lily* by James Brough. (Hodder and Stoughton. 1975)

CATHERINE WALTERS. *Skittles, The Last Victorian Courtesan* by Henry Blyth. (Rupert Hart Davis. 1970)

KITTY FISHER. *Ladies Fair and Frail* by Horace Bleackley. (John Lane, The Bodley Head. 1909)

LOLA MONTEZ. *Lola Montez* by Helen Holdredge. (Alvin Redman. 1957)

ELIZABETH HOWARD. *The Mistresses* by Betty Kelen. (W.H. Allen. 1966)

MARY ROBINSON. *The Green Dragoon* by Robert D. Bass. (Alvin Redman. 1957)

Chapter 6: Bloomsbury and Fitzrovia

IGNATIUS TREBICH LINCOLN. *The Self-made Villain* by David Lampe and Laslo Szenasi. (Cassells. 1961)

MAY CHURCHILL. Also FRANK DUTTON JACKSON and EDITHA LOLETA JACKSON. *The World's Worst Women* by Bernard O'Donnell. (W.H. Allen. 1953)

REVD HAROLD DAVIDSON. *The Age Of Illusion* by Ronald Blythe. (Hamish Hamilton. 1963)

FREDERICK CALVERT, LORD BALTIMORE. *Six Ventures in Villainy* by Jack Smith-Hughes. (Cassell. 1955)

THERESA BERKLEY. *A Worm in the Bud* by Ronald Pearsall. (Weidenfeld & Nicolson. 1969)

LORD ARTHUR SOMERSET. *The Cleveland Street Scandal* by H. Montgomery Hyde. (W.H. Allen. 1976)

CHARLES WELLS. *Crime within the Square Mile* by Ernest Nicholls. (John Long. 1935)

Chapter 7: North of Trafalgar Square

MARY RICHARDSON. *Laugh a Defiance* by Mary Richardson. (Weidenfeld & Nicolson. 1953)

MARY TOFTS. *Mid-Georgian London* by Hugh Phillips. (Collins. 1964)

MRS KATE MEYRICK. *Secrets of the 43* by Mrs Meyrick. (John Long. 1933)

CHEVALIER D'EON. *The Enigma of the Age: Chevalier D'Eon* by Cynthia Cox. (Longman. 1966)

JOHN HENRY ST JOHN, VISCOUNT BOLING BROKE. *Viscount Bolingbroke* by Jeffrey Hart. (Routledge and Kegan Paul. 1965)

CASANOVA. *Casanova* by John Masters. (George Rainbird. 1969)

Chapter 8: Marylebone

JANE DIGBY. *Passion's Child* by Margaret Fox Schmidt. (Hamish Hamilton. 1976)

LADY FLORA PAGET. *The Pocket Venus* by Henry Blyth. (Weidenfeld & Nicolson. 1966)

JOANNA SOUTHCOTT. *The Second Coming* by J.F.C. Harrison. (Routledge and Kegan Paul. 1979)

ANTHONY BLUNT. *A Conspiracy of Silence: the Secret Life of Anthony Blunt* by Barrie Penrose and Simon Freeman. (Grafton Books. 1986)

GUY BURGESS. *The Fourth Man* by Douglas Sutherland. (Martin Secker & Warburg. 1980)

DR STEPHEN WARD. *Scandal '63* by Clive Irving, Ron Hall and Jeremy Wallington. (William Heinemann. 1963)

CHRISTINE KEELER. *Sex Scandals* by Christine Keeler and Robert Meadley. (Xanadu Publications. 1985)

MANDY RICE-DAVIES. *Mandy* by Mandy Rice-Davies and Shirley Flack. (Michael Joseph. 1980)

THE DUCHESS OF WINDSOR. *The Windsor Story* by Charles J.V. Murphy and Joseph Bryan. (Granada. 1979)

BISHOP OF CLOGHER. *Celebrated Trials Vol VI.* (Knight & Lacey. 1825)

MARY ANNE CLARKE. *By Royal Appointment* by Paul Berry. (Femina. 1970)

ARTHUR ORTON. *The Tichborne Claimant* by Douglas Woodruff. (Hollis & Carter. 1957)

ARTHUR THISTLEWOOD. *The Cato Street Conspiracy* by John Stanhope. (Cape. 1962)

Chapter 9: Belgravia and Pimlico

ROGER CASEMENT. *The Black Diaries* by Peter Singleton-Gates and Maurice Girodias. (Olympia Press. Paris. 1959)

LORD LUCAN. *The Lucan Mystery* by Norman Lucas. (W.H. Allen. 1975)

LADY MORDAUNT. *Painful Details* by Michael Harrison. (Max Parrish. 1952)

LORD AND LADY COLIN CAMPBELL. *The Mayfair Calendar* by Horace Wyndham. (Hutchinson. 1925)

SIR CHARLES DILKE. *Sir Charles Dilke* by Roy Jenkins. (Collins. 1958)

OSCAR WILDE. *Oscar Wilde* by H. Montgomery Hyde. (Eyre Methuen. 1976)

ADELAIDE BARTLETT. *Poison and Adelaide Bartlett* by Yseult Bridges. (Macmillan. 1962)

Chapter 10: Knightsbridge and Kensington

GEORGE HUDSON. *Enter Rumour* by R.B. Martin. (Faber & Faber. 1962)

OSCAR MERRIL HARTZELL. *The Confident Tricksters* edited by Colin Rose. (Topaz Books. 1977)

HARRIETTE WILSON. *The Game of Hearts* by Lesley Blanch. (Gryphon Books. 1957)

THOMAS LEY. *Forty Years of Murder* by Keith Simpson. (Geo. G. Harrap. 1978)

RUTH ELLIS. *The Trial of Ruth Ellis* by Jonathan Goodman & Patrick Pringle. (David & Charles. 1974)

ELIZABETH CHUDLEIGH, DUCHESS OF KINGSTON. *The Virgin Mistress* by Eleanor Mavor. (Chatto & Windus. 1964)

OAN ('SALIM'). *Siege: Six Days at the Iranian Embassy* by George Brock. (Macmillan. 1980)

FRANK HARRIS. *Frank Harris* by Hugh Kingsmill. (Biographia. 1987)

RADCLYFFE HALL. *Radclyffe Hall at the Well of Loneliness* by Lovat Dickson. (Collins. 1979)

Chapter 11: Gloucester Road to Chelsea

JOHN HAIGH. *Forty Years of Murder* by Keith Simpson. (Geo. G. Harrap. 1978)

WILLIAM JOYCE. *The Trial of William Joyce* edited by C.E. Bechhofer Roberts. (Jarrolds. 1946)

KIM PHILBY. *The Long Road to Moscow* by Patrick Searle and Maureen McConville. (Hamish Hamilton. 1973)

MARY JEFFRIES. *The Age of Consent* by Michael Pearson. (David & Charles. 1972)

ALEISTER CROWLEY. *The Great Beast: The Life and Magic of Aleister Crowley* by John Symonds. (Macdonald. 1971)

Chapter 12: The City

SIR WILLIAM TURNER and SIR JAMES EDWARDS. *The History of The Temple* by J. Bruce Williamson. (John Murray. 1924)

ELIZABETH BROWNRIGG. *Lives of Twelve Bad Women* edited by Arthur Vincent. (T. Fisher Unwin. 1938)

SIR WILLIAM NECHTONE. *The Phoenix of Fleet Street* by Dewi Morgan. (Charles Knight. 1973)

MARY FRITH. *The Elizabethan Underworld* by Gamini Salgado. (Dent. 1977)

JONATHAN WILD. *It Takes a Thief* by Gerald Howson. (The Cresset Library. 1987)

WILLIAM FITZOSBERT. *A Survey of London* by John Stow edited by Charles Lethbridge Kingsford. (Oxford University Press. 1971)

RICHARD PARSONS. *Haunted London* by Peter Underwood. (Harrap. 1973)

LORD GEORGE GORDON. *The City of London* by Mary Cathcart Borer. (Constable. 1977)

KITTY BYRON. *Lord Darling and His Famous Trials* by Evelyn
Graham. (Hutchinson. 1929)

THOMAS FARRINOR. *The Great Fire of London* by Walter George Bell.
(Bodley Head. 1951)

Chapter 13: Whitechapel and the East End

JACK THE RIPPER. *The Complete Jack the Ripper* by Donald
Rumbelow. (W.H. Allen. 1975)

DICK TURPIN. *Immortal Turpin* by Arty Ashe and Julius E. Day.
(Staples Press. 1948)

HENRY WAINWRIGHT. *The Verdict of the Court* edited by J. Michael
Hardwick. (Herbert Jenkins. 1960)

PETER PIATKOW (PETER THE PAINTER), FRITZ SVAARS and JOSEF. *The
Battle of Stepney: the Sidney Street Siege* by Colin Rogers. (Robert
Hale. 1981)

FRANZ MÜLLER. *Trial of Franz Müller* edited by H.B. Irving.
(William Hodge. 1911)

RONNIE KRAY. *The Profession of Violence* by John Pearson.
(Weidenfeld and Nicolson. 1972)

Chapter 14: North-East London

DENNIS NILSEN. *Killing for Company* by Brian Masters. (Jonathan
Cape. 1985)

GEORGE J. SMITH. *Famous Trials:* edited by Harry Hodge and James
H. Hodge. Selected and introduced by John Mortimer. (Viking.
1984)

FREDERICK SEDDON. *Notable British Trials Series: Trial of the Seddons*
edited by Filson Young. (Hodge. 1914)

DR HAWLEY HARVEY CRIPPEN. *Crippen: The Mild Murderer* by Tom
Cullen. (The Bodley Head. 1977)

JOHN SMYTH PIGOTT. *Abodes of Love* by John Montgomery.
(Putnam. 1962)

KENNETH HALLIWELL. *Prick Up your Ears* by John Lahr. (Allen
Lane. 1978)

Chapter 15: South-East London

INGRAM FREZER. *The Muses' Darling* by Charles Norman. (Falcon Press. 1947)

EDMUND POOK. *Unfair Comment* by Jack Smith-Hughes. (Cassell. 1951)

PRINCESS CAROLINE. *The Disastrous Marriage* by Joanna Richardson. (Jonathan Cape. 1960)

CHARLES PEACE. *Notable British Trials Series. Trials of Charles Frederick Peace* edited by W. Teignmouth. (Hodge. 1926)

ELIZA ROBERTSON. *The History of the Paragon, Paragon House and their Residents* by W. Bonwit. (The Bookshop, Blackheath. 1976)

CHARLES STEWART PARNELL, KATHERINE O'SHEA and CAPT. WILLIAM O'SHEA. *The Face of Parnell* by F.S.L. Lyons. (Routledge & Kegan Paul. 1962)

REV. ARTHUR TOOTH. *Judgement on Hatchem* by Joyce Coombs. (Faith Press. 1969)

LOUIS STAUNTON, PATRICK STAUNTON, ALICE RHODES. *Trial of the Stauntons* edited by J.B. Atlay. (Hodge. 1911)

DR EDWARD AVELING. *The Life of Eleanor Marx* by Isuzuki Chushichi. (Oxford. 1967)

Chapter 16: South-West London

ARTHUR and NIZAMODEEN HOSEIN. *Shall We Ever Know?* by William Cooper. (Hutchinson. 1971)

CYNTHIA PAYNE. *An English Madam* by Paul Bailey. (Fontana. 1983)

MRS CHARLES BRAVO. *How Charles Bravo Died* by Yseult Bridges. (Jarrolds. 1956)

FREDERICK ROBINSON. *Search for the Truth: My Life for Psychical Research* by Harry Price. (Collins. 1942)

KATE WEBSTER. *Trial of Kate Webster* edited by Elliot O'Donnell. (William Hodge. 1925)

BUSTER EDWARDS. *The Trian Robbers* by Piers Paul Read. (W.H. Allen. 1978)

Chapter 17: North-East London

BARBARA VILLIERS, DUCHESS OF CLEVELAND. *The Illustrious Lady* by Elizabeth Hamilton. (Hamish Hamilton. 1980)

FRANCES HOWARD. *Black Sheep* by Christopher Simon Sykes. (Chatto & Windus. 1982)

PETER AND HELEN KROGER, GORDON LONSDALE, HARRY HOUGHTON and ETHEL GEE. *Spycatcher* by Norman Lucas. (W.H. Allen. 1973)

GEORGE BLAKE. *George Blake, Superspy* by H. Montgomery Hyde. (Constable. 1987)

JOHN REGINALD HALLIDAY CHRISTIE. *10 Rillington Place* by Ludovic Kennedy. (Gollancz. 1961)

HORACE RAYNOR. *The Universal Provider* by Richard S. Lambert. (Harrap. 1938)

BRIAN DONALD HUME. *Famous Criminal Cases: Vol VI.* by Rupert Furneaux. (Odhams Press. 1960)

THOMAS WISE. *Thomas Wise in the Original Cloth* by Wilfred Partington. (Robert Hale. 1954)

ETHEL LE NEVE. *Crippen: The Mild Murderer* by Tom Cullen. (The Bodley Head. 1977)

PETER RACHMAN. *Rachman* by Shirley Green. (Michael Joseph. 1979)

EMIL SAVUNDRA. *Fraud: The Amazing Career of Dr Savundra* by John Connell and Douglas Sutherland. (Hodder & Stoughton. 1978)

Illustration credits

Category Index

Page numbers will be found under the person's name in the main index. Some names appear under more than one heading.

Adulterers
Byron, Lord
Campbell, Lady Colin
Campbell, Lord Colin
Casanova, Giacomo
Crippen, Harvey Hawley
Dilke, Sir Charles
Digby, Jane
Hamilton, Emma Lady
Kean, Edmund
Lamb, Lady Caroline
Mordaunt, Lady Harriet
Nechtone, Sir William
O'Shea, Katherine
O'Shea, Capt. William
Parnell, Charles Stewart
Wainwright, Henry

Agitators
Burdett, Sir Francis
Camelford, Lord
Edwards, Sir James
FitzOsbert, William
Gordon, Lord George
Josef
Mosley, Sir Oswald
Piatkow, Peter
Svaars, Fritz
Trebich-Lincoln, Ignatius
Turner, Sir William

Arsonist
Hubert, Stephen

Assassins
Bellingham, John
Boroski
Frezer, Ingram
Konigsmarck, Count Charles
Stern, Lieut.
Vratz, Capt.

Bigamists
Chudleigh, Elizabeth, Duchess of
    Kingston
Montez, Lola
Smith, George Joseph
Villiers, Barbara Duchess of
    Cleveland

Blackmailers
Chaffers, Alexander
Levenson, Sarah Rachel
Paget, Lord William
Phillips, Teresia Constantia
Pole-Tynley-Long-Wellesley, William
Wild, Jonathan
Wilson, Harriette

Blasphemers
Smyth Pigott, Revd John
Wilkes, John

Brothel-keepers
Berkley, Theresa
Hayes, Charlotte
Jeffries, Mary
O'Kelly, Dennis

Burglars
Peace, Charles
Wild, Jonathan

Con-men
Gregory, J. Maundy
Hartzell, Oscar Merril

Conspirators
Berenger, Charles Random de
Bolingbroke, Henry St John,
   Viscount
Cochrane, Lord Thomas 10th Earl of
   Dundonald
Fawkes, Guy
Oates, Titus
Thistlewood, Arthur

Courtesans
Bell, Laura
Fisher, Kitty
Howard, Elizabeth
Montez, Lola
Pearl, Cora
Phillips, Teresia Constantia
Walters, Catherine 'Skittles'

Deceivers
Tofts, Mary
Twiss, Lady

Deviants
Fahmy, Ali Kamel
Halliwell, Kenneth
Radclyffe Hall, Marguerite

Eloper
Paget, Lady Flora

Embezzlers
Escoffier, Auguste
Ritz, César

Extortionists
Clarke, Mary Anne
Levenson, Sarah Rachel

Fanatics
Gordon, Lord George
Tooth, Revd Arthur

Trebich-Lincoln, Ignatius
Smyth Pigott, Revd John
Southcott, Joanna

Forgers
Dodd, Dr William
Ireland, William Henry
Trebich-Lincoln, Ignatius
Wise, Thomas J.

Frauds
Bottomley, Horatio
Hudson, George
Savundra, Emil
Wells, Charles
Wright, Whitaker

Gangsters
Churchill, May
Kray, Ronnie
Wild, Jonathan

Hoaxers
Hartzell, Oscar Merril
Parsons, Richard

Highwaymen
Duval, Claude
Turpin, Dick

Imposters
Orton, Arthur
Twiss, Lady
Serres, Olivia

Kidnappers
Calvert, Frederick, Lord Baltimore
Hosein, Arthur
Hosein, Nizamadeen
Pole-Tylney-Long-Wellesley, William
Stoney-Bowes, Capt. Andrew

Malcontents
FitzOsbert, William
Gordon, Lord George
Oates, Titus

Mistresses
Bell, Laura
Churchill, Arabella

Index